A Torah Minute

A Treasury of

Torah Gems & Practical Laws

The Hakham Rabbi Ya'aqob Menashe

Published by

Midrash BEN ISH HAI

P.O. Box 220133

Great Neck, NY 11022

USA

(516) 487-6676

www.midrash.org

ISBN 978-0-9841828-1-7

Cover design by

Lorene Sasson (917) 767-8884

Printed in Canada

לע"נ

איוב בן שכראלה

יוחנן בן ניסן הלוי

אברהם בן חיים יצחק

יוסף בן בבא הלוי

משה בן יעקב

הושע בן יוסף הלוי

מרדכי בן יצחק

ע"ה

פוראן בת אברהם

בומון בת נבת

רבקה בת אסתר

מרים בת פנחס גד

נבת בת פנחס גד

סלתנת בת יוחנן

טובה בת חיים

פארי בת יוסף הלוי

ע"ה

יוסף ואנג'לה מותהדה

In honor of

Rabbi Ya'aqob Menashe

Dedicated by
the

Toobian family

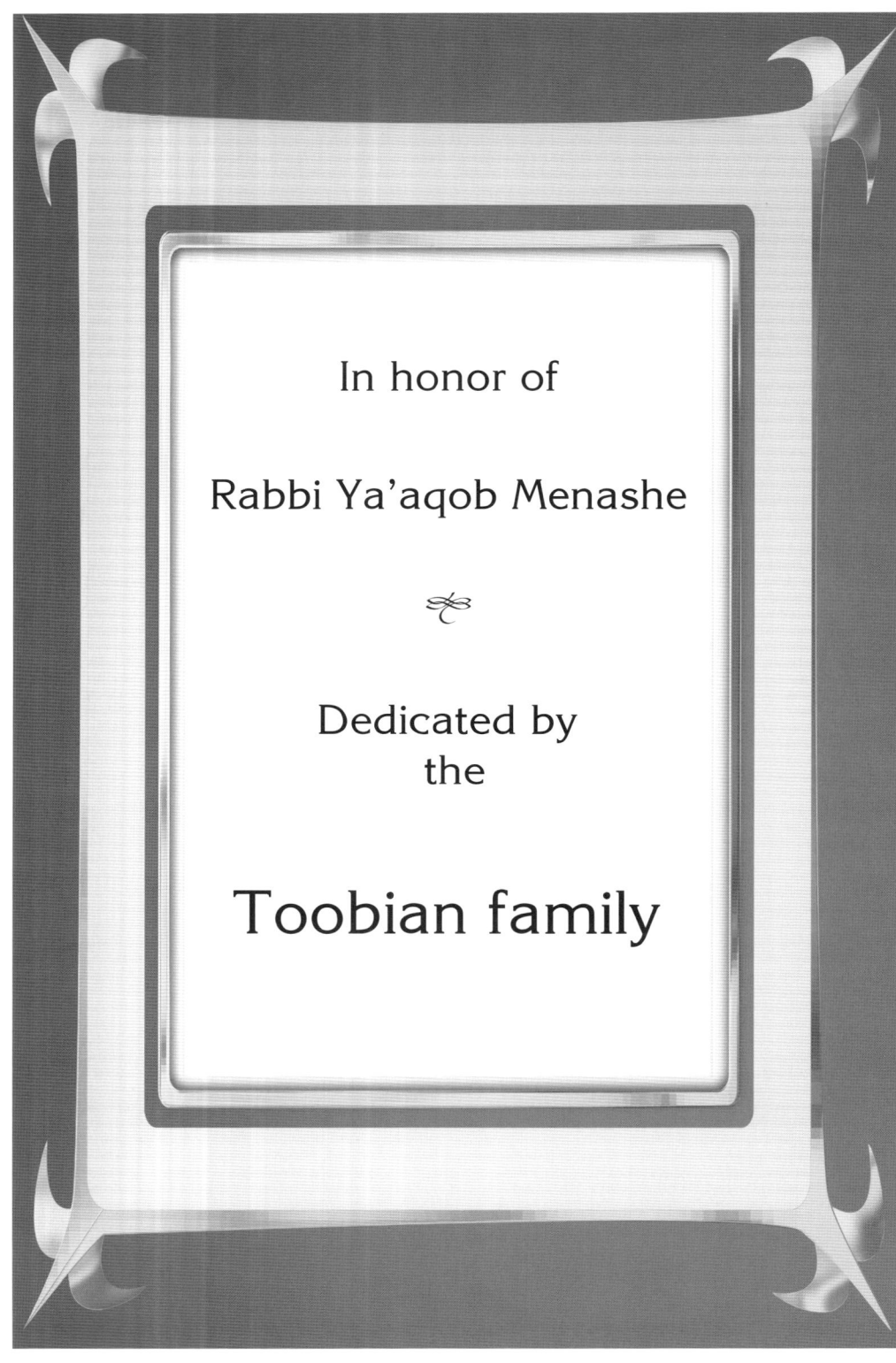

In memory of

Moshe Ben Yaakov

Pari Bat Saltanat

Yosef Ben Baba

Saltanat Bat Yahya

Houshang Ben Yosef

Yitzhak Ben David

ע״ה

Dedicated by

Mr. & Mrs. Parviz Lavi

In Honor of

Rabbi Dovid Shapiro

Rosh Yeshiva
The Maimonides School
Brookline, MA

Dedicated by

Drs. Meira & Peter
Pernicone

In honor of

Rabbi and Rabbanith Menashe

Dedicated by

The Ghermezian family

In honor of

Hakham Ya'aqob &
Rabbanith Ruth
Menashe

Dedicated by

The Mottahedeh Family

In memory of

Najia Muallem Bath Chahla

Dedicated by

Abe & Rita Lerner

For the blessings and success of

Elimelech & Susan
Goldstein

and family

In memory of
Avraham Ben Haiim
and
Rachel Bat Yehuda
'a"h

Dedicated by
Mr. & Mrs. Hertsel
Akhavan

In memory of
Gurjiyah and
Nissim Sheena
'a"h

Dedicated by
The Sheena
family

In memory of

Shemuel Ben
Aharon
Baradaran
'a"h

In memory of

Ezra Ben Naima
'a"h

Dedicated by
Roni Mualem

In memory of

Aharon Ben Pinhas

'a"h

2nd Shebat, 5764 (תשס"ד)

Dedicated by

The Rayhanian Family

Johnny & Edwina Khedouri

In memory of

Yehudah Ben Ephraim Fattal, 'a"h

Dedicated by

Leah & Fredy Menahem & Ephraim Iny

לע"נ

ראובן בן דוד
מוצפי בן סביחה
יוסף בן גורג'יה

ע"ה

In memory of

Mordechai Ben Adina
Hiski Ben Sara
Avraham Ben Heftzi
Sara Bat Zulaicha
Estam Bat Tuvia
Abo Ben Beluria
Adina Bat Yeshou

Dedicated by

Mierov David Nisan
Itzhak Mirzayev

Leiluy Neshamot

Serach Bat Eliezer
Nomi Bat Alta Leah
Shem Tov Ben Benyahu

May each soul soar up to Hashem! Amen! May Hashem save us from the hands of our enemies. Amen!

Anonymous

In memory of
David Ben Moshe
'a"h

Dedicated by
Mr. & Mrs. Farhad Azizzadeh

For the success and well-being of our dear children
Debbie, Lisa & Jennifer

Dedicated by
Mr. & Mrs. Rony Zelouf

In honor of
Meir & Dina Silverberg

Dedicated by
Yoni Dreisen

This dedication is for the following:
In memory of my father Harav Shimon ben Haghai and for the health of my mother
Goltaj Bat Khanom
and my daughters
Sarah, Rivkah and Esther
and Sholom for K'lal Israel and Jewish nation as a whole - we need Moshiach Now

Anonymous

For the Refuah Shelamah of Dora Bat Zilpa
Dedicated by Shoshana Masturov

In honor of Kamy Avraham Baradarian &
Jackie Nagila Baradarian

In memory of Janet Schapira.
Dedicated by Sami Sheena

In memory of Neria Ben Michael
Dedicated by Penina Spinrad

In memory of Naim Ben Haron Dallal & Haiim Ben
Hesqel Kattan

David & Maxine Yeroshalmi

Rubin & Irena Masturov

In memory Ezer Haim Ben Ester Benaim z"l

IMO our dear father Egal Shasho Ben Zakeyeh &
grandmother Chana Light Bat Pearl. Your legacies will
continue to shine forever. Ohev Shalom veRodeph
Shalom, Olam Hesed Yibaneh

The Sellers Depot, inc., Hiski & Avi
212 768 GOLD - thesellersdepot@ymail.com

סדר ההסכמות לפי תאריך כתיבתן

RABBI YAAKOV HILLEL
ROSH YESHIVAT
HEVRAT AHAVAT SHALOM
45 ARZEY HABIRA ST. JERUSALEM

יעקב משה הלל
ראש ישיבת
חברת אהבת שלום
רח' ארזי הבירה 45 ירושלים

בס"ד

21 Adar I 5771

Approbation and Congratulations

To my dear friend, Rabbi Yaakov Menashe,

Mazal tov! I was very glad to hear the good news of your son Menashe's upcoming wedding, and about your plans to publish a work of Torah in honor of the occasion.

I browsed through Volume Two of "Torah Minute Book" and was truly impressed by the concept, and by the wealth of valuable information made available to readers on the basis of "one single minute" of study.

You have succeeded in presenting basic, vital halachic rulings and information in the framework of minute-long study sessions. By studying your book, those who are not well versed in *halachah* can acquire essential knowledge of crucial daily *halachot*.

Of special significance is the source of these *halachot*: the works of the great Ben Ish Hai, whose rulings are definitive in the Sephardic community, and those of later rabbinic authorities who follow in his footsteps. Abiding by their teachings ensures proper fulfillment of our sacred obligations as Jews.

My blessings to you and your family on this joyous occasion. May you go from strength to strength and enjoy great success in all your praiseworthy endeavors for the benefit of our people. May it be His Will that you merit to "study and teach, observe and fulfill," bringing increased honor to Torah, and be blessed with success in all you do.

With best wishes,

R Y. Hillel

Rabbi Yaakov Hillel

יעקב משה הלל
YAAKOV MOSHE HILLEL
ישיבת חברת אהבת שלום
YESHIVAT HEVRAT AHAVAT SHALOM JERUSALEM

בס"ד

Yeshivat ישיבת
Mikdash Melech מקדש מלך

The Judah A. Safdeye Rabbinical College

Roshei Hayeshiva
Rabbi Haim Benoliel
Rabbi David Lopian

President
Mal Cohen

עש"ק ויקהל תשע"א
25 Feb. '11

לכבוד ידידי רב פעלים לתורה ותעודה
הרה"ג רבי יצחק מנשה שליט"א ריש מתיבתא
מדרש בן איש חי
שלום רב —

ראיתי גליונות מספרו אשר עומד בע"ה
להוציא לאור, הלכות ומנהגים על פי
בעל הבן איש חי זצוק"ל כת"ע –

ואמינא יישר חילך לאורייתא, ויצליח
במטרתו הקדושה לזכות הרבים ולקרב
הלבבות לאבינו שבשמים.

יהי"ר שיאריך מלאת כבוד הרב שליט"א על ממלכתו
בבריות גופא ונהורא מעליא מתוך נחת וישוב הדעת,
כלבבו הטוב וכברכת ידידו מכבדו ומוקירו,

הצב"י חיים בנוליאל

1326 Ocean Parkway, Brooklyn, NY 11230 ~ Phone 718.339.1090 ~ Fax 718.998.9321 ~ Mikdash@verizon.net

סדר ההסכמות לפי תאריך כתיבתן

סיני הלברשטאם

בלאאמו"ר הרה"צ רבי ישראל זצללה"ה
אבד"ק זמיגראד יע"א
ורב דק"ק "דברי חיים", ברוקלין, נוא יארק יצ"ו

בס"ד

כ"ד אדר א' ה'תשע"א

כבר איתמחי האי גברא רבא ונודע בשערים הוד תפארת גדולתו ה"ה כבוד הרב הגדול בתורה וביראה טהורה באר מלא פלג אוצר בלום מעוז ומגדול מוה"ר יעקב אליהו מנשה שליט"א בן ח"ר עבדא-ללה פרג' חיים ע"ה. מסדר השיטות בסדר נכון ובטוב טעם ודעת הפליא עצה הגדיל תושיה ברוב חכמה ותבונה, וחפץ ה' בידו יצלח.

שמח לבי ותעלוזנה כליותי לחזות פרי קדש הלולים, את ספרו הבהיר בשחקים של ידידי היקר. הצצתי בהגאות והביאורים והציונים וראיתי ציונים חשובים, הרבה מהם מוכרחים וקצתם מובנים, ועל כולם שהם נבנו בהשכל ודעת קולעים אל השערה.

מה נכבד היום בהגלות אור יקרות הספר היוצא לאור בצורה מתוקנת ומדוקדקת ובו דברי תורתם של רבותינו הקדושים ערוכים בתכלית היופי וההידור, הערות מאירות עינים ולב, בלולים ממקורות הראשונים והאחרונים ללבן ולזקק את ההלכה היומית. וניכר העמל הרב שהושקע בדבר למען יצא מתחת ידו דבר מתוקן להעלות על שולחן מלכים.

ולכן באתי לברכו על מלאכה נאה שעשה להגדיל תורה ולהאדירה, ויה"ר שחפץ ה' בידו יצלח שיתקבל מלאכתו הנאה בכל תפוצות ישראל, ויזכה להוציא לאור עולם שאר חיבורים נאים לזכות את הרבים.

כאות נפשו ונפש מוקירו
המצפה לרחמי שמים
כי לא כלו רחמיו

סדר ההסכמות לפי תאריך כתיבתן

בס"ד

שמואל אליהו
רב עיה"ק צפת ת"ו

Shmuel Eliyahu
Chief Rabbi of Safad
Israel

ראיתי את הספר שכתב חכם רבי יעקב מנשה שליט"א על פי פסקיו של מרן בעל הבן איש חי זיע"א ובאתי בדברים אלו לעודד ולחזק אתכם שאתם מפיצים תורתו של גאון עוזנו ותפארתנו בעל הבן איש חי. המחבר בין החכמה הפנימית לתורת הנגלה. קדושה, יראת שמים ומידות לפשט והלכה.

מרן רבי יוסף קארו זיע"א כינס לשולחן ערוך אחד את כל חכמי ישראל. ואף כי בימיו, לא היה אפשר לכנס אותם פיזית לשולחן אחד, הוא כינס אותם רוחנית, והיה זה ראשית כינוסם המעשי שעתיד להחזיר לנו את השראת השכינה. "אלוקים ניצב בעדת אל".

כינוס וחיבור מביא כוח ועוצמה, הרבה יותר מסך כל הפרטים. חז"ל למדו זאת מהפסוק שאומר: "ורדפו מכן חמשה מאה ומאה מכם רבבה ירדופו". ושאלו: וכי כך הוא החשבון? והלא לא היה צריך לומר אלא מאה מכם שני אלפים ירדופו? אלא אינו דומה מועטין העושין את התורה למרובים העושין את התורה".

רבי יוסף קארו - "המחבר" הראה לנו את נכונותו של הכלל הזה בחכמת הפשט. גאון עוזנו ותפארתנו בעל הבן איש חי הראה לנו את נכונות הכלל הזה בחיבור תורת האר"י ותורת השו"ע לספר הלכה אחד לשיטה אחת.

מו"ר אבא ז"ל, הריני כפרת משכבו, שהיה מקורב מאוד לבבא סאלי זיע"א סיפר כי זאת הייתה הסיבה שבגללה הייתה נוהגת המשפחה הקדושה הזהו לפסוק על פי דעת בעל הבן איש חי זיע"א. שחיבר בפסקיו את כלל תורת חכמי ישראל, הפשט והסוד שעסקו בלימודם והפצתם כל ימיהם, ביחד עם קדושה וטהרה, מידות ושכינה ששרתה בכל מעשי ידיהם.

התורה הזאת היא המשך לשיטתם של חכמי ספרד מדורי דורות ובראשם החיד"א זיע"א, שבעשרות ספריו השונים שילב את כל חלקי התורה בכל פסקי ההלכה שלו. תורה זו של בעל הבן איש חי וממשיכי דרכו מחברת אותנו גם לגדולי פוסקי ההלכה מדורי דורות.

תבורכו במפעלכם הגדול והחשוב שאתם עושים בארצות הברית. להגדיל תורה ולהאדירה. להרבות כבוד שמים וכבוד חכמים ינחלו. ויהי רצון שיתקיים בכם "יָפוּצוּ מַעְיְנֹתֶיךָ חוּצָה בָּרְחֹבוֹת פַּלְגֵי מָיִם". ונזכה לראות אתכם עם כל קהלכם כאן בארץ הקודש על אדמת הקודש. אמן כן יהי רצון.

בכבוד רב

[signature]

שמואל אליהו
רב עיה"ק צפת

צפת 13200, רח' הפלמ"ח, ת.ד. 1189, טלפון 04-6971633, 04-6972438,
פקס. 04-6921311 Aaa5252@gmail.com

Acknowledgements

With deep gratitude, I thank the Al-mighty for giving me the זכות, and for blessing me with the assistance of so many good people in my life, to enable me to prepare and publish this book.

I have been blessed with the help of many who have assisted me through life in different ways. First and foremost I owe a debt of eternal gratitude to my dear late father, ע"ה, my teacher, who led by example, imbuing in me, since I was very young, a love and respect for our holy religion and commitment to even the minutiae of the Minhagim it embodies. To my mother, מב"ת, I owe the many skills that she taught me that I need and use through life, with constant encouragement. I pray that הקב"ה will grant her long life, with health and happiness, to continue to guide me.

My wife shares in the זכות of this holy work, not only for the women's section that she presents in her pleasant manner, and the many Shi'urim she gives to women where she speaks to their hearts, but also for the constant support she gives me to fulfill the goal of reaching out to our Jewish brethren, near and far. Happy are her parents who brought her up.

My sister and my children have been involved in all my endeavors in serving the community, even when it was at the expense of their own interests. Each one, in their own unique way, has been a source of support and encouragement and has always been willing to assist in whatever way possible. I am grateful that the path of their forefathers is important to them.

The encouragement and guidance of the Gaon, Rabbi Sinai Halberstam, Shlit"a, from the early years till today, have been a source of motivation to continue the holy work that we have undertaken. I owe him a debt of gratitude.

I would like to say a special word of thanks to the many generous individuals who have supported us in all our endeavors, and those for whom this work was so important, that they generously donated, volunteered or otherwise contributed towards the project. Without your support this work would not have been possible.

May הקב"ה grant you all health, prosperity and much blessing, and may you merit to see all your descendants follow in the path of our Holy Torah, Amen.

YM
18th Adar II, 5771

Table of Contents

Parasha	***23***	
Shabbath	***69***	
Holidays	***99***	
Yom Tob		101
Nissan & Pesaḥ		105
Ḥol Hamo'ed		118
'Omer		120
Shabu'oth		123
The 22 days		127
Elul		131
Rosh Hashanah		133
Yom Kippur		139
Sukkoth		143
Hosha'na Rabba		148
Shemini 'Aṣereth / Simḥath Torah		149
Tu Bishbaṭ		150
Ḥanukkah		152
Adar / Purim		159
Rosh Ḥodesh		167
Fasts	***170***	
Synagogue	***175***	

Prayer	*183*
Ṣiṣṣith & Tefillin	*209*
Blessings	*219*
Eating	*241*
Life Cycle	*249*
Financial	*257*
Mussar	*263*
Various Torah Minutes	*273*
Pirqei Aboth	*287*
Women's Corner	*295*
Transliteration Table	*347*

Introduction

When we started our daily Torah minutes, providing A Torah Minute every day, we felt that the pearls of Torah wisdom and Halakhoth would be an important tool in the spreading of the Torah. Our motivation was to give an opportunity to any and every Jewish individual to be inspired spiritually daily, with an investment of just one minute of his or her time. What we could not anticipate was just how popular this would prove to be.

It is truly a blessing from Shamayim to see so many people depend on receiving the daily ATorahMinute email every day — people from all backgrounds and origins. Indeed, the challenge often is to ensure that they contain something for everybody. Publishing the Torah minutes in a book enables us to reach a wider audience.

The book, like the daily Torah minutes published on ATorahMinute.com, contains many pearls of wisdom gleaned from our Ḥakhamim who commented on the entire *Pardes* of the Torah. The Halakhoth cover a wide range of topics and often include laws not commonly talked about.

My main purpose in publishing this work, is to sanctify the Name of the Holy One Blessed Be He. There is always a fear when putting such a work together that errors will creep in the work which may cause others to stumble, Heaven forbid. I pray that Haqqadosh Barukh Hu will accept this work as a tool for the furthering of the study of the Holy Torah and not let me be the cause of others' transgressions, ח"ו.

It is hard to imagine that only one minute a day has already resulted in two fully-fledged books in a short period of time. There is a message here to all of us. Although one minute may seem insignificant to us, this book is clear proof that the opposite is, in fact, the case. Minutes make up days, which make up years, which make up a lifetime. Minutes, when spent learning, lead us to eternity.

A Torah Minute (volume 2):

A Treasury of Torah Gems and Practical Laws.

By Rabbi Ya'aqob Menashe

With a **Women's Corner**

by Rabbanith Ruth Menashe

מדרש בן איש חי
Midrash BEN ISH HAI™

1

פרשה

Parasha

Bereshith: Studying Torah with humility

When we finish reading the last portion of the Torah (Wezoth Habberakha) on Simḥath Torah, we begin reading Bereshith immediately, so that the Torah will be continuous, with no interruption. The Torah, which was the blueprint for the Creation of the world, is also the blueprint for our lives as Jews and it is only by delving into it constantly that we can hope to have even a small understanding of it.

Just the first word in the Torah, Bereshith, has a myriad of explanations. When we consider that the Torah contains close to 80,000 words, we realize the colossal wealth of information it holds for those who seek it.

One explanation given to us by Rabbenu the Ḥida, 'a"h, on the word Bereshith, which is made up of two words which mean in the beginning or at first, is that the Torah was given to the Jewish people because of their humility. We know this because the word BeReshith has the same letters in Hebrew as the words BeShe-erith which means the Remnants (of Israel). From this we see that the Torah was given to the Jewish people who are called Reshith (the first) on account of the fact that they are humble as in She-erith (remnants).

It is also a hint to us that if we wish to understand the depths of the Torah it must be done BeShe-erith, in humility.

(See Naḥal Qedumim, Bereshith)

Bereshith: Shabbath is the spiritual soul of the world

In the Parasha of Bereshith we read that G-d rested on the Seventh day and blessed it and sanctified it.

The Alshikh Haqqadosh mentions that anything physical that is devoid of a spiritual dimension will surely perish. A perfect example is a human being who cannot survive once the spiritual soul leaves him. This is true of all that G-d created in this world.

The world that G-d created was purely physical and would, therefore, have not been able to exist. But when the Holy One Blessed Be He, imbued the abundance of holiness and blessing of the holy Shabbath into the world, it now had its required element of spirituality to permit it to survive. As it says in Ki Thissa: *Shabath Wayinnafash* (He ceased from work and was rested [lit. and obtained a soul]).

The world, at first, was like a body lacking a soul. But what gave it a soul and the ability to exist was the Shabbath, which gave abundance and holiness to everything that was created.

(See Rabbenu Moshe Alshikh, Parashath Bereshith)

Parashath Nowaḥ: Why did Noah not pray to save his generation?

Rabbenu Beḥayye (Baḥya) states that the question begging to be asked, is why didn't Noah, who is described by the Torah as being righteous, pray on behalf of the people of his generation to save them. We see that Abraham Abinu 'a"h, prayed repeatedly on behalf of the wicked people of Sedom (Sodom). Indeed, we see that the Prophets and others prayed on behalf of their generations.

The answer is that Noah was not remiss in not praying for the people of his generation. Rather, it was because Noah understood that for the world to exist there must be at least 10 righteous people, as Ḥazal (our Rabbis of Blessed memory) tell us. Indeed, G-d would not have brought the Mabbul (the great flood) on the earth had there been ten righteous individuals.

In fact, the only people permitted to enter the Ark were Noah and his family, who were a total of only eight. As a matter of fact, Abraham Abinu also stopped praying to G-d when he realized that there were not ten righteous people in Sedom. Not only that, but the people in Noah's time had been given 120 years warning to change their ways (which was the time it took to build the Ark), but paid no heed.

(See Rabbenu Beḥayye on the Torah, 6:14)

Lekha Lekha: the righteous are called Holekh

Angels are called 'Omdim (standing still) because they do not have a Yeṣer Hara' (evil inclination) which pulls them down the wrong path. A righteous individual (Ṣaddiq), on the other hand, is called Holekh (one who goes), and constantly ascends from one level to the next.

The fact that G-d tells Abraham Abinu,'a"h, Lekh Lekha (go), means that He is saying to him: "You have the title of Lekh, not 'Omed". This means that G-d is informing Abraham Abinu that he still has not reached his highest level of perfection but rather, must keep going down his long path towards his ultimate goal.

It is best illustrated by a parable about a man who dreamt that the king was climbing a ladder which had 1000 rungs, but only reached the 500th rung. The man went and related his dream to the king who gave him 500 gold coins.

When the man's neighbor's wife heard this she told her husband to go and tell the king that he dreamt the king reached the 1000th rung. The king would surely be delighted and reward him with 1000 gold coins. But when the man told the king about his supposed dream the king had him physically thrown out of the palace. The reason was that the dream indicated that the king had reached the top of the ladder of his career and would, perforce, only have the option of descending. However, the dream showing that he was only half way up the ladder indicated that he was only half way up to the power and position that he would eventually have.

(See 'Od Yoseph Ḥai Derashoth, Parashath Lekh Lekha)

Wayyera: Changing the truth for peace

In the Parasha of Wayyera Sara Immenu says וַאדֹנִי זָקֵן *"... and my husband is old"*. When G-d repeats this to Abraham Abinu, He says "Sara says... and I (Sara) am old". It says in the

Gemara that peace is so dear to G-d that He even made a change for it (when He changed what Sara Immenu said).

The Ben Ish Ḥai states in 'Od Yoseph Ḥai, that there are two specific areas where we must also make a change. One area is in a case of life and death. He gives an example of someone who is critically ill, and you see in his face that it appears to be the end. If he asks you what you see and you tell him the truth, if it will affect him so badly that it will hasten his death, G-d forbid, then you must not tell him the truth but must give him hope. As a result you will give him the possibility of living longer, whereas by telling him that it looks to you that there is no hope, you may be guilty of causing his death prematurely, Heaven forbid.

The second area is for the sake of making peace between two people. For instance, if A is speaking to B and curses C, if C asks B, "What did A say about me?", B must push away the truth and say something that will not inflame C.

This does not mean that we can change more than is absolutely necessary, nor may we make or extend the changes simply because it is to our personal advantage to do so. Lying, by definition, is forbidden by the Jewish religion and only specifically to create peace and harmony must we change what is absolutely necessary to ensure peace.

(See Wayyera, ch 18, vs 12-13. Baba Meṣia 87a. 'Od Yoseph Ḥai Derashoth, Parashath Shofṭim)

Wayyera: Getting help with humility

It says in Parashath Wayyera, וַיִּשָּׂא עֵינָיו וַיַּרְא וְהִנֵּה שְׁלֹשָׁה אֲנָשִׁים נִצָּבִים עָלָיו *Wayyissa 'Einaw Wayyar, Wehinnei Shelosha*

Anashim Niṣabim 'Alaw (And he lifted his eyes and saw, and behold, three men were standing over him).

This gives us a hint that if a person looks at those who are below him, it will be impossible for him to be humble, because he will always see that he is superior to the other in one or more areas and will become arrogant. If, however, he looks only at people who are greater or more important than he is, he will be able to be humble because he will see that he is lacking in one or more areas vis-a-vis the others.

We are told that when a person does a Miṣwah (commandment) that one of the righteous people from early times was very particular about, a spark from that righteous person enters him and assists him in the performance of that Miṣwah.

We can now explain the verse "And he lifted his eyes and saw", as telling us that we should look at those who are greater than we are and, as a result, we will surely become humble. The words "And behold three men were standing over him" refers to the three Ṣaddiqim (righteous) who were known for their humility, Abraham Abinu (our father Abraham), Moshe Rabbenu and Dawid Hammelekh (King David), 'a"h. When a person starts going down the path of humility, these three Ṣaddiqim stand over him to assist him.

(See Benayahu, Parashath Wayyera)

Ḥayyei Sara: Why did Eliezer have to swear and not Isaac?

In the Parasha of Ḥayyei Sara it says: וְאַבְרָהָם זָקֵן בָּא בַּיָּמִים וַה׳ בֵּרַךְ אֶת־אַבְרָהָם בַּכֹּל: *And Abraham was old, advanced in years, and G-d blessed Abraham with everything*. Rabbenu Baḥya says that Abraham Abinu (the Patriarch Abraham), 'a"h, was blessed with much, including a long life. However, he had not yet been blessed with grandchildren, which is something he desired very much. He, therefore, made his servant Eli'ezer swear that he would find an appropriate wife for his son Isaac (Yiṣḥaq Abinu, 'a"h).

The reason for requiring an oath from him was that Abraham Abinu was afraid that he might die before Eli'ezer accomplished his task. By making Eli'ezer swear, he felt that Eli'ezer would fulfill the task and he knew that his son Yiṣḥaq would always listen to Eli'ezer and would, therefore, marry the girl.

The question is, why did Abraham Abinu not make Yiṣḥaq Abinu swear instead? The answer is that he was concerned that if he did not place the servant Eli'ezer under an oath, he would find numerous excuses as to why he could not go get a suitable wife for Yiṣḥaq Abinu. He made Eli'ezer swear, therefore, to ensure that he would take the responsibility seriously and find a wife for his son Yiṣḥaq, who in turn would, as we mentioned, do Eliezer's bidding and would have no need to swear also.

(See Rabbenu Baḥya on the Torah, Ḥayyei Sara)

Toldoth: Why did Isaac want to bless Esau?

Yiṣḥaq Abinu (Isaac) 'a"h, asks 'Esaw (Esau) to bring him delicacies, and says: בַּעֲבוּר תְּבָרֶכְךָ נַפְשִׁי *Ba'abur Tebarekhekha Nafshi* (so that my soul will bless you).

People often question what Yiṣḥaq Abinu's (Isaac's) intention was when he blessed Esau. Didn't he know who Esau really was? Did Esau really manage to fool him? Why else would Yiṣḥaq Abinu, 'a"h, wish to bless him?

According to Rabbenu Ḥayyim Wiṭṭal, z"l, his intention in blessing Esau was to correct his ways and to bring him into the path of holiness, and to bestow blessings upon him so that he would become a G-d fearing individual and do Teshubah (repentance).

Rabbenu Ḥayyim Wiṭṭal, z"l, adds that G-d's will, however, was that only Ya'aqob Abinu (Jacob) would be blessed and that Esau would remain the way he was. That is why Ya'aqob Abinu, 'a"h, was the one to receive the blessings.

(See Midbar Qadmuth, Yiṣḥaq)

Wayyeṣe: Why did Jacob need to make a vow?

וַיִּדַּר יַעֲקֹב נֶדֶר לֵאמֹר *Wayyiddar Ya'aqob Neder Lemor* (and Jacob made a vow saying). Ya'aqob Abinu, 'a"h, was in distress and made a vow that if G-d would take care of him, he would give a tithe, from everything he receives, to G-d.

What was the necessity to make a Neder (vow)? G-d had already promised Ya'aqob Abinu, 'a"h, in his dream, that he would take care of him in every respect. Also, apart from not being necessary, why did Ya'aqob Abinu have to be in distress? He was certainly not deserving of it.

This was all done for the needs of his future generations. Whenever they are in distress and make a Neder and turn to go G-d, they will be told "Whoever answered your father Ya'aqob, will answer you". As it says in the Midrash, when a woman has a difficult time giving birth we say to her, "...Whoever answered your mother at the time of her hardship will answer you in your time of hardship".

So too, the only purpose in Ya'aqob Abinu, 'a"h, making the Neder is so that it will be said to his future generations when they are undergoing difficulties, "Whoever answered your father Ya'aqob, will answer you".

(See Ben Ish Ḥai Derashoth, Wayyeṣe)

Wayyishlaḥ: Ya'aqob and 'Esaw (Esau) - Mordekhai and Haman

Ya'aqob Abinu, 'a"h, (Jacob) says to G-d, הַצִּילֵנִי נָא מִיַּד אָחִי *Haṣileni Na Miyyad Aḥi* (please save me from the hand of my brother, from the hand of Esau). The acronym (first letter of each) of the first three words forms the name Haman. (Haman was a descendent of Esau).

This hints to us that Ya'aqob Abinu, 'a"h, prayed to be saved from the affliction of Haman. The Gurei HaAri say that Mordekhai's soul had a spark of Ya'aqob Abinu, 'a"h. It was, of course, Mordekhai who was behind the reversal of Haman's wicked intentions against the Jewish people.

The Ḥida, 'a"h, tells us that the Gemaṭria of the the last letters of each of the three words is 15. This hints at the fifteen years that the three Patriarchs (Aboth) studied Torah together. The fact that the three Patriarchs studied together helps the world exist. In addition, it is a hint, that in this merit, Ya'aqob Abinu, 'a"h, would be saved from the hands of the wicked Esau.

(See Naḥal Qedumim)

Wayyesheb: Joseph represents all the Jewish people

אֵלֶּה | תֹּלְדוֹת יַעֲקֹב יוֹסֵף *Elleh Toldoth Ya'aqob, Yosef* (these are the generations of Jacob, Joseph). When the Torah says these are the generations of Ya'aqob, it would seem appropriate to then list all his sons. Instead the Torah only mentions Yoseph. The simple meaning is that all the brothers' characteristics were included in Yoseph Haṣṣaddiq, 'a"h.

We know that Joseph was Ya'aqob Abinu's, 'a"h, favorite son and even though Reuben was acually the first born, Joseph was the one who carried the distinction of being the son of Ya'aqob Abinu. According to the Midrash, Yoseph Haṣṣaddiq is compared to Ya'aqob Abinu, 'a"h, because they were alike. Whatever befell Ya'aqob Abinu, also befell Joseph. For instance, just like Ya'aqob Abinu, 'a"h, was chased away by his brother 'Esaw (Esau) who wished to kill him, so too Yoseph Haṣṣaddiq was chased away by his brothers. Just as Ya'aaqob Abinu was elevated through a dream (of the ladder) so too Yoseph was elevated by his dream.

When the Torah states that Joseph was *Ben Zequnim Hu Lo* (the son of his old age), it is referring to the fact that they looked similar and does not mean that Joseph was the youngest, because, in fact, Benyamin (Benjamin) was six years younger than Yoseph Haṣṣaddiq, 'a"h.

(See Rabbenu Beḥayye, 37: 2)

Miqqeṣ: It was part of G-d's master plan

לֹא־אַתֶּ֞ם שְׁלַחְתֶּ֤ם אֹתִי֙ הֵ֔נָּה כִּ֖י הָאֱ' *Lo Attem Shelaḥtem Othi Henna, Ki HaElokim* (It was not you who sent me here, but G-d [Bereshith 45:8]).

If people trouble someone or cause him pain, even if later on he overcomes the pain and even becomes very important, nevertheless, he still remembers the pain and the anguish that was caused him. Thinking about it still causes him sadness and feelings of anger towards those who were responsible.

Even if he is a righteous person who does not bear a grudge, nevertheless, he is still a human being and it is not possible for him to feel no anger or pain. However, if it was precisely the anguish that was the catalyst for his success, then obviously he will not remember the pain. On the contrary, since he realizes that it was for his own good, it causes him joy.

This is exactly what happened to Yoseph Haṣṣaddiq, 'a"h, (Joseph). G-d caused the wrongs that his brothers intended to do to him to be the launching pad for his success and rise to greatness. Joseph's happiness at achieving greatness was less, in fact, than the happiness he felt because he was saved from bearing a grudge or feeling sad over the past. Had he not achieved success he knew he might have failed in this area since he was, after all, a human being.

(See Benayahu, Parashath Miqqeṣ)

Wayyiggash: When praise is really an insult

Yehudah (Judah) says to Yoseph (Joseph), not knowing that he is his brother, כִּ֥י כָמ֖וֹךָ כְּפַרְעֹֽה *Ki Khamokha KePhar'oh* (For you are like Pharaoh). He appears to be praising him but, sometimes, even though it seems that someone is being praised, those who understand realize that it is an insult.

There is a story about a man who was devoid of any wisdom and went to an important Ḥakham requesting that he write a letter of recommendation. The man was travelling to another city and wanted to show this letter full of his praises, to the Rabbi of the other city, so that he would be received there with much honor and respect.

The Rabbi wrote the following:"You must know that had the bearer of this letter lived at the time of the prophet Elisha, the oil would not have stopped flowing". The man was deliriously happy that the Ḥakham had written such praises about him, that the oil would not have stopped flowing.

When he arrived at his destination, he rushed to give the letter to the Rabbi who understood the meaning immediately. In this city, there were seven levels of hospitality, those who were at the lowest level were hosted at the house of the Shammash of the Synagogue. He sent the man to the Shammash's house to be hosted.

The man was confused. How could the Rabbi receive such a letter full of praise and send him to the house of the Shammash? He asked the Shammash to explain to him the meaning of what transpired. The Shammash explained that the oil at the time of the prophet Elisha', 'a"h, did not stop flowing as long as there were still empty vessels. This man was considered to be such an empty vessel, that had he lived at the time of the prophet Elisha, the oil would never have stopped flowing.

Yehudah, in saying to Yoseph, You are just like Pharaoh, was not saying how great he was, but rather, just as Pharaoh lies, so do you.

(See 'Od Yoseph Ḥai, Parashath Wayyiggash)

Wayḥi: Hoping for salvation above and beyond the course of Nature

In his blessing to his son Dan, Ya'aqob Abinu (our father Jacob) 'a"h says: לִישׁוּעָתְךָ קִוִּיתִי ה׳: *Lishu'athkha Qiwwithi H'* (for Your salvation have I hoped, O G-d [Bereshith 49:18]).

Ḥakham Yoseph Ḥayyim, 'a"h, says that there are two different types of salvation, natural and miraculous. As long as the average person can be saved from his trials and tribulations in a natural way, G-d will not perform miracles for him. However, that is not the case for the righteous. They receive both kinds of salvation.

Someone who is going through a difficult period and hopes for salvation in a natural way, does not receive any reward or praise for his hopes. This is because it is the ordinary course of nature for circumstances to change and is not something extraordinary. If, on the other hand, he hopes for salvation in a way that is beyond the norms of nature, it is considered praiseworthy. This is because it shows that he has the important requirement of Emunah (faith), because he fully believes in G-d's ability to do that which is above nature.

As the prophet Habbaquq stated, "The righteous one shall live by his faith". So when it says For Your Salvation have I hoped O L-rd, it means that I did not hope for the natural occurence which the Holy Name Elokim symbolizes, but rather,

I hoped for the miraculous salvation which is connected with the Holy name Hashem, which is the one used in this Pasuq.

(See Sefer Benayahu on the Torah, Parashath Wayḥi, Habbaquq 2: 4)

Shemoth: The Strategy of the Egyptians

וְכַאֲשֶׁר֙ יְעַנּ֣וּ אֹת֔וֹ כֵּ֥ן יִרְבֶּ֖ה *Wekha-asher Ye'annu Otham Ken Yirbeh*, (As much as they would afflict them, so would they increase [Shemoth 1:12]). Depending on the level of the affliction, the numbers of the Children of Israel increased proportionately. Through this, the Egyptians recognized that this was not a natural act but emanated from G-d, because they were the Children of Israel who came from a Holy source. The Egyptians, therefore, were fearful of retribution.

As a result, they changed their strategy from a heavy hand to Parekh (Peh Rakh) – they spoke with soft words. There was no doubt in their minds that when the Jewish nation cling to G-d their intervention is Divine and not natural. That is why it says "they were disgusted because of the Children of Israel" – meaning, because they merited to be called by the term Children of Israel which is the term used when they cleave to their G-d.

The use of Peh Rakh was in order to cause them to willingly follow the wrong path, to sin and lose Divine intervention. This is the same tactic used by 'Esaw (Esau) against his brother Jacob (Ya'aqob Abinu, 'a"h), and the same one used by our enemies at different times in our history.

We must be aware of this tactic and never fall into the trap of our enemies, but rather, constantly cleave to the Holy One Blessed be He and the path He has laid out for us in His holy Torah. And those who would do us harm must also realize that while, in the short term, they might succeed in causing pain (Heaven forbid), in the long run their wicked plans invariably backfire just as they have throughout history. We must always remember that we are the Children of Israel who come from a Holy source as we await the coming of Mashiyaḥ Ṣidqenu speedily in our days, Amen.

(See Alshikh, Shemoth 1: 12)

Wa-era: Why did G-d punish the Egyptians if He hardened Pharaoh's heart?

It says in Parashath Wa-era: וַאֲנִי אַקְשֶׁה אֶת־לֵב פַּרְעֹה *Wa-ani Aqshei Eth Leb Par'oh* (and I will harden Pharaoh's heart [Shemoth 7:3]). Many people ask if G-d was the One who hardened Pharaoh's heart, why did He bring so many plagues upon him if it wasn't his fault? We know that G-d is righteous and will not do any injustice.

One of the explanations is given by Rabbenu Baḥya who states that Pharaoh was already wicked and a sinner. For instance, when he saw that the Children of Israel were multiplying so rapidly, he gave the order to have the newborn boys killed. Since he was wicked and this wickedness was his own doing (as was the case with his people), it was appropriate that the right to repent not be given him. That is why the Holy One Blessed Be He put it into his heart not to allow them to leave, because had the Egyptians repented, G-d would not have been able to punish them.

(See Rabbenu Baḥya, Parashath Wa-era)

Bo: Why did the sun shine on the night we left Egypt?

'לֵיל שִׁמֻּרִים הוּא לַה' *Leil Shimurim Hu LaShem'* (it is a night of watching for G-d [Shemoth 12:42]).

It says in the holy Zohar that the light on the night we left Egypt was like a day in the month of Tammuz. Why is it that G-d illuminated that particular night? The answer is that the sun came to disprove three of the statements made by scorners.

1. From the sun we see that there is something or someone that causes it to move. It can't just happen by itself. There clearly was a Creator that was behind it.

2. There are those who claim that G-d does not watch over individuals in this world. Perhaps he created the world, but is not involved with its people (Hashgaḥa Peraṭith). However, the fact that the sun gives its light to the earth and its inhabitants, is a repudiation of that claim.

3. Those who say that there must be two different forces, one that is in charge of the good and the other is in charge of the bad, are proven wrong by the sun. The sun can dry that which is wet and melt something that is hard, thereby proving that two opposite actions can emanate from the same source.

That is why, G-d caused the sun to shine at night on the night of Pesaḥ (Passover), so that there would be no darkness. From this everyone can learn that He is G-d in Heaven and earth and there is none other.

(See Penei Dawid)

Yithro: What Yithro understood that others didn't

וַיִּשְׁמַע יִתְרוֹ כֹהֵן מִדְיָן חֹתֵן מֹשֶׁה אֵת כָּל־אֲשֶׁר עָשָׂה אֱ׳ לְמֹשֶׁה וּלְיִשְׂרָאֵל עַמּוֹ *Wayishma' Yithro Khohen Midian Ḥothen Moshe Eth Kol Asher 'Asah Eloqim Le Moshe UlYisrael 'Ammo* (Jethro, the priest of Midian, the father-in-law of Moses, heard everything that G-d did to Moses and His people Israel [Shemoth 18:1]).

Why did it specifically say that Yithro heard when we know that the majority of the the world heard? Additionally, the word Kol (all) seems unnecessary. The meaning would have been clear without it.

It comes to teach us that the other nations did not fully comprehend all the plagues that occurred, nor did they understand the order in which they took place. Whoever heard each Makkah (plague) separately, even though he would understand the greatness of G-d, might still mistakenly have given importance to the Sar (protecting angel) of Egypt, because the destruction in each plague was not complete. For instance, in the Makkah of Deber (pestilence), not all the animals died. In the Makkah of Barad (hail), not all the livestock and vegetation perished. This might have caused people to think that it was a result of the power of the Sar of Egypt.

One who would consider all the plagues together, however, would understand that each one was connected to the other in a specific order. For example, the animals that were saved in Makkath 'Arob (the plague of the wild animals) were killed in the following plague (Deber). And whichever was saved from the Deber was killed in the Barad (hail).

Wayishma' Yithro means that Yithro had a deeper understanding than did the others, and knew everything that took place and understood the order in which they occurred. That is why is says he heard (as in understood), and it adds the word Kol (all), to tell us that he comprehended everything.

(See 'Od Yoseph Ḥai, Parashath Yithro)

Mishpaṭim/Sheqalim: Why proclaim the Sheqel in Adar

וְהָיָה֙ כִּֽי־יִצְעַ֣ק אֵלַ֔י וְשָׁמַעְתִּ֖י כִּֽי־חַנּ֥וּן אָֽנִי׃ *Wehaya Ki Yiṣ'aq Elai weshama'ti Ki Ḥannun Ani* (And it shall come to pass when you cry out unto me, I shall hear, because I am compassionate [Shemoth 22:26]).

Prayer must be said in happiness. If a person prays with joy, his prayer is accepted willingly (Beraṣon). Whenever the term Wehaya is used, it denotes happiness. That is why when it says "And it shall come to pass (Wehaya) when you cry out to me", we learn that when a person cries out to G-d in prayer, his prayers will be accepted.

This is why Razal said that on the first of Adar a proclamation is made concerning the giving of the half Sheqel (Maḥaṣith Hasheqel) for the Beth Hamiqdash (Temple). Maran z"l brought down as Halakha in the Shulḥan 'Arukh, *Mishenikhnas Adar, Marbin Besimḥa* (from when Adar starts, we increase our happiness). Since every Miṣwah (commandment) performed with happiness is accepted more readily, it is most important to perform the commandment of the Maḥaṣith Hasheqel (half Sheqel) in the month of Adar when the Jewish people increase their happiness. That is why the proclamation of the Sheqalim is made on the first of Adar.

(See Addereth Eliyahu, Parashath Mishpaṭim)

Terumah: Charity can change the negative into positive.

G-d tells the Children of Israel וְיִקְחוּ־לִי תְּרוּמָה *Weyiqḥu Li Terumah* (and you shall take a donation for Me [Shemoth 25:2]). Why does it specifically use the term Terumah, which implies that it is a fixed amount separated from a larger quantity, as opposed to Nedabah which is a donation that has no fixed amount?

The power of charity (Ṣedaqa) is that it changes something negative into positive. It is not that the bad disappears and is then replaced by good, but rather, the bad remains, but instead of harming, does good to the person. An example of this is King Ahashwerosh, who was known to be a hater of the Jewish people. Despite this, G-d did not kill him or otherwise do away with him, but rather, caused the salvation of the Jewish people to come via him.

This is the power of charity. If there was a decree that there should be Neghef (a plague), the letters of the word become switched to read Gefen (vine). Similarly Negha' (disease) becomes 'Onegh (a delight). Now we can uderstand the use of the word Terumah. Switching the order of the letters creates the word Temurah which means 'to exchange', which hints at the great power that the giving of charity has, that it changes the bad into something positive.

(See 'Od Yoseph Ḥai, Derashoth, Parashath Terumah)

Teṣawweh: The final Temple will stand forever

וְיִקְחוּ אֵלֶיךָ שֶׁמֶן זַיִת זָךְ כָּתִית לַמָּאוֹר לְהַעֲלֹת נֵר תָּמִיד *And they shall take for you pure olive oil, pressed for the illumination (Kathith Lammaor), to kindle the light perpetually.*

The Torah is likened to oil. Through the study of the Torah, Benei Yisrael (the Children of Israel) will merit the Geullah (redemption). The word Kathith (pressed) hints at the two Temples. The Gemaṭria (numerical value) of the word Kathith is 830, which is the total amount of years that the two Temples stood. The first stood for 410 years and the second stood for 420 years.

Through the study of the Torah they will be rebuilt and become Lammaor (for illumination). However, unlike the first two Temples which were destroyed, the third Beth Hamiqdash (Temple) will stand forever. A hint to this is seen in the words Leha'aloth Ner Tamid - to kindle the light 'perpetually'.

(See Kether Ṣaddiq, Parashath Teṣawweh)

Wayyaqhel/Pequdei: What did Moshe Rabbenu's blessing mean?

Beṣalel... did everything that G-d commanded Moshe. Even things that Moshe Rabbenu, 'a"h, (Moses) had not conveyed to Beṣalel, he still did intuitively and, therefore, Moshe Rabbenu blessed him and those who were involved in the building of the Mishkan.

What did Moshe Rabbenu bless them with? They were already physically strong, wise and wealthy. He said to them: "May it be G-d's will that the Shekhinah (G-d's Holy Presence) will rest upon the works of your hands". What did this mean?

The following parable in the Gemara of Ta'anith explains it. It says:

To what may this be compared? To a man who was travelling in the desert. He was hungry, weary and thirsty. He came upon a tree whose fruits were sweet, whose shade was pleasant, and had a stream of water flowing beneath it. He partook of its fruits, drank the water, and rested beneath its shade. When he was ready to continue his journey he said to the tree: "O tree, what can I bless you with? If I would say to you, "May your fruits be sweet", they are sweet already, "May your shade be pleasant", it is already, "May a stream of water flow below you", the stream already flows below you. Therefore I bless you by saying "May it be His Will that all the shoots that come from you will be like you".

So too, in this case, they were already strong, wise and wealthy. Moshe Rabbenu, 'a"h, blessed them that just as the Shekhinah rested upon them, so too may it rest on the works of their hand, which were their children.

(See Kether Ṣaddiq, Parashath Pequdei)

Wayyiqra: How to bring G-d closer to us

אָדָם כִּי־יַקְרִיב מִכֶּם קָרְבָּן לַה׳ *When a man from among you (Mikkem) brings an offering (Yaqrib) to G-d* (Wayyiqra 1:2). The word Mikkem (from among you) seems superfluous. The following parable will give us an insight to better understand this Pasuq (verse).

A man went to a store to buy a mirror. The store owner showed him a beautiful one but the customer glanced at it and immediately said that he was not interested. When asked why, he responded that there was a very odd picture in it. He saw an image of a man who was disheveled, with messy clothes and dirt on his face. That was because he saw his own reflection. The storekeeper said to him, "You foolish man. The 'picture' that you see is a reflection of yourself. If you go and tidy yourself up, the picture will improve accordingly".

The moral is that the way that G-d deals with us is the way that we deal with Him. If we follow His instructions and go down the right path, He deals with us accordingly. If, however, we do not do that which He asks, then G-d does not deal with us the way we wish. This is an explanation of the verse *Ani Ledodi Wedodi Li* (I am for my beloved and my beloved is for me) the amount of attachment that I have to G-d is the attachment that G-d has to me.

We can now read our verse, "When a man wishes to bring himself closer (Yaqrib) to G-d , the extent to which G-d comes close to him comes 'from you' (Mikkem)". There is a direct correlation between how close you come to G-d and how close He comes to you.

(See 'Od Yoseph Ḥai, Parashath Wayyiqra)

Parashath Ṣaw: Only studying Torah for its own sake

זֹאת תּוֹרַת הָעֹלָה הִוא הָעֹלָה עַל מוֹקְדָה *Zoth Torath Ha'Olah Hee Ha'Olah 'Al Moqdah* (This is the law [Torah] of the elevation offering [Wayyiqra 6:2]), this is the elevation offering on the fire). Why is the word 'Olah (elevation offering) mentioned twice?

There is a story in Ben Ish Ḥai Derashoth about a Ḥakham who once entered a Beth Midrash where the students were arguing points of Gemara with acuity and excitement. He realized that their studies were not Lishmah̲ (for the sake of learning) but for the purpose of winning the argument. So he said to them, "I see that this Beth Midrash is filled with Torah". The students were delighted because they thought that he was praising them.

When he saw that they did not understand his meaning he said, "You should know that when Torah is learned for its own sake, it goes immediately up to Heaven. That is why Torah is referred to as fire, because the nature of fire is to constantly rise. But if the learning is not done for the sake of the Torah then it remains in the Beth Midrash. That is why I stated that this Beth Midrash is full of Torah". The students were embarrassed by his words.

We can translate the Pasuq verse above as follows: *Zoth Torath Ha'Olah* can be translated as meaning "which type of Torah is the most elevated (choicest)?" The answer is *Hee Ha'Olah*, which can be read to mean "the one that rises and does not remain below". From this we see how important it is to study Torah Lishmah̲ (for its own sake) and not for any ulterior motive, whatever it may be.

(See Ben Ish Ḥai Derashoth, Parashath Ṣaw)

Shemini and Aboth 1: forbidden foods block the heart

In Pirqei Aboth (Ethics of the Fathers) Yose Ben Yoḥanan says, "Let your home be open wide". One's body is also called a home (Bayith) and like a home a body has several gates/openings such as the eyes, ears and mouth. A person should always open them for a good purpose and shut them to prevent them for being used for any transgression.

In the Parasha of Shemini it says, "Do not contaminate yourself through [creeping creatures], lest you become contaminated through them". One of the gates of the body, as we mentioned, is the mouth. We must refrain from eating food which is forbidden because it contaminates us. The word used in the Hebrew for becoming contaminated is Weniṭmethem which is written here without an Aleph. This alludes to another word Ṭimṭum which means blockage.

The letter Aleph, which is missing, has a numerical value of 1, which alludes to the oneness of G-d. We learn from here that one who eats forbidden foods creates a blockage of the heart and the Shekhinah (G-d's Holy Presence) cannot rest on him.

(See Birkath Aboth 1, Mishnah 5. Penei Dawid, Shemini)

Tazriya'/Ṭaharoth: G-d gives us so we can give others

It says in Parashath Ṭaharoth (Meṣora') כִּי תָבֹאוּ אֶל־אֶרֶץ כְּנַעַן אֲשֶׁר אֲנִי נֹתֵן לָכֶם לַאֲחֻזָּה וְנָתַתִּי נֶגַע צָרַעַת בְּבֵית אֶרֶץ אֲחֻזַּתְכֶם׃ *When you arrive in the Land of Canaan that I am giving you as a possession, and I shall place the disease of Ṣara'ath (often translated as a form of leprosy) in a house in the land of your possession*. Rabbenu the Ḥida states that the phrase that I give to you as a possession sounds unnecessary. Additionally the phrase in a house in the land of your possession could be simply stated as in your house.

When G-d blesses a person with a home filled with only blessings as a possession, He does it to test the person to see if he will benefit others also with part of the blessings that he has received. Whatever a person gives to others is not taken from what is his, but from what was given to him from Heaven. That is why it says that I am giving you as a possession so that you should not think that it is your strength and capabilities that brought it to you. In addition, there is no room for selfishness, because the reason that G-d gives it to you is so that you can give to others.

If you are selfish and consider the possession to be yours, G-d will place the disease of Ṣara'ath in a house in the land of your possession, meaning, in the place that you consider to be exclusively your possession.

(See Wayyiqra, Parashath Ṭaharoth, 14: 34. Ḥomath Anakh, Ṭaharoth)

Aḥarei Moth: For the merit of the Torah, the Temple stood

It says in the Parasha of Aḥarei Moth, "With this (Be'Zoth') Aaron shall enter the sanctuary". This can be explained that in the merit of the Torah which is called Zoth, Aharon Hakkohen (Aaron the High Priest) was able to enter the Sanctuary. The word Bezoth has the numerical equivalent of 410 which comes to inform us that the first Temple would stand for 410 years and the Kohanim (who were the descendants of Aaron) would enter the sanctuary during that time.

If not for the merit of the Torah that they studied, the Temple would not have stood that long. Seven Bathei Dinim (High Courts) performed idolatry, yet G-d did not destroy the Temple. Once they stopped studying Torah, however, the Temple was destroyed. G-d was prepared to forgo the judgement for the idolatry but was not willing to overlook the lack of Torah study.

This explains why Ribbi Ḥananya Ben Teradyon says in Pirqei Aboth (Ethics of the Father), when two people sit together and speak words of Torah, the Shekhinah (G-d's holy Presence) rests between them.

(Alshikh on the Torah, Aḥarei Moth, 16: 3, Aboth 3: 3)

Emor: G-d is constantly giving

כִּֽי־תָבֹ֣אוּ אֶל־הָאָ֗רֶץ אֲשֶׁ֤ר אֲנִי֙ נֹתֵ֣ן לָכֶ֔ם וּקְצַרְתֶּ֖ם אֶת־קְצִירָ֑הּ *When you enter the Land that I am giving you, and you shall reap its harvest* (Wayyiqra 23:9).

Nothing causes a person to become arrogant and sin more than being blessed with an abundance of everything. This abundance causes people to think that it was their own wisdom and capabilities that brought them their success. This shows a lack of gratitude to the Creator for His blessings which, in turn, causes people to go astray and not follow G-d.

Just like a father wishes to direct his son in the right path, our Father in Heaven, before we have the chance to develop feelings of haughtiness when we see the abundance of blessings (such as an abundant crop of wheat in the field), commands us to bring an offering from the first harvest to the Kohen.

By bringing it the Kohen the person shows that he recognizes that everything he receives is from G-d. That is why it says, "the land that I am giving you" in the present tense, to show that it is not something that G-d gave once as a permanent gift and you inherited it, but rather that He gives it constantly at all times. In addition to making us realize that He is the source of all blessings, it also shows the importance of following the right path to guarantee that it will always be given.

(See Alshekh, Parashath Emor, 23: 10)

Behar Ṣion/Beḥuqqothai: Picking and choosing commandments

אִם־בְּחֻקֹּתַי תֵּלֵכוּ *Im Beḥuqqothai Telekhu* (if you follow my decrees [Beḥuqqothai, 26: 3]).

One commonly hears from people that they are only willing to keep the commandments (Miṣwoth) that are logical in their eyes. If one does not make sense they will not keep it.

Rabbenu the Ḥida states in his explanation on Parashath Beḥuqqothai that the Mefarshim speak at length about the fact that when a person is quick to perform the commandments which fall under the category of Ḥuqqim (decrees for which no reason whatsoever was given) Haqqadosh Barukh Hu (the Holy One blessed be He) gives him reward also for the commandments that make sense logically (Miṣwoth Sikhlioth). The reason being that when he keeps the Ḥuqqim he shows that his purpose is to do the will of the King. Therefore, when he keeps the logical commandments we can likewise assume that he is doing them for the same noble reason.

One who is only willing to perform the logical Miṣwoth, does not get any reward, because he demonstrates by this that he is not performing it to fulfil the commandment of G-d, but is only doing it because it makes sense to him.

(See Ḥida on the Torah, Parashath Beḥuqqothai, 26: 3)

Bamidbar: Why does the Torah use the word Se-oo (to count)

שְׂאוּ אֶת־רֹאשׁ כָּל־עֲדַת בְּנֵי־יִשְׂרָאֵל לְמִשְׁפְּחֹתָם *Take a census of the heads of all the congregation of Israe*l (Bamidbar 1:2).

Why does the Torah uses the word Se-oo for the performance of the census when other words may seem more appropriate? The word Se-oo has two opposite meanings. One has the meaning of elevating a person, in the sense of promoting him to a higher position. The other implies the removal of the head (decapitation) of a person.

The spritual uplifting of the Jewish nation depends entirely on their performance of the Torah. It is in their hands as to whether they will have a spiritual elevation or whether, Heaven forfend, they will lose the spiritual elevation that they have.

In Midrash Tanḥuma it says that G-d says to the Jewish people that He does not love any nation more than the Jewish people. Therefore, he says, "I have elevated you to be the head, just as I am the Head of the whole world".

(Rabbenu Beḥayye on the Torah, Bamidbar 1:2)

Naso: Raising the prayers of others together with yours

יָאֵר ה׳ | פָּנָיו אֵלֶיךָ וִיחֻנֶּךָּ׃ *Yaer H' Panaw Elekha Wiyḥonnekka* (G-d will shine His Countenance upon you and be gracious to you [Bamidbar 6: 25]). The Mefarshim explain that Wiyḥonnekka means that you will find favor in the eyes of G-d, and that He will grant you your desires.

A person who prays with great intent and holiness of thought has the merit to pull along with his prayer the prayers of others which get left behind and cannot make it on their own steam to Heaven. This is in accordance with what our Rabbis of blessed memory tell us, that when G-d remembered Sara (Immenu 'a"h) to allow her to conceive, other barren women were remembered along with her. The same happened when Yiṣḥaq Abinu, 'a"h, (Isaac) prayed for Ribqa Immenu, 'a"h (Rebecca), that G-d remembered other barren women who did not have enough merits to be answered in their own right.

We can understand Wiyḥonnekka as meaning you will find favor in the eyes of G-d to grant you your desires and allow your prayers to raise and pull along with them the prayers of others.

(See Ben Ish Ḥai Derashoth, Parashath Naso)

Beha'alothkha: Moshe Rabbenu epitomized humility

וְהָאִ֥ישׁ מֹשֶׁ֖ה עָנָ֣ו [עָנָ֣יו] מְאֹ֑ד מִכֹּל֙ הָֽאָדָ֔ם אֲשֶׁ֖ר עַל־פְּנֵ֥י הָאֲדָמָֽה׃ *And the man Moses was exceedingly humble ('Anaw), more than any man on the face of the earth.* Moshe Rabbenu, 'a"h, epitomized what it means to be humble, despite his enormous position among the Jewish people. Rabbenu the Ḥida, 'a"h, provides several Gemaṭrioth to demonstrate the essence and extreme importance of humility.

The Gemaṭria of the word 'Anaw (humble) is 126. If we take the last words of the Five Books of Moses and add the numerical value of the last letters of those words (BeMisrayim, Mas'eihem, Sinai, Yereho, Yisrael) they also total 126. We learn from this that the essence of the Torah is humility.

The word 'Anaw has the same letters in Hebrew as the word 'Awon (transgression). When one manages to overcome his inborn traits, G-d forgoes his transgressions. In addition, the numerical value of the last letter of each word of the verse Moshe 'Anaw Me-od (Moses was exceedingly humble) is fifteen which is the same value as one of G-d's holy names.

(See Naḥal Qedumim, Parashath Beha'alothkha, 12:3)

Shelaḥ Lekha: 613 commandments to give us life

Our Rabbis tell us that the Miṣwah (commandment) of Ṣiṣṣith (the wearing of fringes) is equal to the entire Torah. There are a total of 613 commandments which are hinted at in the commandment of Ṣiṣṣith as follows:

The word Ṣiṣṣith in Gemaṭria (Jewish numerology) is equal to 600. To this we add the 8 strings and 5 knots which make a total of 613. That is why the Torah tells us Ur-eethem Otho Uzkhartem Eth Kol Miṣwoth H' (you shall see them and remember all G-d's commandments).

The 613 commandments cover every aspect of our lives and are, in fact, what give us life. It can be likened to a man who was thrown overboard into the sea. The captain, seeing this, throws him a rope and instructs him not to let go of the rope, because as long as he holds on to it he will not drown and will live.

So too, Haqqadosh Barukh Hu threw us a line, which are His holy commandments, and instructed us not to let go of them. Because we are told that as long as we cleave to G-d, we will have life – *Ḥayyim Kullekhem Hayyom.*

(See Rashi, Parashath Shelaḥ Lekha, Rabbenu Baḥya, ibid. Midrash Tanḥuma, ibid)

Qoraḥ: Unity and diligence are key

וַיֹּצֵא פֶרַח וַיָּצֵץ צִיץ וַיִּגְמֹל שְׁקֵדִים׃ *It brought forth a blossom, sprouted a bud, and almonds ripened* (Bamidbar 17:23).

It says in Ben Ish Ḥai Derashoth that the reason why these three miracles happened to Aharon Hakkohen's staff – it blossomed, sprouted a bud and bore fruit – is because the Jewish people have three types, Kohanim (priests), Lewiim (Levites) and Yisraelim, which form an acronym in Hebrew of the word Keli (vessel).

If there is unity and a connection among the Jewish people then we have a complete vessel to receive the blessings from Heaven in, as it says, the only vessel that Haqqadosh Barukh Hu (the Holy One Blessed Be He) found fit for the purpose of receiving blessings for the Jewish people is Shalom (peace). Controversy and argument break the vessel into separate segments, and it will be unfit to hold the abundance and blessings.

Rabbenu the Ḥida, 'a"h, explains that a fruit tree has either the blossom or the fruit on it at any given time, but in this case they were both present together, and this was a miracle. The reason why there were almonds on it is because the people were diligent in the study of the Torah. The Hebrew word for almond (Shaqed) is similar to the word Shoqed which means showing diligence.

We see from this that unity amongst each other and diligence in Torah study bring much blessing to the Jewish people.

(See Parashath Qoraḥ, Ben Ish Ḥai Derashoth. Ḥida, Ḥomath Anakh)

Ḥuqqath: New Ḥiddushim on the Torah are always possible

בְּאֵר חֲפָרוּהָ שָׂרִים כָּרוּהָ נְדִיבֵי הָעָם *A well that the rulers dug, the nobility of the people excavated.*

Razal explain that the well refers to the Torah which is called Be-er Mayim Ḥayyim (well of living water). The rulers are the great scholars of Israel who dug deep into the Torah. The Torah has no limit. Even after the greatest Torah minds and scholars formed the Halakha (laws) and made Ḥiddushim and asked and answered deep questions on the Torah, whenever a Talmid Ḥakham delves into the depths of the Torah, he can still add to the understanding and make new Ḥiddushim and delve even deeper.

The reason is that every Talmid Ḥakham who studies Lishmah̲ (for the sake of the Torah without any ulterior motive), has a spark of Moshe Rabbenu, 'a"h. Through the power of this spark, he can continue to make new Ḥiddushim on the Torah. The Hebrew letters of the word Lishmah̲ are the same as the word LeMoshe (to Moshe).

The Niṣṣuṣ (spark) of Moshe Rabbenu, 'a"h, therefore, will rest upon him.

(Pene Dawid, Parashath Ḥuqqath)

Balaq: How do I treat a fellow Jew who follows a different path?

כִּנְחָלִים נִטָּיוּ כְּגַנֹּת עֲלֵי נָהָר כַּאֲהָלִים נָטַע ה׳ כַּאֲרָזִים עֲלֵי־מָיִם׃
Stretching out like brooks, like gardens alongside a river, like aloes which were planted by G-d, like cedars next to water (Ba<u>m</u>idbar 24:6).

We know that there are four types of people in the Jewish nation as is mentioned in connection with the four species in Sukkoth. This is similarly hinted at in the Parasha of Balaq. The streams of water which have a taste but no smell, hint at those who have Torah but no good deeds (Miṣwoth). The gardens are a place where fruit trees are found, and hint at those who have both Torah and good deeds. Aloes have a smell but lack any taste and hint at those who have good deeds but no Torah. Finally, the cedars have neither smell nor taste and are a hint to those who are devoid of both Torah and Miṣwoth.

In Sukkoth the four species are bound together and signify the need for unity. Similarly in this case, the Parasha shows us that this is the make up of the Jewish people, from which it seems obvious that we must treat each other with respect and unity whichever category our neighbor falls into.

(See Addereth Eliyahu, Parashath Balaq)

Pinḥas: Why the extra harsh language towards the Midianites?

צָרוֹר אֶת־הַמִּדְיָנִים וְהִכִּיתֶם אוֹתָם׃ *Harass the Midianites and smite them*. What is the necessity to say harass them when the Pasuq (verse) anyway says smite them? Furthermore, why is it that when the Egyptians enslaved the Jewish people and slaughtered their children, G-d commanded us not to hate them, yet,when dealing with the Midianites who did not enslave Israel nor raise their hands against them, we are commanded to harass them forever and smite them?

Ḥakham Yoseph Ḥayyim, 'a"h', in 'Od Yoseph Ḥai explains that even though the Egyptians enslaved and afflicted us, the final result was the purification of the Jewish people, which was only possible through the affliction. The Midianites, on the other hand, caused impurity to be infused into the Jewish people through their idolatry and immoral practices.

This can be compared to a snake and a leech who were discussing. The snake complained to the leech that they both have a similar "professions", that of biting humans. Yet human kind wish to crush the head of the snake but are willing to spend money to buy the leech. The leech explained that the difference is that even though they both bite humans, the leech is used to let blood from the sick and heal them. The snake, however, infuses its poisonous venom into the one it bites.

An additional reason is that the Egyptians wished to harm the Jewish nation physically, whereas, the Midianites gave physical pleasure to us which caused great spiritual harm.

(See 'Od Yoseph Ḥai Derashoth, Parashath Pinḥas)

Maṭṭoth/Mas'ei: forbidden words feed the Siṭra Aḥara

לֹ֥א יַחֵ֖ל דְּבָר֑וֹ כְּכָל־הַיֹּצֵ֥א מִפִּ֖יו יַעֲשֶֽׂה׃, *He shall not desecrate (Yaḥel) his word, whatever comes forth from his mouth shall he do.*

If a person guards his tongue from speaking any forbidden speech and is equally careful not to speak idle talk and sanctifies his mouth, he will find that G-d will answer his prayers. The root of the word Yaḥel (desecrate) in Hebrew, is the same as the word Ḥullin (profane). This verse can then be read that he should sanctify his mouth by not speaking profane matters. As a result, whatever comes forth from his mouth, He (G-d) shall do.

It mentions in the writings of Rabbenu Ḥayyim Wiṭṭal, 'a"h, that any type of speech that a person does on earth, has a corresponding effect in Heaven. If he speaks words of Torah and holiness, it awakens the spirituality and holiness above. The opposite is also true. If a person speaks Lashon Hara' and forbidden words, his words feed the Siṭra Aḥara (the evil side).

We are told that in the merit of watching what we speak, Mashiyaḥ (the Messiah) will come and G-d's throne and Name will be complete.

(See Ba<u>m</u>idbar, 30:3. Homath Anakh, Parashath Maṭṭoth)

Debarim: Why does it say heads and not judges?

הָבְוּ לָכֶ֣ם אֲנָשִׁ֨ים חֲכָמִ֧ים... וַאֲשִׂימֵ֖ם בְּרָאשֵׁיכֶֽם׃ *Provide for yourself men who are wise... and I shall appoint them as your heads* (Debarim 1:13). In Ben Ish Ḥai Derashoth it says that it would have been more appropriate to have said, "I shall appoint them as your *judges*". Ḥakham Yoseph Ḥayyim, 'a"h, answers as follows:

The Ḥakhamim are called the eyes of Israel because they are the ones who look closely at the deeds of the Jewish people and examine them. Our Rabbis of blessed memory say,

"A wise man's eyes are in his head". This is a difficult statement to comprehend. Do not all people have their eyes in their head?

The answer is that a fool does not see his own shortcomings, but only the shortcomings of others. Therefore, he is likened to a person whose eyes are in his feet because he does not look at his entire body. A wise person, on the other hand, has his eyes in his head and can see his whole body and all that it does. That is why the Holy One Blessed Be He created us with our eyes in our heads to hint at the fact that a person must examine himself from head to toe, in order for him to realize his failings.

The reason it uses the word heads, is because, since the Ḥakhamim are the eyes of the people, they will observe closely the deeds of the entire community. This is in contrast to those judges who do not examine the deeds of all the community, and whose eyes appear to be in their feet.

(See Ben Ish Ḥai Derashoth, Debarim)

Nahamu/Wa-eth-ḥannan: We can feel confident about the impending Geullah

Several times in the past, the Geullah (redemption) could have taken place. Because of our sins, however, the redemption was postponed and the Galuth (exile) became lengthened. As it is said: *Bishnath Zoth* (in this year), which refers to the year 5408, which was supposed to be the year of the redemption as is mentioned in the holy Zohar.

Instead of the Geullah, however, many people were killed that year in Poland, for our sins. When the real final redemption takes place, people may question whether our sins will again nullify the redemption so that it will not take place,

Heaven forbid. The answer to this doubt comes from the words of the Prophet when he says: *"Nahamu Nahamu"* (comfort, comfort), doubling the word Nahamu. One Nahamu is for the Galuth itself and the other is for the fact that the Galuth was extended and the Geullah postponed.

The prophecy continues: The time of the exile has been fulfilled (כי מלאה צבאה). This comes to teach us that once the final time has come, it cannot be postponed further because this is the time of the true Geullah.

(Naḥal Soreq, Haftarath WaEth-ḥannan)

Parashath 'Eqeb: A difficult word to translate

The Parasha of 'Eqeb begins by telling us that 'Eqeb (when/as soon as) we hear G-d's ordinances (Mishpaṭim) and we perform and keep his commandments (Miṣwoth)... He will protect us and give us all the blessings that He promised the Patriarchs.

The truth is that the word 'Eqeb (which literally means heel) is not so easy to translate. It says in Ben Ish Ḥai Derashoth, that many Mefarshim (commentators) have struggled with the meaning of the word and offered various explanations.

One explanation is that keeping the Torah and the observance of the commandments is dependant on the love and unity that the Jewish people have between them. The number of words in the 10 commandments is 172 which in Gemaṭria (Jewish numerology) is equal to the numerical value of the word 'Eqeb.

The last word in the 10 commandments is the word Lere'ekha (to your friend/neighbor). This is a word which has connotations of love and friendship. This comes to tell us that if love and friendship (which is connected to the word Lere'ekha) is a quality that you have when you hear G-d's ordinances, then it is certain that you will be able to do and keep the commandments (Miṣwoth). And this, in turn, will bring us the blessings G-d promised our forefathers.

(See Ben Ish Ḥai Derashoth, Parashath 'Eqeb)

Parashath Re-eh: We must be happy

It says in Parashath Re-eh, וְהָיִיתָ אַךְ שָׂמֵחַ *Wehayeetha Akh Sameyaḥ* (and you shall be totally happy). We see from this how dear happiness is to G-d and to what extent we must be careful to perform this Miṣwah (commandment).

When a person performs any commandment, he should not say "what difference does it make if the performance is accompanied by happiness or sadness". Rather, he must know that happiness is, first and foremost, a commandment in its own right. In addition, when joy is lacking, it also detracts from the Miṣwah that was performed, and actually hurts it.

That is why we have a specific commandment here of happiness, to teach us that it is a Miṣwah on its own, and that a person gets reward specifically for it. For this reason the Anshei Kenesseth Haggedolah (Rabbis of the Great Assembly) instituted individual Berakhoth (blessings) connected to Simḥa (happiness), such as Sheheḥeyanu that we recite on new clothing and the like.

(See Ben Ish Ḥai, 1st year, Parashath Re-eh, Introduction)

Shofṭim: When telling a lie is an obligation

It says in Parashath Shofṭim: צֶדֶק צֶדֶק תִּרְדֹּף *Justice, justice Shall you pursue*. Why is the word Justice doubled?

It says in 'Od Yoseph Ḥai that, obviously, a person must cleave to truth and justice and distance him/herself from lies and falsehoods. This is a fundamental in Judaism. But just as a person must normally keep away from lying, there are times when he must keep away from the truth. As our Rabbis of blessed memory tell us: we must change [the facts] for the sake of peace.

This comes to teach us that a person should never say, "I am very righteous and only speak the truth and will never lie, even for the sake of peace". We must know that lying for the sake of peace is not only permitted, but is an obligation.

That is why the word justice is doubled. The first time it means righteousness, and the second time truth. When the verse tells us that we must pursue it, it is coming to tell us that in order to do righteousness in the world there are times you have to be in pursuit of (run after) truth to chase it away.

(See 'Od Yoseph Ḥai Derashoth, Parashath Shofṭim)

Parashath Ki Theṣe: Building fences around ourselves

It says in Parashath Ki Theṣe: כִּי תִבְנֶה בַּיִת חָדָשׁ וְעָשִׂיתָ מַעֲקֶה לְגַגֶּךָ *If you build a new house, you must make a fence for your roof.*

This can be understood on a different level. The month of Elul is a time for introspection and Teshubah (repentance). Our bodies are like the house in which the soul dwells.

Someone who repents properly becomes a new entity – a new house for the soul.

The danger that anyone who repents faces, is the prospect of regressing. The best advice one could give someone who repents correctly not to regress, is to build a fence for the roof. Our Ḥakhamim made fences for us around the Torah, by forbidding us to do something which is similar to a Torah prohibition but, nevertheless, permitted by the Torah, lest we should inadvertently come to do that which is forbidden by the Torah. We, in turn, should go one step further and make additional fences for ourselves by building fences to forbid even that which was permitted by the Ḥakhamim.

In this way, if a person stumbles and transgresses one of his self built fences, he does not transgress an actual law from the Torah or the Ḥakhamim, but only the fence that he built for himself.

(See Addereth Eliyahu, Parashath Ki Theṣe)

Parashath Ki Thabo: Blessings will happen against all logic

It says in the Parasha of Ki Thabo, וּבָ֧אוּ עָלֶ֛יךָ כָּל־הַבְּרָכ֥וֹת הָאֵ֖לֶּה וְהִשִּׂיגֻ֑ךָ *"And all these blessings shall come upon you and overtake you, if you listen to the voice of the L-rd your G-d".*

Sometimes a person is so blessed by G-d that whatever he does he succeeds in, even if logically his business venture should fail. A story that illustrates this well is the story of Timothy Dexter who, in the 18th century, exported two shiploads of coal from Virginia to Newcastle in England, which was a famous coal producing town. Everyone was expecting to hear of his ruin because of this foolish act. When his ships arrived in England, a miners' strike was in progress. Dexter sold all his coal for a handsome profit.

Even if a person runs away from success, if G-d wishes him to have it, success will run after him as it says, *"all these blessings shall come upon you and overtake you"*. But, as far as the Jewish people are concerned, we must know that there is a condition. Our blessings are dependant on the keeping of the Torah, as the Pasuq (verse) says, *"if you listen to the voice of the L-rd your G-d"*.

(See Addereth Eliyahu, Parashath Ki Thabo)

Niṣabim/Wayyelekh: Elul, Repentance and Shabbath

The month of Elul is a time for Teshubah (repentance) and introspection. Each night it is appropriate for us to examine all our deeds closely. In truth, this must be done throughout the year, but at the very least from Elul till Yom Kippur.

It says in Parashath Niṣabim, וְשַׁבְתָּ֞ עַד־ה' א' *WeShabta 'Ad H' Elokekha* (And you shall return [repent] to the L-rd your G-d). The word Shabta (you shall repent), in Hebrew, has the same letters as the word Shabbath. From this we can learn that repentance will not happen unless there is keeping of Shabbath. And keeping Shabbath, we are taught, is equal to keeping the whole Torah.

Each one of the Miṣwoth corresponds to a particular part of our body. Each time we transgress, the corresponding part of the body is affected and rectifying the damage done to all the various parts of the body can be a very lengthy and cumbersome process, requiring us to do heaps of Miṣwoth.

However, if a person keeps Shabbath correctly, in all its detail, it is as if the person did indeed do bundles of Miṣwoth.

We see from this how careful we must be to ensure that we study the laws of Shabbath to be able to keep it as required, since the benefit and reward is very great indeed.

(See Kaf Haḥayyim, 581, Oth 24. Ḥida, Naḥal Qedummim, Parashath Niṣabim)

Parashath Ha-azinu: How to speak to Heaven and earth

It says in the Torah (Ha-azinu, 32: 1) that Moshe Rabbenu called on the Heavens and the earth as witnesses when he spoke to the Children of Israel: הַאֲזִינוּ הַשָּׁמַיִם וַאֲדַבֵּרָה וְתִשְׁמַע הָאָרֶץ אִמְרֵי־פִי׃ *Ha-azinu Hashamayim Wa-adabbera, Wethishma' Ha-areṣ Imrei Fi* (Lend me your ear O Heavens, and the earth shall hear the words of my mouth).

Moshe Rabbenu tells Heaven to first listen and then he will speak. The Hebrew word for speak that he uses is the relatively strong term of *Wa-adabbera* (I shall speak). When addressing the earth, however, he tells it to hear the words of his mouth (*Imrei Fi*), which is a softer way of saying it. In addition, the sentence implies that first the words will emanate from his mouth and then the earth will hear.

We see from this that a righteous individual is able to dictate to and command celestial beings, even in harsh terms, since they have no freedom of choice. Speaking to human beings, however, is a different matter. We cannot dictate to people or order them around.

If we want a person to do something specific, that person must be persuaded that it is the best option. This can only be achieved by first speaking to the individual in quiet and convincing terms.

(See the Alshikh on the Torah, Ha-azinu)

Wezoth Habberakha: Moshe Rabbenu's intense love for the Jewish people

The Parasha of Wezoth Habberakha starts with the words: וְזֹאת הַבְּרָכָה אֲשֶׁר בֵּרַךְ מֹשֶׁה אִישׁ הָא׳ אֶת־בְּנֵי יִשְׂרָאֵל לִפְנֵי מוֹתוֹ׃ And this is the blessing that Moses, the man of G-d, blessed the Children of Israel with, before his death (*Wezoth Habberakha Asher Berakh Moshe Ish HaElokim, Eth Benei Yisrael Lifnei Motho*).

There are a couple of questions concerning this Pasuq (verse).

1. Why does it mention the Children of Israel? It is obviously about them because the Torah proceeds to mention the names of the tribes that are blessed.

2. Why is it necessary to mention that it is before his death? We are aware from elsewhere in the Parasha that this was before he passed away.

The nature of the world is that when a person passes from this earth, he thinks of what is dearest to him and usually blesses his own family. In the case of Moshe Rabbenu, 'a"h, his love for the Jewish people was so great that he blessed all the tribes of Israel. His own children were not mentioned individually, but rather, included in the all encompassing blessings, proving that his love for all his people was very great.

There is a Pasuq (verse): *Sof Dabar Hakkol Nishma'* (the end explains everything). The Torah by mentioning these two points stresses that since it was mentioned at the end of his life, this proves the immense love he had for all Israel throughout his life.

(See Ben Ish Ḥai Drashoth, Parshath Wezoth Habberakha)

2

שבת

Shabbath

How early can Shabbath be started?

In the summer months it is common for families to start Shabbath early. What is the earliest one may start?

The Shabbath candles may be lit from Pelagh Haminḥa (10.75 halachic hours into the day), 'Arbith may be prayed and the Friday night Shabbath meal may be eaten right away.

When praying early, one must be careful to read the Shema' again at the correct time, which is after the stars come out, even though one already read it as part of 'Arbith. The blessings of the Shema' are not repeated.

This rule holds true even on weekdays, that whenever 'Arbith is prayed early, the Shema' must be recited again after nightfall.

(See Shulḥan 'Arukh 267: 2, and 235: 1)

Does Shabbath start with candle lighting?

When a woman completes the lighting of the Shabbath candles, Shabbath has started for her. If a man should light them (even with a Berakha [blessing]) Shabbath does not start till he recites Boee Kallah and Mizmor Shir Yom Hashabbath in the prayer. (This assumes that he prayed at the correct time, i.e. before sunset. Shabbath obviously starts by sunset, whether or not one has prayed).

Therefore, a woman is not permitted to do any Melakha (labor forbidden on Shabbath) once she has lit, but a man may. However, even in the case of a man, if he makes a condition before lighting, that he does not intend to accept Shabbath at that time, it is preferable.

Even though a woman automatically accepts Shabbath with the lighting of the candles, if she knows that she still has a forbidden labor to do after lighting – obviously to be completed before sunset, or before the community accepts Shabbath in the Synagogue (whichever comes first) – she must verbalize the condition before lighting, that she is not accepting Shabbath with the lighting of the candles. (This situation is commonly found before Kol Nidre on Yom Kippur, when a woman who lives some distance from a Synagogue, wishes to be taken by car to the Synagogue before Yom Kippur starts).

(See Ben Ish Ḥai, 2nd year, Parashath Nowaḥ, Oth 8, and Rab Pe'alim, Ḥeleq 2, Oraḥ Ḥayyim, 44)

A woman's opportunity for prayer when she lights the Shabbath candles

When the Ba'alath Habbayith (lady of the house) lights the Shabbath lights, it is appropriate for her to pray that G-d will give her sons who study the Torah, because prayers are accepted better at the time of the performance of the commandment. And in the merit of lighting Shabbath candles she will merit that her sons will be Torah scholars because the Torah is called light.

If a woman is finding bringing up her children to be very difficult and challenging, or if she doesn't have any children at all, it is considered to be a Seghulla (good omen) to read the Haphṭarah of the first day of Rosh Hashanah, after she lights the candles (about Ḥannah who prayed for a son). She should read it with understanding and intent (Ka<u>w</u>anah). It is also good to give three coins in charity (before lighting) because there are Qabbalistic reasons for this.

(See Kaf Haḥayyim 263, Oth 34)

If a woman forgot to say the blessing at candle lighting

When the lady of the house lights the Shabbath candles, as we know, she first lights and then recites the Berakha (blessing).

If, after she lit the Shabbath candles, she forgot to say the Berakha (blessing), she can say it when she remembers, provided it is at a time when one is still permitted to light candles. If, however, she remembers at a time when one is no longer permitted to light, she may not recite the Berakha.

If she cannot remember if she recited the blessing after the lighting or not, she should say it without Shem Umalkhuth (without mentioning G-d's name and Kingdom in the blessing).

(See Kaf Haḥayyim 263, Oth 36)

Having Shabbath candles burn during the day also

A Rabbinical question (She-elah) was asked concerning those who light the Shabbath candles using oil instead of candles. Some people would put in a lot of oil, so that they would burn throughout the day of Shabbath into the following evening. Is there a basis for this custom?

It says in a responsum in Torah Lishmah̲ that there does not appear to be any source for this custom. The reason a light is kept burning throughout the day in a Synagogue is for the honor of the Synagogue. A memorial (Yahrzeit) candle remains burning throughout the day for the soul of the one who passed away. However, keeping a light burning throughout the day on Shabbath in a person's home, serves no purpose.

On the contrary, it comes under the prohibition of Bal Tash-ḥith (wasting), and should be stopped.

(See Torah Lishmah̲, Oraḥ Ḥayyim, She-elah 'Ahn Waw)

A woman who forgot to cut her nails for Ṭebilah on Friday night

On Shabbath, one is not permitted to cut one's nails either by hand or with an instrument. Part of the preparation before a woman goes for Ṭebilah (ritual immersion) is the cutting of her nails. If she is to do the immersion on a Friday night (Shabbath) but realizes, after Shabbath has entered, that she forgot to cut her nails, what are her options?

The Mishnah Berurah mentions the opinion that she may have a non-Jew cut her nails by hand, and if that is not possible, the non-Jew may cut them with an instrument. (He mentions further that if immersion must be done then and there is no non-Jew available, then picking the dirt from under her nails might be an option if she checks thoroughly to ensure that no dirt remains).

Ḥakham Yoseph Ḥayyim, 'a"h, states in Ben Ish Ḥai that the custom is to have a woman who is not Jewish cut the nails. She must be taught to pull the Jewish woman's hand towards her in order to cut the nails, but the Jewish woman may not stretch her hand out to the non-Jewess. In fact, she may not assist the non-Jewess at all in the entire process of having her nails cut.

(See Shulḥan 'Arukh, 340:1. Ben Ish Ḥai, Ki Thissa, 2nd year, Cth 16, Parashath Shemini, 5. Mishnah Berurah 340, 3.)

Not interrupting between the Friday night prayer and Qiddush

After the 'Arbith prayer of Leil Shabbath (Friday night) one must go to one's house immediately in order to make the Qiddush. One must not be like those who sit for an hour or two with their friends or speak idle talk, thereby casting away the sanctity of the Shabbath. As Shelomo HaMelekh, 'a"h, (king Solomon) said in Mishlei (Proverbs, 1:14) בְּנִי אַל־תֵּלֵךְ בְּדֶרֶךְ אִתָּם מְנַע רַגְלְךָ מִנְּתִיבָתָם׃ *Do not walk with them in their way, refrain from placing your foot in their path.*

One must be careful to connect one Qedusha (holiness) with another. One should not interrupt between the holiness of 'Arbith and the holiness of the Se'uddah (the Shabbath meal) with quarrelsome words that cause pain to the Nefesh Yethera (additional soul that one receives on Shabbath).

One should have in mind that the first Se'uddah represents Yiṣḥaq Abinu (Isaac), 'a"h, and saves us from the pain of Mashiyaḥ. The second represents Abraham Abinu (Abraham), 'a"h, and saves us from the punishment of Gehinnam (hell). The third represents Ya'aqob Abinu (Jacob), 'a"h, and saves us from the war of Gogh Umaghogh.

(See Ben Ish Ḥai, 2nd yr, Wayyera, Oth 11. Moreh Be'eṣba', 147)

Can a frozen loaf be used for Leḥem Mishneh?

The Shabbath meals require Leḥem Mishneh (two loaves of bread) to be brought to the table. This is because of the double portions of manna that fell on Fridays in the desert because of Shabbath. (According to Rabbenu the Ari z"l, however, twelve loaves must be placed on the table.)

If one has only one loaf of bread but has another frozen loaf in the freezer, can the frozen loaf be used together with the first loaf as Leḥem Mishneh? According to the Ohr LeṢion, the frozen loaf may be combined with the other one to form Leḥem Mishneh. The rationale is that since if one were to separate Ḥallah from the frozen bread it would be considered to be a valid separation, and additionally, frozen bread has the same rules concerning the contracting of ritual impurity as does non-frozen bread, this shows that frozen bread is considered to be bread.

As such, he considers that frozen bread may, indeed, be combined together with the edible loaf to form Leḥem Mishneh.

(See Ohr LeṢion, Ḥeleq 2, Ch. 21, Oth 2)

Making a mark on the bread before the Berakha

When breaking the Bread for Ha<u>m</u>oṣi on Shabbath, the Ashkenazi custom is to cut the bread with a knife. Sephardim do not bring a knife to the Ha<u>m</u>oṣi bread but break it with their hands.

The Mishnah Berurah states that those who are particular in the performance of the commandments, first make a mark with their knife where they intend to cut the bread after reciting the Berakha (blessing). This avoids any delay between the Berakha and the cutting of the bread. This is the prevalent custom amongst Ashkenazim, to make a mark, recite the blessing and cut the bread where the mark is.

The Kaf Haḥayyim quotes the opinion that one should not make a mark with the knife as well as the opinion that one should apply the principle of Sheb We'Al Ta'aseh 'Adif (it is better to abstain from doing so). Ḥakham Yoseph Ḥayyim, 'a"h, states in Ben Ish Ḥai simply that one should take the top two loaves in one's hand and recite the blessing. This is the custom of Sephardim, to take the bread without making a mark, to recite the blessing and break it with one's hands.

(See Mishnah Berurah 274: 2. Kaf Haḥayyim, ibid, 11. Ben Ish Ḥai, 2nd year, Parashath Wayyera, Oth 15)

Skipping a Pasuq during the Shabbath Torah reading

If, for some reason, when reading the Torah on Shabbath morning, a Pasuq (verse) was skipped, the congregation has to go back to read the missing Pasuq, even if the Torah was already put away and even if Musaf was prayed.

They must read the Pasuq that was missed plus two adjacent Pesuqim (verses).

If, however, the Pasuq which was skipped was one of those that was read the previous Shabbath at Minḥa and during the week on Monday and Thursday, then there is no need to repeat it. If someone, nevertheless, wishes to be strict and read it, it must be read without the blessings.

In a congregation where there are probably many people present who will not have heard the readings during the previous week, it is preferable to go back to the portion missed and to say it without a blessing.

(See Sh.'A. 137:3. Kaf Haḥayyim ibid: Oth 16. Qiṣur Shulḥan 'Arukh, Ḥ"R Rafael Barukh Toledano, 124:9)

The correct time to pray Musaf

The Musaf (additional) prayer can technically be prayed throughout the day. However, the correct time is right after Shaḥrith (the morning prayer) since the Musaf sacrifice was offered right after the Tamid sacrifice of the morning.

It should not be prayed after the end of the seventh hour of the day calculating from daybreak. One who prays Musaf after this time is considered to have wilfully transgressed. Nevertheless, he has still fulfilled his obligation, provided he prayed it during the daytime hours since it can technically be prayed throughout the day, as we have mentioned.

If a person were to pray Musaf before Shaḥrith in error, he would still have fulfilled his obligation. However, this is not the correct way to do it because, in addition to the reason mentioned above, according to the Ari z"l, for Qabbalistic reasons, it is important to pray Shaḥrith before Musaf (because of the correct order of the 'Olamoth).

(Sh. A. 286: 1, with Rama. M.B. ibid, 1, 5. Kaf Haḥayyim ibid 12, 9)

Praying for Refuah (healing) on Shabbath

In general, one may not ask for one's personal needs on Shabbath. There are various reasons for this, one of them being that one may become sad and cry on Shabbath.

Included in this is praying for one who is ill. Even though it is commonly done nowadays, nevertheless, there is a difference of opinion among the Posqim and there are those who rule that one may not recite a Misheberakh (blessing) for a Ḥoleh She-eino Mesukkan (one who's life is not in danger) on Shabbath. If reciting a Misheberakh for one who's life is not in danger, it is appropriate to minimize the blessing to "May G-d have mercy upon him among all the sick of His people Israel". It is appropriate to add the sentence: Shabbath Hi Milliz'oq ...

In the case of a Ḥoleh Sheyesh Bo Sakkanah (one who is critically ill - whose life is in danger), however, all agree that a blessing may be recited, on Shabbath, as is mentioned in the Shulḥan 'Arukh. A woman who is having difficulties during labor, is considered to be in this category.

(See Shabbath 12 a&b. Shulḥan 'Arukh, 287: 1 & 288: 10. Kaf Ḥayyim 288: 76, 78, 80. M.B. ibid, 28.)

Not eating till after noon on Shabbath

The Shulḥan 'Arukh states that it is forbidden to fast on Shabbath until the (end of the) sixth hour, which is midday in Halakhic time. The Rama adds that even if one was studying Torah or praying, it is still forbidden. This assumes that the person simply went without eating, but if his intention was to fast, then even one hour is forbidden.

This can cause difficulties for Minyanim that start and end late on Shabbath morning. There is an opinion, however, that in some cases the sixth hour can be calculated from when one got out of bed. Also, the Bighdei Yesha' states that if one is studying or praying, it is permissible.

In any case, an effort should be made not to lengthen the prayers unnecessarily, especially in the winter, so as to avoid getting into this situation.

(See Shulḥan 'Arukh, 288: 1 with Rama. Kaf Haḥayyim ibid, Oth 1 and 3. M.B. ibid 2.)

Treating the morning Qiddush with respect

The Shabbath morning Qiddush is of lesser importance than the one on Friday night, because the source for the Friday night Qiddush is from the Torah, whereas the morning Qiddush is by Rabbinical enactment. Nevertheless, the table must be set and a fine table-cloth placed upon it, in the same way that is required at night.

The morning Qiddush is euphemistically referred to as Qidusha Rabba (the Great Qiddush). This is the same way that a blind person is referred to, with deference, as *Saghi Nahor* (having an abundance of light). Despite the fact that it is the smaller one, it's honor is greater than that of the night (in certain respects) and if one has a limited amount of delicacies, they should be saved for the morning Se'uddah (festive meal).

(Shulḥan 'Arukh 271:3, 289:1. M.B. 271, 9. Kaf Haḥayyim, 289, 3, 7)

Eating Se'uddah Shelishith on Shabbath

The Gemara of Shabbath states that one should be particular to eat Se'uddah Shelishith (the third Shabbath meal). Both men and women are obligated to eat this meal. The time for it is from when one can pray Minḥa. If one completes the meal before that time one does not fulfill his obligation.

One should eat the meal with at least 2 ounces of bread. Therefore, one should be careful not to eat so much during the previous meal that one will still feel satiated during Se'uddah Shelishith. One who did the wrong thing and over ate is not required to force himself to eat again, but should eat in accordance with what he is able to.

The meal should be eaten after the Minḥa prayer, but if one ate it before Minḥa one has still fulfilled one's obligation. According to the Ari z"l, however, if the meal was eaten before Minḥa one has not fulfilled his obligation of eating Se'uddah Shelishith at all.

(See Mas. Shabbath, 118a. Shulḥan 'Arukh 291:1 & 2. Ben Ish Ḥai, 2nd year, Parashath Ḥayyei Sara, Oth 13 & 14)

How many loaves for the third Shabbath meal?

The Shulḥan 'Arukh states that we must break bread over two loaves at Se'uddah Shelishith (the third Shabbath meal). The Rama mentions that while it is appropriate to break bread over two loaves, the prevalent custom is to use only one loaf for Se'uddah Shelishith. The Mishnah Berurah adds that, Lekhatteḥilla (a priori), it is preferable to have two loaves. The above is the custom of Ashkenazim as mentioned by the Rama and Mishnah Berurah.

The Ben Ish Ḥai states that twelve loaves of bread must be placed on the table, according to the Sod (Qabbalah) as revealed by Rabbenu the Ari z"l, in the same way that twelve loaves are used on Friday night and Shabbath morning. In all cases, only two of the loaves are lifted for the Berakha (blessing). This is the custom of Sephardim and Ashkenazim who follow the Sod. In a case where twelve loaves are not available, it can obviously be made on less.

(See Shulḥan 'Arukh291: 4, with Rama. Ben Ish Ḥai, 2nd yr. Ḥayyei Sara, Oth 12. 'Od Yoseph Ḥai, Wayyera, Oth 15. Mishnah Berurah 291, 21).

Coloring food on Shabbath

Painting/coloring is forbidden on Shabbath. However, the Shulḥan 'Arukh states that one may put saffron into food (which will have the effect of making it orange or yellow) without compunction, since coloring does not apply to food.

According to the Mishnah Berurah, one may do so even if one's intention was to color the food. He quotes an opinion, however, that it is preferable to refrain from doing so.

It says in Ben Ish Ḥai, however, that even though one may dip one's bread in colored liquid, despite the fact that the bread will become colored, and one may similarly put something into the food even though it will color it, this only applies if it was not added for the purpose of coloring it. However, if one's intention was to color it, it is forbidden to do so. As such, Sephardim must refrain from intentionally coloring food on Shabbath.

(See Shulḥan 'Arukh 320: 19. M.B. ibid, 56. Ben Ish Ḥai, 2nd year, Parashath Pequdei, Oth . Kaf Haḥayyim 113, Oth 320, 115)

Complications with coloring drinks on Shabbath

Even though we mentioned previously that coloring food on Shabbath is permitted, nevertheless when it comes to coloring liquids, there is a substantial difference of opinion.

The Mishnah Berurah permits pouring red wine into white on Shabbath, even though the white wine will become red. This is the Halakha for Ashkenazim. The Mishnah Berurah adds that this is permissible even when it was the person's intention to color it. He quotes an opinion, however, that says that it is preferable to avoid doing so.

It says in Ben Ish Ḥai that coloring water or other drinks is forbidden on Shabbath, even though it was not the person's intention to color the liquid, because it resembles making dye, which is a Torah prohibition according to the Rambam (Maimonides). He mentions a custom in his city of mixing red and white alcoholic beverages and says that one must be careful not to pour the red into the white.

Pouring white into red is permissible, however, provided that it was not one's intention to color the liquid. Sephardim should follow this stricter opinion in accordance with the Ben Ish Ḥai, Kaf Haḥayyim and others.

(See Ben Ish Ḥai, 2nd year, Parashath Pequdei, Oth 3 & 4. Mishnah Berurah 320:56. Kaf Haḥayyim ibid, Oth 116 & 117)

Separating bad lettuce leaves from good ones on Shabbath

On Shabbath, because of the Melakha of Borer (the forbidden activity of separating), we are forbidden to separate bad food from good, but rather, must take the good and leave the bad behind.

If you have vegetables such as celery, lettuce or scallions, which have portions (such as some leaves or part of the stalk) which are rotten, you have to remove the good from the bad as we have mentioned. However, this only applies when the leaves are separated and not still connected to the whole vegetable.

In a case, however, where they are all still connected and the outer leaves are rotten, we are permitted to remove the inedible leaves first in order to take the good leaves which are on the inside, since that is the way it is normally done.

It is important to mention that this is only permitted if the food is to be eaten Le-altar (within the hour). It is forbidden to keep it aside for later.

(See Ben Ish Ḥai, 2nd year, Parashath Beshallaḥ, Oth 6)

Filling a Thermos with hot water on Shabbath

Haṭmanah, which is the act of insulating food by covering, is forbidden on Shabbath, when the food is in the vessel that it was cooked in. The Shulḥan 'Arukh states that if the food was poured into a second pot (Keli Sheni), Haṭmanah is permitted provided that it does not cause the heat to increase.

The reason why it is permitted is because Haṭmanah is only forbidden with regard to hot food which is in the vessel in which it was cooked. The Ohr LeṢion states, therefore, that a Thermos flask (which is a Keli Sheni and does not increase heat), may be filled with hot water on Shabbath and we need not be concerned about Haṭmanah.

(See Shulḥan 'Arukh 257: 5. Mishnah Berurah ibid 28,29. Kaf Haḥayyim ibid, Oth 33. Ohr LeṢion 2: 17, Oth 11)

If a non-Jew boils water on Shabbath for a Jew

If a non-Jew boils water for a Jew on Shabbath, the Jew may not benefit from it on Shabbath. It only becomes permitted when Shabbath is over, plus the time it took to heat it up (Bikhdei Sheya'asu).

If the non-Jew boiled the water and the water then became cold again, so that the Jew gains nothing from the act of boiling, he still may not benefit from the water on Shabbath itself, since a forbidden action was, nevertheless, done to it, but may benefit from it immediately after Shabbath without the need to wait the time it took to boil it.

If, however, the reason for boiling it was for a purpose that benefits the Jew, such as boiling water in a place where the water must always be boiled prior to drinking for health reasons (as is the case in many countries), then he must wait till Shabbath is over plus the time it took to boil it.

(Note: the above assumes that Moṣei Shabbath is not Yom Ṭob.)

(See Qiṣur Shulḥan 'Arukh, Rabbi Rafael Barukh Toledano, Siman 296, Oth 11)

May powdered baby formula be prepared on Shabbath?

Lash (kneading) is forbidden on Shabbath. The question is whether mixing powdered baby formula with water on Shabbath falls into the category of kneading, which would cause it to be forbidden to be made on Shabbath.

The nature of the baby formula powder is that when it is mixed with water it does not solidify like flour that is kneaded but rather, it melts in the water. Therefore, this does not appear to fall into the category of kneading. Nevertheless, one should not add only a little water to the powder to begin with, but rather should pour onto it a substantial amount of water, more than the quantity of the powder itself. When it is done in such a manner, there can be no concern about kneading.

In addition, there can be no issue about the hot water cooking the powder on Shabbath, since the powder is already fully pre-cooked and we apply the concept that there is no cooking after cooking with regards to food that is dry, as is the case with this powder.

(See Ohr LeṢion vol.2, 33: 8)

Washing dishes on Shabbath

The Shulḥan 'Arukh writes that cutlery, crockery and the like may be washed on Shabbath, provided that they will be needed for that Shabbath, such as when there are other S'euddoth (Shabbath meals) remaining. However, after

Se'uddah Shelishith (the third Shabbat meal which is eaten after Minḥa), they may not be washed.

This implies that one may wash utensils after the Friday night meal for the Shabbath morning meal, or even for Se'uddah Shelishith, if they are needed. In addition, even if one requires only one cup, he may wash several since each of the ones washed would be fit to be used. However, if one has other clean utensils that could be used it is good to use the clean ones and not wash the dirty dishes on Shabbath because of the effort it requires.

The reason why we may not wash dishes and the like after Se'uddah Shelishith is because one does not normally eat after this, but if someone wishes to eat more, or guests are expected, then it is permitted.

(See Shulḥan 'Arukh, 323: 6. Kaf Haḥayyim ibid, Oth 39-42)

Making one's bed during the day on Shabbath

One may not make one's bed during the day on Shabbath in order for it to be ready on Moṣei Shabbath (Saturday night). This is because one may not prepare something on Shabbath for after Shabbath.

If, however, it would be a disgrace or an embarrassment to Shabbath for the bed to remain unmade, then one is permitted to make it, because it is considered that it was made for the purpose of Shabbath itself. If the bed is in a place where people pass to go from one room to another, it may be made in honor of Shabbath.

In a case, however, where the beds are located in a separate room where people do not ordinarily go, they should not be made on Shabbath.

(See Kaf Haḥayyim, 302, Oth 23)

Erasing writing on one's hand on Shabbath

There are those who write notes and messages on their hand. If someone does this before Shabbath, he should remember to erase it before Shabbath starts, because erasing is not permitted on Shabbath.

If someone forgot to remove it before Shabbath he is still permitted to wash for Hamoṣi (eating bread) on Shabbath, provided he pours at least a Reb'ith* of water on his hand in one shot (or immerses his hands in water that is fit for the ritual immersion of hands), because the Shulḥan 'Arukh states that when he washes in this way, he does not need to dry his hands afterwards. Drying one's hands with a towel would, of course, cause the ink to be erased. However, there is an opinion that it is better to wrap a piece of cloth around one's hands where the letters are.

There is also an opinion that one is required to dry one's hands even when immersing one's hands or pouring a Rebi'ith in one shot. In view of this, one should wrap a piece of cloth around it or dry it in the sun or breeze, so as not to come to erase the letters with a towel on Shabbath.

(*There are different opinions as to the quantity of a Reb'ith, starting at 3 fl. oz.)

(See Kaf Haḥayyim 340: Oth 25. Shulḥan 'Arukh, 158: 13. K. H. ibid Oth 89. See also Ben Ish Ḥai, 2nd year, Tazriya' Ṭaharoth, Oth 12)

Making a mark on a book with a fingernail, on Shabbath

It says in the Shulḥan 'Arukh that one may make a mark with one's finger nail in a book on Shabbath, the way that people make marks as a sign, because a mark of this nature does not last.

The Mishnah Berurah comments that there are those who do not permit it, and in any case this refers to just a mark and not a letter. Making a shape of even one letter with one's fingernail is prohibited. He adds that this Halakha is about making a mark on parchment, as they did in the times of the Talmud, however making a mark with a fingernail on paper is permanent and forbidden.

The Ben Ish Ḥai also states that it is forbidden to mark paper with a fingernail on Shabbath. He adds that it is important to caution people about this because people often make marks on their books with their fingernails for various reasons (most commonly to find the place easily later). This is not permitted, even though it is just a mark and not the shape of actual letters.

(See Shulḥan 'Arukh, 340: 5. M.B. ibid, 23-25 and Beur Halakha. Ben Ish Ḥai, Parashath Pequdei, Oth 2.)

Using a door-knocker on Shabbath

The Shulḥan 'Arukh states that making a sound on Shabbath with a musical instrument is forbidden. However, to knock on a door and the like, which is not for a musical purpose is permitted.

The Rama, however, adds that knocking on a door with a door-knocker, even though it is not made for musical purposes, is forbidden, since it is an instrument made specifically for that purpose. The Halakha for Ashkenazim, therefore, is that it is forbidden to use a door-knocker on Shabbath. (Using another device, such as a dead bolt to knock with, would be permitted).

The situation is different for Sephardim. The Ohr LeṢion states that the intention of the Shulḥan 'Arukh is in accordance with the Rif and the Rambam, which is to permit the use of a door knocker on Shabbath, even if it is not one specifically intended for Shabbath use, since it is not for a musical purpose. Sephardim, therefore, may use a door-knocker to knock on a door on Shabbath.

(See Shulḥan 'Arukh 338:1 with Rama. Mishnah Berurah ibid, 2, 4. Ohr LeṢion 39: 1.)

Asking a non-Jew to effect a transaction on Shabbath

A Jew is forbidden from giving a non-Jew money during the week in order to buy him something on Shabbath. Similarly, a Jewish individual is forbidden from giving a non-Jew an article any day of the week, including Sunday, if it is to be sold on Shabbath.

If a Jew gives a non-Jew money to purchase something for him, or gives him an item to sell on his behalf, and the transaction can only take place on Shabbath, it is forbidden even if he did not specify that it should occur on Shabbath. Since the transaction has to take place on Shabbath because there is no other day, it is as if he specified that it should be done on Shabbath. Buying or selling in auctions or flea markets and the like that are only open on Shabbath would fall into this category and are forbidden.

In a case, however, where the non-Jew could effect the transaction on a weekday or on Shabbath, and was not told to conduct the transaction on Shabbath, but because it was convenient for him conducted the business on Shabbath, it is permitted, provided he was not told specifically to transact the business on Shabbath.

The required conditions for such a transaction to be permitted, then, are that:

1. the Jew must not specify that it is to be done on Shabbath and

2. the non-Jew must have the opportunity to do it on another day of the week.

(See Shulḥan 'Arukh, 307:4. Kaf Haḥayyim, ibid, 20,24,25)

Renting premises to a non Jew if he will conduct business there on Shabbath

A Jewish landlord may rent his premises to a non Jew, even though the landlord knows that the non Jew will be transacting business in his building on Shabbath. (The rental may not be made by the day but must be made annually and the like).

The reason he may do this is because it is common practice to rent out premises to others and no one suspects that the Jew is involved in the business that the non Jew will be transacting on Shabbath. However, a Jew may not rent out premises to a non Jew if people will think that the Jew is involved in the business being conducted on Shabbath.

In the days when people used bath houses, a Jew could not rent a bath house to a non Jew, because bath houses were known by their owners' names and people would assume that the non Jew was hired for the day to transact business on behalf of the Jew on Shabbath. Similarly today, one could not rent out any property if it was known that the owner was Jewish and it would appear that the non Jew was actually conducting his business on behalf of the Jew on Shabbath.

(See Abodah Zara 21b. Shulḥan 'Arukh, 243: 1 & 2)

Touching a tree on Shabbath

One is permitted to touch a tree on Shabbath provided it does not move or sway as a result. Leaning on a tree is more complicated.

In order for leaning on a tree to be permitted, two conditions must be met:

1. The person must be strong and not need to lean heavily on the tree. Leaning on it is considered to be using the tree which is forbidden. Therefore, someone who is weak and needs to lean heavily on the tree is forbidden from doing so (as this comes into the category of using that which is attached, which is forbidden on Shabbath).

2. The tree must be strong and wide and not sway when one leans on it. If the tree is not that sturdy and rocks as a result, leaning on it is forbidden.

Unless both these conditions are fully met, leaning on a tree on Shabbath is forbidden.

(See Rama 336: 13. Kaf Haḥayyim ibid, Oth 89 & 90)

A swing or hammock attached to a tree on Shabbath

One may not make use of a tree on Shabbath for fear that we may come to break off part of the tree. As such it is forbidden to lean a ladder against the side of a tree and use it on Shabbath. But the "sides of the sides" of the tree are permitted. Therefore, if there is a hook or handle attached to a tree from before Shabbath and the ladder was attached to the hook, also from before Shabbath, it is permitted to be used.

Similarly, a swing or a Hammock which is tied directly to a tree may not be used on Shabbath. However, if there is a hook or pole attached to the tree and the swing or hammock is attached to the hook or pole and not to the tree itself, then it may be used on Shabbath.

Two conditions must be met, however. Both the hook and the swing or hammock must be attached from before Shabbath and the tree must be solid so that it will not sway with the weight or movement of the swing or the hammock.

(See Shulḥan 'Arukh, 336: 13. Kaf Haḥayyim ibid, Oth 85. Mishnah Berurah ibid, S.Q. 59)

Clearing broken pieces on Shabbath

One may carry the pieces of a vessel or utensil that breaks on Shabbath, provided the broken pieces themselves can be used for some purpose. An example would be a piece of broken earthenware that can be used to cover a cask.

If one cannot use the broken pieces for any purpose or does not need the place where they are, they may not be carried on Shabbath.

If the broken pieces are in a place where it is dangerous, however, such as if a vessel broke and the pieces are on the kitchen floor where children walk without shoes, one may carry them to clear the area. This is so even though they are not fit for any purpose whatsoever.

(See Shulḥan 'Arukh, 308: 6 with Rama. Kaf Haḥayyim ibid 62)

Walking on snow on Shabbath

The Shulḥan 'Arukh (Code of Jewish Law) prohibits crushing snow or hail on Shabbath. This means that they may not be broken into little pieces so that the water will flow out from them. (This is different to a case of placing them in a glass of wine or water where they will melt by themselves, and which is permitted). However, walking on snow and trampling it underfoot is permitted.

This is so, even though the snow will become squashed and might melt, because it is not the person's intention to melt the snow when he walks on it, and it is also not certain that it will melt. In fact, even in places where there is a substantial amount of snow which covers all open areas, even though it is certain that walking on the snow will cause it to melt because one's shoes are damp, it is nevertheless still permitted, because we have no other option.

(See Shulḥan 'Arukh, 320: 9, 13. Ben Ish Ḥai, 2nd year, Yithro, 11)

Why were Zakhor and Shamor said together?

Razal tell us that the words Zakhor and Shamor (remember and keep [the Sabbath]) were said in one utterance.

Ḥakham Rafael Barukh Toledano asks why Razal felt it necessary to stress that it was in one utterance. Whether it was said in one or two utterances, it has the same effect. We are still obligated to both remember and keep the Shabbath.

He answers that one possible reason is that many people today keep the commandment of remember, by readying themselves for Shabbath with their preparations and clothes they wear, and even lighting the Shabbath candles. But when it comes to keeping, many are not particular. There are even those, he adds, who do all the preparations for Shabbath but desecrate it once it starts.

When Razal mention that Zakhor and Shamor were said in one utterance, they are letting us know that if you keep the laws (Shamor), then you also get reward for the preparation (Zakhor). But if you do not keep the Shabbath then you get no reward for the preparation. They were said in one utterance to show us that they are both just one commandment.

(See Qiṣṣur Shulḥan 'Arukh of Ḥakham Rafael Barukh Toledano, Siman 233, Oth 8)

Answering what Torah we learned on Shabbath

The entire week, a person is preoccupied with the daily concerns of making a living and all the other preoccupations of the week. Nevertheless, one must set aside time to study the Torah every day. But if one was unable to study during the week then, at the very least, on Shabbath one must make the effort to study Torah and not spend the entire day simply eating, drinking and sleeping. Our Rabbis of blessed memory tell us that Shabbath and Yom Ṭob (Holy days) were only given to us in order to study Torah and one who does not waste time has time for everything.

The importance of learning Ḥiddushei Torah (new Torah insights) on Shabbath is great. It says in the holy Zohar that on Moṣei Shabbath (when Shabbath finishes) the Neshamah Yethera (additional soul that we receive on Shabbath) returns to Heaven. The Holy One Blessed Be He asks it: "What Ḥiddush Torah did you learn today?" After which the soul is seated in the Yeshibah on high.

(See 'Abodath Haqqodesh - Morei Be'eṣba' 153. Kaf Haḥayyim 300, Oth 13.)

Was Shabbath given for eating and drinking or studying Torah?

It says in the Talmud Yerushalmi that Ribbi Ḥaggai said that Shabbath and Yom Ṭob were given for the purpose of eating and drinking. Ribbi Berakhia said that they were given exclusively for the study of Torah.

The Tanḥuma explains that there is no contradiction between the two. When Ribbi Berakhia states that they were given for the purpose of studying Torah, this refers to workers and business people who are busy at their work the whole week, and on Shabbath they spend their time involved in the study of Torah.

Ribbi Haggai's comment that it is for pleasure refers to Talmidei Ḥakhamim (Torah scholars) who toil in the Torah every day of the week. When Shabbath comes they enjoy its pleasures.

From this we see, that contrary to popular belief, business people and workers who are involved with their jobs throughout the week, have a greater obligation to study Torah on Shabbath than do Torah scholars who are involved in the study of Torah every day. But, obviously, even Talmidei Ḥakhamim must spend the majority of the day involved in Torah.

(See Kaf Haḥayyim 288: Oth 6, Qiṣṣur Shulḥan 'Arukh, Ḥakham Rafael B Toledano, 266:4)

Dieting on Shabbath or not eating meat or drinking wine

And you shall call Shabbath a delight (Onegh). Part of the delight on Shabbath is eating meals with meat and wine. The Shulḥan 'Arukh states that there is an opinion that if food harms an individual, then not eating is considered Onegh (Shabbath delight) for him, and he his permitted to not eat. This means that one should not eat and suffer as a result, on Shabbath.

The Ohr LeṢion states that this appears to apply only if the food actually harms him, but if he simply wants to diet, he must not nullify the commandment of 'Onegh Shabbath and is required to eat at least a Kebesa (2 oz.) of bread, and should not refrain from eating other food.

Someone who only eats natural or vegetarian food, since his intention is not to deprive himself from [the pleasure of] meat and wine, is permitted to do so on Shabbath also. The same applies if someone does not get pleasure from consuming meat and wine, that he is not obligated to have them but can partake of other foods instead.

(See Shulḥan 'Arukh, 288: 2. See also Kaf Haḥayyim ibid, Oth 7 & 8 regarding not requiring a make up fast. Ohr LeṢion 2, 21:3)

3

ימים טובים וחגים

Holidays

Yom Ṭob (Holidays)

Honoring holidays like Shabbath

All Jewish holidays (Yamim Ṭobim) are called holy convocations (Miqraei Qodesh). Just as we are commanded to honor Shabbath and to call it a delight, we are likewise obligated to honor and delight in the holidays. We must also eat a meal at night and again during the day with bread and wine. However, unlike Shabbath, we are not required to eat Se'uddah Shelishith (a third meal).

The Ḥakhamim stated that honoring the holidays is done by cutting one's hair ('Ereb Yom Ṭob) in honor of the holiday, to wash, and to cut one's nails as one does before Shabbath. On Yom Ṭob one should also wear finer clothes than one wears on Shabbath (provided one can afford it).

(Shulḥan 'Arukh, 529:1 Kaf Haḥayyim ibid, Oth 4, 7, 12, 23. M.B. ibid: 12)

Any labor forbidden on Shabbath is forbidden on Yom Ṭob

Any labor that is forbidden on Shabbath is likewise forbidden on Yom Ṭob (with a few exceptions). The reason for this is so that the Jewish people will remember the great miracles that G-d did for them and their forefathers and will speak about them and recount them to their children and grand children.

Since the Jewish people must keep away from daily worldly matters, they have the time for this. Had we been permitted to do any form of Melakha (servile work), however light, each person would take care of his matters and the honor of the holy day would be forgotten by all, young and old.

There are many additional benefits to the fact that we may not do any work. All the people gather in Synagogues and houses of learning to hear words of Torah and be to guided and taught. Our Rabbis of blessed memory state that this is in accordance with the dictum of Moshe Rabbenu, 'a"h, that the Jewish people must study the laws pertaining to Pesaḥ (Passover) on Pesaḥ and the laws of Shabu'oth on Shabu'oth.

(Sh. A. 495:1. Ben Ish Ḥai, 1st year, Bamidbar, Oth 8. Kaf Haḥayyim ibid, oth 1. Meghilla 4: 1)

The order of candle lighting on a Holiday

The order of the blessings and candle lighting on Yom Ṭob (a Holy Day) which does not fall on Shabbath is different to the order on Friday evening. On Yom Ṭob, the Ba'alath

Habbayith (lady of the house) first recites the blessings and then lights. She must be careful not to put out the match after lighting since extinguishing a flame is not permitted once a person has accepted the sanctity of Yom Ṭob.

When Yom Ṭob falls on Shabbath, however, the order of the candle lighting is the same as for a regular Shabbath. The custom, as mentioned by the Ashkenazi and the vast majority of Sephardi Posqim (deciders of Halakha), which applies to both Sephardim and Ashkenazim, is that when the Ba'alath Habbayith lights the Shabbath candles, or the candles for when Shabbath and Yom Ṭob fall together, she first lights the candles, closes her eyes and then says the blessing.

(See Maamar Mordekhai, Hilkhoth Ḥaggim of Ḥ"R Mordekhai Eliyahu, ch. 15:9)

Carrying from one domain to another on a Holiday

Since carrying out from one domain to another on Yom Ṭob was permitted for the purposes of food, it was likewise permitted for any need. Even carrying into the public domain is permitted. The only proviso is that there must be some need, however small, for the object which is being carried.

As such, one can take out a child, even if one is merely going for a walk, since it serves the purpose of *Simḥath Yom Ṭob* (the happiness of the Holiday). Similarly, a Lulab may be carried out on Sukkoth or a Sefer Torah may be taken out to be read from. In fact, any item which is permitted to be carried on Yom Ṭob and for which there is some use may be taken from one domain to another.

In a place which has a valid 'Erub, one may carry out any item which may be handled on Yom Ṭob, even if there is no need for it at that time.

(See Shulḥan 'Arukh, 518:1 with Rama. Ben Ish Ḥai, 1st year, Bamidbar, Oth 9. Kaf Haḥayyim 518, Oth 1,2,3,5)

No candle or spices at Habdalah of a Holiday

At the conclusion of a Holiday (Yom Ṭob), both when it becomes Ḥol Hamo'ed or an ordinary day (Ḥol), the Habdalah prayer is recited during the 'Amidah and again after the prayers with a cup of wine. The difference between a Holiday and Shabbath, however, is that Habdalah after a Holiday does not include a candle or Besamim (sweet smelling spices).

A candle serves no purpose during the habdalah of Yom Ṭob because lighting candles (in the prescribed manner) is permitted on Yom Ṭob. The reason the Besamim are required for Habdalah after Shabbath is because of the additional soul (Neshamah Yetherah) that we receive on Shabbath which leaves us after it. On Yom Ṭob there is no additional soul. When Yom Ṭob falls on the completion of Shabbath we do not use Besamim in the Habdalah. The reason being that the joy of the Holiday and the eating and drinking that we do, serves in place of the Besamim.

(See Shulḥan 'Arukh 491: 1. Kaf Haḥayyim ibi, 2-3.)

Nissan & Pesaḥ

The Parah Adummah in today's world

Shabbath Parah, about the Parah Adummah (red heiffer), always falls on the Shabbath preceding Shabbath HaḤodesh (the Shabbath before the month of Nissan). This is because the Parah Adummah was burnt in the wilderness close to the month of Nissan, in order to purify Benei Yisrael so that they could offer the Pesaḥ (Passover sacrifice) at the correct time.

Every year, through the reading of the portion of the Parah Adummah with the congregation, the roots of this precept are re-awakened in Heaven. Therefore, if we read this portion every year and connect it to Teshubah (repentance) we purify our souls. It is considered, in fact, as if we performed the actual act of the Parah Adummah, as it says: *Unshallemah Farim Sefathenu* (the words of our lips shall be instead of oxen).

Every person, therefore, while Parashath Parah is being read in the Synagoue, should pay close attention, and request from G-d that He will accept his repentance and then purify him. The repentance has to come first, because it is like a case of a robber. There is no point locking the door while he is still inside. First we must remove him, and then we lock the door.

(See Dabar Be'Itto, Derush Parashath Parah)

Studying the laws of Pesaḥ 30 days before the Holiday

Thirty days before Pesaḥ, one should inquire about the Halakhoth (laws) of Pesaḥ. We learn this from the fact that Moshe Rabbenu, 'a"h, explained the laws pertaining to Pesaḥ Sheni (which takes place one month after Passover) on Pesaḥ (Passover) itself.

From this, there are those who learn that the laws of all Holidays must be learnt a month before the Holiday, whereas others say that this only applies to Pesaḥ. Pesaḥ has an additional reason as to why one must study one month in advance, and that is because its laws are complex and numerous.

Even though the Gemara (Talmud) also mentions that one must give Derashoth (homilies) from a month before Pesaḥ, the Shulḥan 'Arukh (Code of Jewish Law) does not mention this aspect. The custom nowadays is that the Derashoth are given on Shabbath Haggadol (usually the Shabbath before Pesaḥ) when the Rabbis of the communities expound on the Holiday and then give Halakhoth (laws) pertaining to Pesaḥ.

(See Shulḥan 'Arukh 429: 1. Mishnah Berurah. ibid 1,2. Kaf Haḥayyim ibid, 1,2)

No Confession/Taḥanun in Nissan because the whole month is considered holy

Widdui (confession) and Taḥanun (supplication prayer) is not recited the entire month of Nissan. The reason for this is that since the majority of the month is holy we consider that the entire month is holy. The breakdown of the days is as follows:

On the first of Nissan the Mishkan (Tabernacle) was erected. and each of the Nesiim (Princes of the Twelve Tribes) brought their offerings. Each Nasi (Prince) brought his offering on one day. This lasted, therefore, for twelve days, and each day was a Yom Ṭob (holy day) for the one who brought that day's offering.

The following day (the thirteenth day) was their Isru Ḥagh (the day after a holiday which also contains holiness). The day after that is 'Ereb Pesaḥ (the eve of Passover) which is also holy. After that we have 8 days of Pesaḥ (Passover), plus the Isru Ḥagh which, as we mentioned, also has holiness attached to it. And since the majority of the month passed in holiness, we consider the entire month to be holy.

There is an opinion, however, that the remaining days of Nissan also have their own Qedusha (holiness).

(See Shulḥan 'Arukh 429:2 and Rama. Kaf Haḥayyim ibid, 21. Mishnah Berurah ibid, 7.)

The final days of Nissan contain their own sanctity

We mentioned that the final days of the month of Nissan are considered to be auspicious days because the majority of the month was spent in Qedusha (holiness).

Additionally, there is an opinion that the final days of Nissan contain their own sanctity.

According to the Ma'aseh Roqeyaḥ, in the future, the third Beth Hamiqdash (Temple) will be built, not during the Yom Ṭob (holy days of Passover), but after the holiday of Pesaḥ, because if it were built during the holiday itself, it would be considered mixing one rejoicing with another. Therefore, the dedication of the Temple, which would take another seven days, would bring us to the end of the month of Nissan.

That is why even the final days of the month are also considered holy, and fasting is not permitted, in recognition of the third Beth Hamiqdash which will be built in the month of Nissan. May we witness it speedily in our days, Amen.

(See Kaf Haḥayyim 429, Oth, 21)

When can Birkath Ha-ilanoth (Blessing on the Trees) be recited?

Once a year, in the month of Nissan, we have the opportunity to say Birkath Ha-ilanoth (the Blessing of the Trees). It must be recited in front of two fruit trees which have blossomed with the blossoms visible on them.

It is preferable to say them at the first opportunity. Therefore, if the trees have blossomed, it is good to recite the blessing on Rosh Ḥodesh (the first day of the month of) Nissan. However, this is not always possible and it is often not even an option in many Western countries where the trees blossom later. In any case, the blessing may be recited at any time during the month of Nissan, including Ḥol Hamo'ed (the intermediate days of the Festival).

On Shabbath and Yom Ṭob (the first and last days of the holiday), however, Birkath Ha-ilanoth may not be recited. If it could not be said during the month of Nissan, it should be recited after Nissan, but without Shem Umalkhuth (without mentioning G-d's name).

(See Shulḥan 'Arukh 226: 1. Kaf Haḥayyim ibid, Oth 1. Haggadah Orah Ḥayyim, Birkath Ha-ilanoth, Oth 7).

Are women obligated to do Birkath Ha-ilanoth (blessing on the trees)?

There is a difference of opinion among the Posqim (deciders of Jewish law) as to whether women are obligated to do Birkath Ha-ilanoth (the blessing on the trees) or not. The difference of opinion centers on whether or not this is a time-bound precept.

Women, as we know, are exempt from performing time-bound precepts. If Birkath Ha-ilanoth is not a time-bound precept, they should recite the Berakha (blessing), but if it is they may not recite the Berakha, because to do so would be to recite G-d's holy name in vain, which is something that must be avoided at all costs.

In view of this, women should not recite this blessing because of the possibility that they would be taking G-d's name in vain. There are those who say that the husband should have his wife in mind when reciting the blessing and that she should stand near him so that she can hear the blessing and have in mind that she is fulfilling her obligation through this. However, this is not the prevalent custom. Ashkenazi women who have the custom of reciting the blessing, should continue to do so.

(See Maamar Mordekhai, Hilkhoth Ḥaggim of Rab Mordekhai Eliyahu, 2: 17).

Bediqah (search for leaven) in multiple locations and with others' help

The Berakha (blessing) that one recites before the Bediqath Ḥameṣ (search for the leaven) can cover his search in multiple houses. The physical going from one house to another is not considered to be a Hefseq (interruption). Despite different opinions, the custom is that even if they are far away from each other, the same blessing covers the other houses or stores or places of business.

If the head of the household wishes, he may have other members of the household stand next to him when he recites the Berakha and they then disperse to different parts of the house to check their own area. They do not recite a separate Berakha but rely on the one made by the householder. The same rule applies if he hires someone not from his household to assist with the Bediqah (checking).

The head of the household must also check at least a portion of the house since his obligation is greater than that of his Shaliyaḥ (agent). There is also an opinion that he is not permitted to recite the blessing if he does not check at all. As such, he should first check a portion of the house after reciting the blessing and then let his Shaliyaḥ continue.

(See Shulḥan 'Arukh, 432: 2. Kaf Haḥayyim ibid, 22-24, 26, Mishnah Berurah ibid 7,8)

What places must be included in the Bediqah (search for leaven)?

Any place where Ḥameṣ (leaven) was known to have been taken, must be checked. Not only that, but any place where there is reason to believe that Ḥameṣ (leaven) might have been taken, must also be included in the Bediqah (search).

All the rooms of one's house, therefore, including the attic, must be checked since, occasionally, people enter them with a piece of bread in their hands. Also included are storerooms where wines and other beverages are stored, because it is not uncommon for people to go there during their meal to get a drink. However, if it is known that no one enters these storerooms during their meal (or at any time) with bread or other leaven in their hands, they do not require checking.

It also goes without saying that if there are children in the house, all areas to which they have access, require checking.

(See Shulḥan 'Arukh, 433: 3. Kaf Haḥayyim ibid, Oth 22-30, 35. M.B. ibid, 13-17.)

Nullifying the Ḥameṣ (leaven) requires comprehension of the words

After doing the Bediqath Ḥameṣ (search for leaven) at night, one should nullify all Ḥameṣ (leaven) that may have remained in one's possession, by reading the first Kol Ḥamira (all leaven that is in my possession...should become nullified).

The nullification process, as ordained by the Torah, can be done in one's heart, but the Ḥakhamim ordained that we should actually utter the words, and the one reciting it must understand what he is saying. Someone who does not understand the language in which it is written (Aramaic) should recite it in the language he understands.

If someone who does not understand Hebrew or Aramaic recites it in one of those languages and does not understand at all what he is saying, thinking he is reciting some kind of a prayer or request, he has clearly not fulfilled his obligation at all. However, in the event that he knew what he was reciting but did not understand the actual words, he has fulfilled his obligation aposteriori (Bedi'abad).

(See Shulḥan 'Arukh, 434: 2. Rama, ibid. Kaf Haḥayyim ibid, Oth 19, 32-33.)

If a person erroneously recites a blessing over the first Neṭilath Yadayim

The first Neṭilath Yadayim (ritual washing of hands) that we do on the night of Pesaḥ is for the Karpas and is made without reciting the Berakha (blessing) of 'Al Neṭilath Yadayim. But what should someone do if, out of force of habit, he mistakenly recited the blessing?

There is an opinion that, he should not take his mind off the fact that he has done Neṭilath Yadayim and that this washing will also count later for the Ha<u>m</u>oṣi without washing again. Another opinion is that he should wash again later for the Ha<u>m</u>oṣi, but not recite the Berakha at that time.

There are those (the Lebush and the Gra), however, who hold that a Berakha is actually required for the first washing. From the words of the Beth Yoseph it appears that it is not forbidden to recite a blessing when washing for the Karpas, but only that it is preferable not to do so. If so, then the first washing would be in accordance with those who say that one should recite a blessing over it and has no connection with the second washing. This is particularly true since the person did not have the second washing in mind when he recited the blessing.

As such, a person should not nullify the enactment of our Rabbis of blessed memory and should wash again with a Berakha for the Ha<u>m</u>oṣi.

(See Kaf Haḥayyim, 473. Oth 106 and 107)

Do women lean at the Seder?

At the Seder on Pesaḥ men are obligated to eat and drink the required quantities of Maṣṣa (unleavened bread) and wine while leaning, as a sign of being a free person. The leaning must be done to the left. Even one who is left-handed leans to the left.

The Shulḥan 'Arukh says that a woman is not required to lean unless she is important. The Rama adds that all our women are considered important, but despite this he mentions that women do not lean, relying on the opinion of the Raabiya (ראבי״ה) that nobody is required to lean nowadays. The custom according to Ashkenazim follows the opinion of the Rama and Ashkenazi women do not lean.

The custom among Sephardim, however, is that the women do lean at the seder in all instances where the men lean.

(See Shulḥan 'Arukh 472: 2, 4. 473: 2. 475: 1. Maamar Mordekhai, Ḥaggim, ch. 11, 17)

To hide or not to hide the Afiqomen

The middle Maṣṣa (unleavened bread) is divided into two pieces and the larger piece is set aside for the Afiqomen at the end of the meal. The custom in Ashkenazi homes is that the Afiqomen is hidden as part of arousing the interest and curiosity of the children during the Seder. In Sephardi homes, however, the Afiqomen is not hidden.

Instead, the Afiqomen is tied onto the back of the youngest child who goes out of the room, usually with the other children, and knocks on the door. He is asked, "Where have you come from?", and he replies, "from Egypt". He is then asked, "And where are you going to?", to which he replies, "Jerusalem". He is finally asked, "And what are you carrying?" which is followed by the singing of Mah Nishtanah.

After that the Afiqomen is placed next to the celebrant who is leading the Seder, till it is used.

(See Ben Ish Ḥai Yr. 1. Parashath Ṣaw, 33. Kaf Haḥayyim 473, Oth 123. M"M, Hilkhoth Ḥaggim, ch. 11, 63 & 65)

If one ate after the Afiqomen

The Afiqomen must be the last item to be eaten on the night of Pesaḥ at the Seder. One may not eat anything after it, not even fruit. The reason for this is that the taste of the Maṣṣa (unleavened bread) must remain in one's mouth. The cups of wine of Birkath Hammazon and Hallel that are drunk after this are not included in this ruling. After this, however, one should not consume anything except water and, some say, coffee.

There are different opinions as to what one should do if one inadvertently did eat some other food after the Afiqomen. There are those who say he is not required to eat the Afiqomen again. However, the Eliyah Rabba states that if he has not yet made Birkath Hammazon, he must eat it again.

The Afiqomen must not be eaten in two different places. The reason for this being that it is in memory of the Qorban Pesaḥ (Passover sacrifice) which had to be eaten in one place, as it says: "In one house shall it be eaten". The Maghen Abraham states that it should not even be eaten at two different tables in the same room.

(See Shulḥan 'Arukh 478:1 with Rama. Ben Ish Ḥai, Yr. 1, Parashath Ṣaw, Oth 35. Kaf Haḥayyim ibid Oth 3-6)

Which blessing on the Hallel? Lighmor or Liqro?

On the first two days of Pesaḥ (Passover), the full Hallel is recited. The question is whether, when the full Hallel is recited, one should recite the Berakha (blessing) of *Lighmor* (to complete) or *Liqro* (to read) the Hallel.

The Maharam MiRotenburg never said *Lighmor* even when completing the Hallel, but always said *Liqro*. He was of the opinion that if, when one said *Lighmor* one left out a word or even one letter, it would be a blessing recited in vain. The Rosh, however, disagreed, saying that *Lighmor* had the same sense as *Liqro*. The Shulḥan 'Arukh ruled in accordance with the Rosh, saying that one should say *Lighmor*, whereas, the Rama was concerned about the opinion of the Maharam of Rotenburg and ruled that one should say *Liqro*.

The final Halakha is that Sephardim only recite a blessing on the Hallel when completing it and recite *Lighmor Eth Hahallel*. Ashkenazim always recite *Liqro*.

(See Kaf Haḥayyim 488, Oth 5)

Pesaḥ Sheni: our make-up day

It says in the Torah that when the laws of the Passover were given, there were those who were unable to keep it because they were defiled from having come in contact with the dead. The Gemara of Sukkah provides different scenarios as to what the exact case was, including the likelihood that it was those who were occupied in the burial of someone who had no relative to take care of it for him. They were unhappy that they did not have the opportunity to perform this commandment (Miṣwah) and brought their case to Moshe Rabbenu 'a"h.

G-d told Moshe Rabbenu that anyone who had been in contact with a dead person or had been traveling, should do the Passover sacrifice (Qorban Pesaḥ) on the fourteenth of the following month (Iyyar) and eat it with unleavened bread and bitter herbs.

There are no remarkable customs for this day nowadays. Sephardim and many Ashkenazim have the custom of not reciting Widdui (confession) and Tehinna (suplication) because it is a happy day. Some have the custom of eating some Maṣṣa (unleavened bread) on this day.

It is, however, a remarkable insight into the mindset of those who came to protest the fact that they could not perform the precept. Many people today would be quite happy to be exempt from having to perform any commandment. It is a lesson for all of us and we see G-d's most unusual response to their request, to let them have a "make up day", something we don't see with other commandments.

(See Ba<u>m</u>idbar 9: 6. Sukkah 25a & b)

G-d will wait till the time comes

Lo Yakhlu Lehithmahmeya<u>h</u> (they were driven out of Egypt and they couldn't delay). It says in the Gemara of Soṭah that G-d does not exact retribution of a nation till its time has come.

We know that the downfall of Egypt was on the seventh day of Pesaḥ (Passover), because this was the day the Egyptians drowned in the Red Sea and their treasures were washed up on the sea shore. This was obviously the day when their time had come. If so, why did Benei Yisrael (the Children of Israel) have to leave in such a rush, seven days before the time and not wait till the seventh day?

This can be compared to a wealthy individual who, together with his son, was walking in the marketplace dressed in expensive clothing. He was accosted by a drunk who grabbed his clothes claiming that he had stolen them from him. The wealthy man spoke to him gently saying that he had only borrowed them from the man's wife to wear till the following day at which time he would return them. The wealthy man's son asked him why he had said that he had borrowed them when they were really his own. The father answered that there was no point in arguing at that moment. The answer he gave would appease the drunk till the following day by which time he will have sobered up and would be embarrassed by what took place.

In the future, just as Pharaoh hardened his heart, so too in the future Geullah (redemption) Gogh will harden his heart against G-d and His Mashiyaḥ (Messiah). G-d, sitting in Heaven, will laugh at him and will wait till the appropriate time comes to act.

(See Soṭah 9a. Kether Ṣaddiq, Derush 9, Parashath Bo)

Ḥol Hamo’ed

Repairing a Sefer Torah on Ḥol Hamo’ed

Fixing a Sefer Torah on Ḥol Hamo’ed is forbidden if it requires a Sofer (scribe) to repair it by adding a letter (as opposed to simply separating letters or repairing it in a way that does not require a professional scribe). This assumes that the Synagogue or Minyan has other Sifrei Torah (Sefer Torahs). If not, it may be repaired on Ḥol Hamo’ed even by a professional scribe.

If the Synagogue only has one Sefer Torah, but another one in the vicinity has several, we do not require them to bring one from the other congregation. Indeed, there are complications with doing this according to the Zohar. As such, they may repair their Torah.

A Synagogue that has exactly three Sifrei Torah, and finds an error in one of them on Ḥol Hamo’ed of Sukkoth, is permitted to fix it, even though the other two are usable. The reason being that on Simḥath Torah we take out three Sifrei Torah. Even though one could make do with two by rolling one of them, this is not the preferred method since it puts a burden on the congregation who have to wait. It is also more honor to the Torah to have three Sifrei Torah and gives more pleasure to the three Ḥathanim who are called up to the Torah on Simḥath Torah, who will each have a Torah to read from.

(See Sh. A. 544:1. Kaf Haḥayyim ibid: 3, 6, 14)

Reading the wrong day's Parasha on Ḥol Hamo'ed

If during the four days of Ḥol Hamo'ed they made a mistake in the Synagogue and read the Torah reading for the following day – such as reading *Im Kesef* instead of *Qaddesh Li*, which is the example we will use – they should read the portion that they skipped in error (*Qaddesh Li*), on the following day. This is because even if they are read in the wrong order, one still fulfills one's obligation.

If, when the first person goes up to the Torah, they realize their error before he says the final blessing, there are many who say that they do not need to roll the Torah to the correct spot and start again, but continue reading the following day's portion that they started. However, this only applies in a place where the entire congregation prays in the same Synagogue every day. If not, those who heard *Im Kesef* in error in the first Synagogue today, who go to pray in a second Synagogue tomorrow, will never hear *Qaddesh Li* – the portion they were supposed to read today – at all on Ḥol Hamo'ed. Similarly, if people who were not in that first Synagogue today should come tomorrow, they will hear *Qaddesh Li* read twice.

As such, this ruling can only apply where there is only one Synagogue in the town, as it is not uncommon for people to pray in different Synagogues on different days. Therefore, when they realize their error, they should roll the Sefer Torah back to *Qaddesh Li* as long as they have not finished the reading.

(See Kaf Haḥayyim 490, Oth 27 and 28)

'Omer

Counting the 'Omer before 'Arbith

The ideal time to count the 'Omer is after the emergence of three stars, even on Friday night. According to the Shulḥan 'Arukh this is the appropriate way to perform the counting of the 'Omer.

One may count the 'Omer after the stars come out even if one has not yet prayed 'Arbith. However, ideally, one should pray 'Arbith first and then count the 'Omer because of the concept of *Tadir WeShe-eino Tadir* – something that takes place regularly ('Arbith) takes precedence over something that only comes occasionally (counting the 'Omer).

(Shulḥan 'Arukh 489:2. Oraḥ Ḥayyim Haggadah, Sefirath Ha'omer 9. Mishnah Berurah ibid, 14. Kaf Haḥayyim ibid, 43)

Does the Ḥazzan or the congregation count first?

In many communities, when the 'Omer is counted in the Synagogue, the Ḥazzan first recites the blessing and counts the 'Omer and then the congregation do the same after he has finished. In others, however, It is done the opposite way.

The Kenesseth Haggedolah writes that the custom of most people is for the congregation to bless and count first followed by the Ḥazzan, whereas in a few places it is done in reverse. The Yafeh Laleb (Ḥakham Yiṣḥaq Falaji, 'a"h) states that in his city of Izmir, there were those who had the custom of the congregation blessing and counting first, followed by the Ḥazzan, while others did the opposite.

The Ben Ish Ḥai (Ḥakham Yosef Ḥayim, 'a"h) writes in Oraḥ Ḥayyim that the custom is for the congregation to first recite the blessing followed by the counting, after which they should say the Haraḥaman. The Ḥazzan then blesses and counts, and then both he and the congregation repeat the Haraḥaman.

Both opinions have sources to rely on. However, since generally a Ḥazzan has the intention to pray on behalf of the congregation and the members of the congregation often intend to fulfill their obligation with his prayer, it is generally safer for the congregation to count first. In places where the Ḥazzan blesses and counts first, the congregation must be particular to have in mind that they are not fulfilling their obligation with his blessing because, otherwise, they would not be able to recite the blessing themselves.

(See Oraḥ Ḥayyim Haggadah, Hilkhoth Sefirath Ha'Omer, Oth 6. Kaf Haḥayyim 489, Oth 14)

When Lagh La'omer falls on Sunday

There are varying customs concerning the laws of the 'Omer on Lagh La'omer (the 33rd day of the 'Omer), especially when it falls on Sunday. The Minhagh (custom) concerning cutting hair according to the Rama, is that it can be cut on Lagh La'omer and when this falls on Sunday, one may take a haircut on the preceding Friday, in honor of Shabbath. This is the custom of Ashkenazim.

Sephardim follow the opinion of Maran in the Shulḥan 'Arukh and do not cut their hair till the 34th day of the 'Omer. From the 34th day on it is permitted. Similarly, Sephardim permit listening to music from the 34th day on. It should be noted, however, that according to Rabbenu the Ari z"l, one may not cut one's hair for the entire period of the 'Omer, i.e. till the morning of 'Ereb Shabu'oth.

Weddings are held by Ashkenazim on Lagh La'omer. Some Sephardim hold them from the 34th day on, however, according to the Ben Ish Ḥai, they are permitted any day from Lagh La'omer on.

(See Shulḥan 'Arukh 493: 1-2, with Rama. Oraḥ Ḥayyim Haggadah, Hilkhoth Ḥol Hamo'ed, 25)

Shabu'oth

Operations on the eve of Shabu'oth

The Gemara of Shabbath (129b) states that it is dangerous to let blood on the eve of Shabu'oth (the Festival of Weeks). The Ḥakhamim forbade blood letting on the eve of every Festival on account of the Festival of Shabu'oth. The reason why it was forbidden on the eve of Shabu'oth is that had the Children of Israel not accepted the Torah they would, Heaven forbid, have been killed.

In those days, letting blood was done as a matter of course for health reasons, and that was what was not permitted. Today, donating blood in a non emergency situation would fall into that category and should be scheduled to a different time. Someone who needs to have an important operation, because a possibility of danger exists, can do so on the eve of Shabu'oth. An operation that is not critical or non life-threatening in nature should be scheduled for a different time.

(See Shabbath 129b. Rama 496:10. M.B. ibid, 38. M.M. Ḥaggim, 21: 20)

Prayers, Qiddush and candle lighting for the holiday

The fiftieth day of the 'Omer is the festival of Shabu'oth. Since there must be seven full weeks between Pesaḥ and

Shabu'oth, Qiddush on the first night of Shabu'oth must be made after the stars come out.

The Mishnah Berurah states that one should not pray the 'Arbith prayer of the commencement of Shabu'oth till the emergence of the stars. This is the prevalent custom in Ashkenazi synagogues, to wait till three stars have emerged before praying 'Arbith.

The prevalent custom amongst Sephardim is to pray 'Arbith earlier, but not make Qiddush till the stars have appeared. The women light the candles, as usual, before the onset of the holiday. It says in Ben Ish Ḥai that the Qiddush on the first night must be made after the stars come out. He mentions, however, that on the second night of Shabu'oth (for those who dwell outside the Land of Israel), Qiddush may be made while it is still day. He adds that there are situations where this is, in fact, preferable.

In such a case, the lady of the house lights the candles for the second night of the holiday just prior to the making of the Qiddush, even though it is still day, since the lighting of the candles is on account of the Qiddush.

(See Shulḥan 'Arukh 494: 1. Mishnah Berurah ibid: 1. Ben Ish Ḥai, 1st year, Ba<u>m</u>idbar, Oth 2. Kaf Haḥayyim 494, Oth 1)

Torah study on the night of Shabu'oth

According to the holy Zohar, the Torah study that one does all night on the night of Shabu'oth crowns the Shekhinah (G-d's Holy Presence) with 24 items of jewelry in preparation for the giving of the Torah during the day of Shabu'oth.

Many have the custom of listening to Torah lectures on the night of Shabu'oth. Others prefer to study Gemara. These are the prevalent customs in Ashkenazi communities. According to the Qabbalah, however, one should only learn the special Tiqqun that was made for the night of Shabu'oth which is in accordance with Rabbenu the Ari, z"l.

It includes excerpts from the Torah, Nebi-im (Prophets) and Kethubim (Writings), as well as the Taryagh Miṣwoth (613 commandments) and Zohar. One should not make any change to the order of the reading nor add to or subtract from it, because there is a Sod (secret) attached to it. This is the custom of Sephardim as well as those Ashkenazim who follow the Sod.

Women have no obligation, whatsoever, to stay up learning on the night of Shabu'oth. However, if they wish to go and study Torah (Tanakh) and the like, they will be blessed.

(See Rab Pe'alim, 1, Oraḥ Ḥayyim, Sod Yesharim, 9. Ben Ish Ḥai, Yr 1, Ba<u>m</u>idbar, 4. Kaf Haḥayyim 494, Oth 6. Mishnah Berurah, ibid, 1)

Stand or sit during the Ten Commandments?

One must be particular to pay close attention to the reading of the Ten Commandments on the morning of Shabu'oth and listen to it in fear and awe as if we were standing at Har Sinai (Mt. Sinai).

The custom in Ashkenazi Synagogues is to stand for the reading of the Ten Commandments. Even though the Shalmei Ṣibbur and Rab Ḥida, 'a"h, bring down this custom, the custom today among Sephardim is to remain seated in accordance with the Minhagh of the Ari z"l.

One reason is that we should not give the opportunity to disbelievers to claim that only the Ten commandments are G-d given. In addition, it is possibly easier to have the appropriate concentration while seated. In any case, this should not be a reason for quarrels in the Synagogue.

If a Sephardi is praying in an Ashkenazi Synagogue, he should not remain seated while all others are standing, but should stand from the beginning of that Torah portion and not just for the Ten Commandments.

(See Kaf Haḥayyim 494: 21, 30. H' M. Eliyahu, Hilkhoth Ḥaggim 22: 54)

The second night of Shabu'oth

For those of us who live outside the Land of Israel, the question arises whether one should do a Limmud (learning session) on the second night of Shabu'oth also. It mentions in Ben Ish Ḥai that one should read the portions of the Tanakh that were read on the first night and then go to sleep.

One who is able to also read the 613 Miṣwoth (commandments) as well as the Adra Rabba and remain awake all night will be blessed. There is a famous story about Maran (Yosef Qaro, 'a"h, the author of the Shulḥan 'Arukh) who stayed up all night on both nights of Shabu'oth, together with his disciples and, as a result, had mystical secrets revealed to them.

One should be particular to sanctify the second day of Shabu'oth with the study of the Torah, because it is greater than the second day of any other holiday.

(See Ben Ish Ḥai, 1st year, Parashath Ba<u>m</u>idbar, Oth 7)

The 22 days

Weddings and engagements during the 22 days

The custom is not to hold weddings from the seventeenth (17th) of Tammuz till the ninth of Ab. This applies even to one who has never married and, therefore, not yet been able to fulfil the Miṣwah (commandment) of Peru Urbu (go forth and multiply).

This is the custom of all Ashkenazim. While there are some Sephardim who only prohibit weddings from Rosh Ḥodesh Ab, the prevalent custom amongst Sephardim also, is to avoid weddings from the seventeenth of Tammuz. The reason is that this is not considered to be a time when one sees Berakha (blessing).

For this reason, there are those who avoid engagements from the seventeenth of Tammuz also, whereas others hold them until Rosh Ḥodesh Ab. In the latter case they are held without a Se'uddah (festive meal) and, it goes without saying, without music, whether with live musical instruments or recorded.

(See Ben Ish Ḥai, 1st year, Parashath Debarim, Oth 4. Ḥ"R Mordekhai Eliyahu, Hilkhoth Ḥaggim, 25, Oth 3)

Music on hold – and between news items

If one is listening to the news during the 22 days (the three weeks), and the station has musical breaks between the news items, strictly speaking, one does not need to turn off the radio. This assumes that they are not inappropriate songs, in which case one is obligated to turn them off at any time.

One who wishes to be strict with himself, however, and turns off the radio during these musical breaks, in order not to hear the music, will be blessed.

The same applies to music on hold when one calls a phone number and is placed on hold. One is permitted to listen to it since it is not for pleasure but simply to make the wait more pleasant.

(See M.M. Hilkhoth Ḥaggim, 25: 9 & 10)

New clothes and shoes

One may not buy any garment that requires the Berakha (blessing) of Sheheḥeyanu from Rosh Ḥodesh Ab, even if one intends to wear them after Tish'ah BeAb. However, if there is a need to purchase items that do not require Sheheḥeyanu, such as socks and undershirts, even though it is preferable to purchase them before Rosh Ḥodesh, they may be purchased even after Rosh Ḥodesh Ab. They should not be worn, however, till after the ninth of Ab.

Non leather shoes must be worn on Tish'ah BeAb. If the only shoes that one has that do not contain leather are brand new, they may be worn for the first time on Tish'ah BeAb. Ideally, however, they should be worn for the first time on Yom Kippur.

(See Hikhoth Ḥaggim - Maamar Mordekhai, ch. 25, Oth 34 and 35)

Buying potted plants and planting trees during the nine days

During the nine days between Rosh Ḥodesh Ab and the ninth of Ab (Tish'ah BeAb), we should not plant or purchase trees or potted plants which are for decorative purposes. Obviously, if one already has plants and trees they may be looked after appropriately.

Someone, such as a farmer, who who depends on fruit trees for his living and finds that the season for planting the fruit trees falls during the nine days, is permitted to plant them then. This is because he is planting them for his livelihood and not merely for decoration.

(See Hikhoth Ḥaggim - Ḥ"R Mordekhai Eliyahu, 'a"h, ch. 25, Oth 31)

Veggie burgers and the like during the nine days

The prohibition of eating meat during the nine days (from Rosh Ḥodesh for Ashkenazim and from after Rosh Ḥodesh for Sephardim) applies also to food that had meat cooked in it. For instance, one may not eat the vegetables and leave out the pieces of meat. Similarly, chicken is included in the prohibition.

Soup made from vegetarian powder or cubes that have the taste of meat are permitted to be consumed during the nine days because they do not actually contain meat. The same rule applies to any other vegetarian food, such as veggie burgers made from soy, that they may be eaten during the nine days. The one proviso, however, is that this must be in a place where people are aware of these products and know that they are not real meat.

(See Hikhoth Ḥaggim - Ḥ"R Mordekhai Eliyahu, 'a"h, ch. 25, Oth 37)

Washing clothes, bed linen and towels

Washing one's clothes during the week of Tish'ah BeAb (Shabuwa' Sheḥal Bo) is not permitted, even if they will not be worn till after Tish'ah BeAb. However, this prohibition does not only apply to the clothes that one wears but also to bed linen and towels and the like.

Some permit washing clothes for little children till the age of three because they are soiled regularly and one may not have enough replacements. Those who follow this leniency must be careful not to wash too many at once and may not do so in public.

Even though, nowadays, washing is generally done in a washing machine and not by hand it is still forbidden. Ironing previously washed clothes and bed linen is similarly prohibited at this time.

The custom of Ashkenazim is to forbid all the above from Rosh Ḥodesh.

(See Shulḥan 'Arukh 551:3, with Rama. Ben Ish Ḥai, 1st year, Parashath Debarim, Oth 6. Maamar Mordekhai of Ḥ"R Mordekhai Eliyahu, 25, Oth 65-67)

Some aspects of the fast start earlier

The fast of Tish'ah BeAb (9th of Ab) starts at night and ends the following day after the emergence of three stars. On the eve of Tish'ah BeAb one may eat till close to sunset. However, once sunset comes one is forbidden to eat.

Not only is eating forbidden once sunset comes, but all items that are forbidden on Tish'ah BeAb are forbidden from sunset. Therefore, one must have finished cleaning one's teeth and removed one's leather shoes before this time.

Studying Torah, however, is not done past midday (Halakhic time) on the eve of Tish'ah BeAb, except for those portions that one is permitted to study on Tish'ah BeAb itself. In years when the eve of Tish'ah BeAb falls on Shabbath, the prevalent custom is to permit the study of Torah even past midday.

If there is a Milah or Pidyon Habben on the eve of Tish'ah BeAb, the Se'uddah (festive meal) should be held before midday.

(See Shulḥan 'Arukh 553:2 with Rama. Ben Ish Ḥai, 1st yr, Parashath Debarim, Oth 18. Kaf Haḥayyim 553, Oth 9, 18, and 551, Oth 168)

Birkath Hallebanah after Tish'ah BeAb

When the fast of Tish'ah BeAb is over if there is a clear and unobstructed view of the moon, Birkath Hallebanah (the blessing on the moon) should be recited. However, since one has been fasting the whole day, it is appropriate to taste something before reciting the blessing since this blessing should be recited in happiness.

Since one did not do a complete Neṭilath Yadayim (ritual washing of the hands) that morning, but only did it up to the knuckles, one should do the complete Neṭilath Yadayim, till the wrists, before reciting Birkath Hallebanah.

(See Ben Ish Ḥai, 1st Year, Parashath Debarim, Oth 28)

Elul

The power of repentance

The month of Elul is when we turn our thoughts to repentance in preparation for the Yamim Noraim, Rosh Hashanah and Yom Kippur which are round the corner. Our Rabbis tell us that one who repents is considered to be on a higher level than one who never sinned. Why is that so?

Let us look at a situation of two people who complained of chest pains. The first was visited by his doctor who immediately gave him various medications and cured him in three days. The second one's doctor felt that his illness was insignificant and did not treat it. As a result, his illness became so serious that he was about to die. At that point the doctor gave him the right care and medication over an extended period of three months till the patient was finally cured. Which doctor can be considered greater?

The answer is the second one, because the fact that he was able to cure someone so seriously ill, proves his capabilities. Even though the first doctor nipped the sickness in the bud, we do not know if he would have been able to cure a sickness as serious as the one the second person had.

So too, one who has sinned and repented — even though he has negatively affected himself with all that he experienced in the past, and has much more difficulty chasing away the impurities in his body and keeping away from sin, but nevertheless manages to sanctify himself — is on a higher level than one who has always followed the right path, because we do not know if the latter would be able to withstand the test that the Ba'al Teshubah passed.

(See Mayim Ḥayyim, Ch. 2, Ma'alath Hatteshubah)

The 25th of Elul and creation of the world

Many people erroneously believe that Rosh Hashanah, the Jewish New Year, falls on the day the world was created. In fact, it falls on the day that man was created which was on the last of the six days of creation. The creation of the world, therefore, took place six days earlier, which corresponds to the Hebrew date of the twenty-fifth of Elul.

It says in Leshon Ḥakhamin, that the twenty-fifth of Elul must be sanctified by us. One should light five candles at night for Qabbalistic reasons. They may be lit by the husband or the wife. As on other special days, one should not fast on this day but, rather, should eat meals with bread and Birkath Hammazon, with meat and desserts.

Anger is considered to be a very bad trait, and one should be particular to overcome it at all times. On Rosh Hashanah, we must make every effort not to get angry at all. Similarly, one should take care not to get angry on the twenty-fifth of Elul. And as part of sanctifying this day, we should increase the amount of charity we give.

There all also several prayers that may be recited which may be found in Leshon Ḥakhamim.

(See Leshon Ḥakhamim, end of Ḥeleq Aleph, Limmud Bekaf Heh BeElul)

Rosh Hashanah

Which one of the two blows the Shofar?

There are Synagogues which have two different people to blow the Shofar every year, one on the first day of Rosh Hashanah and the other on the second day.

What happens in a year when the first day of Rosh Hashanah is Shabbath and, as such, the Shofar is only blown on the second day? Should the one who, normally, blows on the first day and recites the Berakha (blessing) of Sheheḥeyanu be the one to blow? Or should it be the second one whose turn it is always to blow on the second day of Rosh Hashanah?

The answer is that the first one is the one who blows the Shofar that year and recites the blessing of Sheheḥeyanu. The second one does not blow that year.

(See Kaf Haḥayyim, Taw Qof Peh Aleph, Oth Meem Ḥeth)

Women and the blessing on the Shofar

Women are exempt from hearing the Shofar because women are not obligated in positive precepts that must be performed at a specific time. However, the majority of women are considered to have accepted it upon themselves as an obligation.

When a woman goes to the Synagogue, the Toqeya' (the one who blows the Shofar) says the blessing on behalf of the congregation and all present should have in mind that they are fulfilling their obligation through his blessing. A question arises if a woman is unable to go to Synagogue, and someone who has already fulfilled his obligation of the Shofar comes to blow for her. What is done in such a case regarding the blessing?

All agree that the one who blows may not recite a blessing for her. Sephardim follow the opinion of the Shulḥan 'Arukh that the woman may not recite the blessing either. Ashkenazim permit women to recite the blessing, even though they are exempt from the commandment.

(See Ben Ish Ḥai, yr 1, Niṣabim, 17. Shulḥan Arukh/Rama 589:6. Kaf Haḥayyim 589: 23, 27,32)

Sleeping during the day on Rosh Hashanah

One should not sleep during the day on Rosh Hashanah. This includes making the effort to wake up in the morning before daybreak.

Since we are being judged on Rosh Hashanah, it would hardly be appropriate for us to show laziness by sleeping at the time we are being judged. In addition, it is said that if one sleeps during the day on Rosh Hashanah, his Mazzal (good fortune) will sleep the rest of the year.

If someone has a headache or some other similar condition and feels the need to sleep during the day, he should make an effort to stay awake in the morning and sleep in the second half of the day.

(See Ben Ish Ḥai, yr1, Parashath Niṣabim, Oth 11. Rama, 583,2. Kaf Haḥayyim, ibid, oth 35 & 36)

Rosh Hashanah on Shabbath – is something lacking?

When Rosh Hashanah falls on Shabbath, people sometimes feel that something is lacking in view of the fact that we do not blow the Shofar on Shabbath. It says in Tokhaḥath Ḥayyim, that when Rosh Hashanah falls on Shabbath and there is no Shofar, we should rush to make Teshubah (repentance) before G-d, because this will awaken the trait of mercy in G-d, ten times more than the blowing of the Shofar.

Not only that, but we see from the fact that we do not blow the Shofar, how important it is to keep Shabbath in all its detail. Even though blowing the Shofar is a commandment from the Torah, and blowing it is not a Melakha (forbidden Shabbath labor), nevertheless, the Ḥakhamim forbade us to blow it on Shabbath out of the concern that someone may come to carry it in the public domain (which is a forbidden labor). If the Ḥakhamim prevented us from performing a positive commandment from the Torah out of fear that there might possibly be Ḥillul (desecration of) Shabbath, we see how extremely particular we must be to not actually desecrate any Shabbath during the year.

When one keeps Shabbath in all its details, it is as if he has kept the entire Torah and it is worth more than 613 Shofars. So instead of feeling sad that there is no Shofar one should rejoice over the fact that we are keeping Shabbath correctly.

(See Tokhaḥath Ḥayyim, Pereq 54)

Tashlikh on Shabbath

When the first day of Rosh Hashanah falls on Shabbath, there are those who do Tashlikh (the symbolic casting of one's sins into the water) on the first day as usual, whereas others postpone it to the second day. It is understood from the Maharil (a Rishon from Germany) that it should always be done on the first day. The Mishnah Berurah mentions that there are a few communities that have the custom of postponing it to the second day when the first day is Shabbath and that it is possible that the reason why they do this is because the river is outside the city and there is a fear that people will carry prayer books and the like. The prevalent custom amongst Ashkenazim today has become to postpone it to Sunday. We should note that there are those, especially in the Hassidic community, who never do it on Rosh Hashanah in any year, but do it later.

While some Sephardim have also adopted the practice of doing it on Sunday, the prevalent ruling by Sephardi Posqim is that Tashlikh should be done on the first day, even when it falls on Shabbath. It says in Ben Ish Ḥai that it must be done on the first day and only if, for reasons out of one's control, one was unable to do it then, one should do it on the second day after Musaf. The Kaf Haḥayyim states that the custom of the Qabbalists in Beth E-l, who followed the Ari z"l, was to do it on the first day even when it was Shabbath. This is also the custom at Midrash Ben Ish Ḥai.

If the congregation goes outside the 'Erub, one must ensure that nothing is carried. In such a case, only the three main Pesuqim (verses) of Mi E-l Kamokha are recited by heart at the water. The lengthy readings before and after are read in the Synagogue. It says in Maamar Mordekhai (Hilkhoth

Ḥaggim), that in these circumstances, some also say it next to a barrel of water in the Synagogue grounds.

(Mishnah Berurah [PMG] 583: 8 - Kaf Haḥayyim ibid: Oth 31 - Ben Ish Ḥai, yr 1, Oth 12 - Maamar Mordekhai, Hilkhoth Ḥaggim, 40:21)

Abinu Malkenu on Shabbath

The Rama writes that we do not say the prayer of Abinu Malkenu on Rosh Hashanah if it is Shabbath. The Rashbaṣ states that the custom is to say it on Shabbath, but since this is a Minhagh (custom), a person should not change his own custom, whatever it is. There are different opinions supporting both rulings.

The Shulḥan 'Arukh (Code of Jewish Law) did not make a ruling in this matter. It would appear that this is because of what the Rashbaṣ wrote, that it depends on one's custom and, as such, he did not wish to make a definitive ruling, leaving each person to follow his own Minhagh.

In practical terms, Ashkenazim follow the ruling of Rama and do not recite Abinu Malkenu on Shabbath. Some Sephardim do recite it on Shabbath, whereas others do not. The custom followed at *Midrash Ben Ish Ḥai* is not to recite it on Shabbath.

(See Shulḥan 'Arukh 584: 1 with Rama. Kaf Haḥayyim ibid: Oth 8)

Behavior during the Ten Days

During the 'Aṣereth Yemei Teshubah (the Ten Days of Repentance between Rosh Hashanah and Yom Kippur), we should intensify our prayer and supplication. We should increase our giving of charity and good deeds at this time. We should likewise increase the study of the Torah and keeping of the precepts, more than we do the rest of the year.

It is appropriate to observe Ḥumroth (stringencies) that one does not do the rest of the year. For example, one who eats (Kasher) bread baked by a non-Jewish bakery during the year, should make every effort to eat Path Yisrael (bread baked by Jews) during the Ten Days. In view of this, one should consider all one's actions at this time of the year to see where one is following leniencies.

As a result, measure for measure (Middah Keneghed Middah), we are are able to ask G-d to be even more merciful with us this time of year, than he is during the rest of the year.

(See Shulḥan 'Arukh 602:1, 603:1 and Kaf Haḥayyim 602:4)

Yom Kippur

Fasting is prohibited the day before Yom Kippur

It is forbidden to fast the day before Yom Kippur. On the contrary we are required to eat the amount of food that we would consume in two days (if it is possible) on that day. It is considered a serious transgression to fast then, since it may cause one to eat on Yom Kippur, for which the punishment is Kareth (defined as Divine punishment of cutting the soul of the person off from the Jewish people).

Even if one has a dream that is troubling to the person, he may not fast. Instead he should redeem the dream by giving money in charity instead.

If someone fasts in error on 'Ereb (the day before) Yom Kippur, he must fast another fast as a make up fast since he fasted when he was not permitted to. However, this fast should be held after the month of Tashri.

(See Rama 604: 1. Kaf Haḥayyim, ibid: 8-13)

Forgiving others without harboring a grudge

We must ask for forgiveness from others before Yom Kippur because sins between a person and his fellow man are not atoned for on Yom Kippur. We must seek forgiveness from our fellow man before we ask forgiveness from G-d.

A person should be easily appeased and hard to anger. Therefore, when someone comes to ask forgiveness, one should not be cruel but should forgive him with all his heart and soul. Even if the sins against him were substantial, he must not bear a grudge or take revenge, because such is the nature of the Jewish people, to be forgiving.

A person should know that if he does not overcome his nature and does not forgive his neighbor, then he will not be forgiven his transgressions either. The only exception is if his intention in not forgiving is for the good of the person, but he should still forgive him in his heart and not bear a grudge.

One who has defamed another person (Moṣi Shem Ra'), does not need to be forgiven. However, it is considered to be an act of humility to do so.

(Sh. 'A 606:1 and Rama. Kaf Haḥayyim ibid 27, 28, 30-32)

Sheheḥeyanu at Kol Nidrei

We must start the holy day (Yom Ṭob) of Yom kippur some time before sunset. On the eve of Shabbath we do this when we say *Boee Kallah* and *Mizmor Shir Leyom Hashabbath.* On Yom Kippur we accept the holiness of the day when we recite the blessing of Sheheḥeyanu.

This assumes, of course, that it is before sunset, because Yom Kippur automatically starts by sunset, even if one did not say Sheheḥeyanu. In addition, if one states after Pelagh Haminḥa, that one is accepting Kippur, even before he says Sheheḥeyanu, then Yom Kippur starts at that time.

The custom is that the one holding the Sefer Kol Nidrei is the one who says the blessing of Sheheḥeyanu loudly on behalf of the congregation (in Ashkenazi communities it is usually the Ḥazzan) and the congregation have in mind that he is saying it on their behalf and answer Amen. The Ben Ish Ḥai states that one who cannot hear him properly should recite his own blessing. There are those who are of the opinion that it is better for each person to say the blessing for themselves, since the one reciting it may not have everybody in mind. It would appear, therefore, in order to satisfy all opinions, that the person who is reciting the blessing should be reminded just prior to saying it, to have everyone in mind and all those who hear him clearly can rely on his blessing and answer Amen.

In any case, a woman who has already recited Sheheḥeyanu when she lit the candles (or anyone who has already recited it, for that matter), must not say it again, but should hear it being recited and answer Amen.

(See Ben Ish Ḥai, 1st yr, Wayyelekh, 11. Kaf Haḥayyim 619:21)

The night of Yom Kippur should be spent in holiness

Even the night of Yom kippur should be spent in a state of holiness. There are those who stay in the Synagaogue the whole night of Yom Kippur reading various songs of praise or Torah. Rabbenu the Ari z"l, used to stay up all night on Yom Kippur, studying Torah. There are those who feel, however, that nowadays we should go home to bed to get proper sleep, in order to be able to pray the next day with complete intent (Lebush).This is especially true of the Ḥazzanim.

Rabbenu the Ḥida, 'a"h, says that at night on Yom Kippur, one should read the entire book of Tehillim, including the Pizmonim (songs of praise) between each book of Tehillim, that are read on Hosha'na Rabba. After that, if he is able, he should read the Adra Zoṭa. And when sleep is about to overpower him, he should read the Shema' with great concentration.

Some men have the custom of sleeping in the Synagogue, but should sleep some distance from the Hekhal or in the women's section when there are no women present.

(See Moreh Be'eṣba', 274, 275, 276. Sh. "A, 619: 6, Kaf Haḥayyim, ibid, 50, 52, 53. MB 15)

Sukkoth

Five blessings when the second night of Sukkoth is Saturday night

When the first day of Sukkoth is Shabbath, those of us who dwell outside the Land of Israel, must make Habdalah as well as Qiddush on the second night of the holiday (Yom Ṭob).

The Habdalah is said during the Qiddush as part of five blessings that are recited then. They form the acronym YaQNeHaZ. These letters stand for:

Yayin - the Berakha (blessing) on the wine

Qiddush - the blessing of Asher Baḥar Banu

Ner - the blessing of Borei Meorei HaEsh

Habdalah - the blessing of Hambdil Ben Qodesh Leqodesh, and

Zeman - the blessing of Sheheḥeyanu.

When the first day of Sukkoth does not fall on Shabbath, there is no Habdalah on the second night.

(See Ḥ"R Mordekhai Eliyahu, Maamar Mordekhai, Hilkhoth Ḥaggim, 51:67)

Using the Synagogue's Arba'ah Minim (four species)

On the first day of Sukkoth, having a Lulab and Ethrogh is a commandment from the Torah (outside the Beth Hamiqdash the requirement for the remaining days was enacted by the Ḥakhamim). Yet there are those who are willing to make large donations in order to open the Hekhal or show the Sefer Torah, but will not purchase their own Lulab and Ethrogh. Instead, they use their friend's or the one that the Synagogue purchases for the congregation to use.

It is important to have one's own Lulab and Ethrogh. Indeed, if the Synagogue has a very special Ethrogh (Mehuddar) and a person sees that his own Ethrogh while Kasher, is not of the same quality, he should still recite the blessing on his own and not on the superior one of the Synagogue.

In fact, if someone does not have his own set of Lulab and Ethrogh, it is preferable for him to borrow one from his friend rather than use the one of the congregation. In such a case, however, since one must bless on his own set, he must be given the Lulab as a *Mattanah 'Al Menath Lehaḥzir* (an outright gift provided he returns it – which means that provided he returns it to its original owner, it will be considered that for the time he had it, it was his).

(See Kaf Haḥayyim 658: 1, 17, 80)

The willow of distinction

The 'Arabah (willow of the brook) has no beauty or smell, does not give any shade, does not produce any fruit and grows alone by the water. Passers by don't even pick it.

There is a parable in Qol Sasson about a king who had many maid-servants. Among them was one who had no beauty, and none of the men-servants wished to marry her. The king seeing this, felt compassion towards her and elevated her and made her part of his royal retinue. As a result, all the other servants became her servants. In addition, the king told the other members of his royal retinue that he would not approach them unless she was among them. This ensured her acceptance by all.

The 'Arabah is likened to the maid-servant. G-d took the 'Arabah and placed it among the regal Lulab (shoot of the palm-tree), the Ethrogh (citron) and the Hadas (myrtle) – three plants of quality and distinction. Despite their importance, without the 'Arabah, we are told that these three are Pesulim (unfit for ritual use).

This is a great message from G-d that all His creatures are equal and we should not push anyone away or reject them, because G-d will not accept us unless we include even the "'Arabah" of His people.

(See Qol Sasson [Ḥakham Sasson Mordekhai Moshe] Ch. 43)

Eating the Ethrogh

Please note: there are those who have mentioned a rumor that Ethroghs are saturated with pesticides more than other fruits and vegetables. We have no knowledge of this one way or the other and this Torah Minute does not refer to it.

Some people have the custom of making jam or other foods from the Ethrogh after Sukkoth. The question is from when are we permitted to eat them?

Even though the last time the Ethrogh is used on Sukkoth is on the morning of Hosha'na Rabba, it is forbidden to be eaten the entire day of Hosha'na Rabba. For those who live in the Land of Israel, it is permitted on Shemini 'Aṣereth. For those of us who dwell outside the Land of Israel, it can not be eaten on Shemini 'Aṣereth, but we must wait till Simḥath Torah, which is the following day and the additional day that we keep outside the Land of Israel (Yom Ṭob Sheni Shel Galuyoth). But this only applies when Shemini 'Aṣereth does not fall on Shabbath.

When Shemini 'Aṣereth falls on Shabbath, one should not eat it on Simḥath Torah either, but only on the following day, in order to cover all opinions.

(See Ben Ish Ḥai, yr 1, Parashath Wezoth Habberakha, Oth 10)

Building a Sukkah on Ḥol Hamo'ed

Since we are commanded to keep Sukkoth for seven days and dwell in booths, there is a question in the Gemara whether a Sukkah that was built on Ḥol Hamo'ed (the intermediate days of the holidays) is valid, since it will not be used for a full seven days.

The opinion of the Ḥakhamim in the Gemara is brought down as Halakha in the Shulḥan 'Arukh (Maran Yoseph Qaro, 'a"h) that if one did not build it prior to Sukkoth, whether for reasons out of one's control, or whether he did not build it then deliberately, it may be built on Ḥol Hamo'ed. So too, if a Sukkah collapses, it may be rebuilt on Ḥol Hamo'ed.

If a boy reaches the age of thirteen (Bar Miṣwah), or a convert is converted on Ḥol Ha<u>m</u>o'ed, he may build it then according to all opinions.

(See Shulḥan 'Arukh, 637: 1. Kaf Haḥayyim, ibid,1-2)

Hosha'na Rabba

The final decisions are handed over on Hosha'na Rabba

It says in Ben Ish Ḥai, based on the writings of the Zohar, that on the night of Hosha'na Rabba, at midnight, the outer seal of our judgement is completed.

This refers to the fact that, according to the Zohar, there are two seals to our judgement - an inner seal which is done on Yom Kippur, and an outer one which is completed on Hosha'na Rabba. When the outer seal is completed, the papers with the decisions are handed over to the angels to be carried out. This is one of the reasons for staying up all night on Hosha'na Rabba.

Even though the decisions have been handed over to the angels, nevertheless, there is still time to have harsh judgements revoked till Shemini 'Aṣereth. Therefore, the whole day of Hosha'na Rabba should be spent in Teshubah (repentance).

(See Ben Ish Ḥai, yr 1, WeZoth Habberakha, Oth 2)

Shemini 'Aṣereth / Simḥath Torah

Torah readings not synchronized between Israel and the Diaspora

There are times when the Torah reading in the Land of Israel and the reading in the Diaspora are not synchronized with each other. A case in point is when Shemini 'Aṣereth falls on Shabbath. Both the Shaḥrith and Minḥa readings are different.

Since both Shemini 'Aṣereth and Simḥath Torah are celebrated on the same day in Israel, the reading in the morning in Israel is Wezoth Habberakha (the last portion in the Torah which is read on Simḥath Torah). In the Diaspora, however, Shemini 'Aṣereth and Simḥath Torah are celebrated on two separate days and Wezoth Habberakha is read on the following day.

As a result, in the Land of Israel, the reading for Minḥa on Shabbath/Shemini 'Aṣereth is Bereishith (which is the next Parasha to be read in Israel). In the Diaspora, however, the reading for Minḥa of that Shabbath is still Wezoth Habberakha, since that Parasha has not yet been read.

(See Shulḥan 'Arukh 668:2. Kaf Haḥayyim ibid:22)

Tu Bishbaṭ

The fruits of Ṭu Bishbaṭ and the Jewish people

There are three types of fruits, and we should attempt to eat some of each type on Ṭu Bishbaṭ. The Jewish people are hinted at in these three types of fruit.

The first type are fruits that are eaten in their entirety, such as grapes and figs. They represent people who do Teshubah Mi-ahaba (repent out of love), which is the highest level of repentance. Their sins, as a result of their returning to G-d, are considered as merits, because the peel which represents one's sins, are eaten together with the fruit which represents one's good deed.

Then there are fruits which have a hard pit inside (which also represents the sins), and are surrounded by the fruit, such as dates and olives. This is likened to someone who repents out of fear, and whose sins are considered as if they were done unintentionally. That is why the fruit covers the pit to symbolize the good covering the bad.

The third type of fruit is one which has a thick and inedible peel, such as a pomegranate. The peel, which represents one's sins, covers the flesh of the fruit, which represents one's good deed, symbolizing that the bad overcomes the good. This is a person who sinned deliberately (Be-mezid) and did not repent.

When the Torah mentions the seven species that the Land of Israel is praised for, all these three types of fruit are included and are considered as one package. The pomegranate is mentioned between the other two types. This comes to show us that it is a great Tiqqun (rectification) for those who found their way to repent, to guide those who have not yet done so, to find the right path to return.

(Dabar Be'itto, 2, Ṭu Bishbaṭ)

When Ṭu Bishbaṭ falls on Shabbath

When Ṭu Bishbaṭ falls on Shabbath, when should the fruits be eaten? There are those who have the custom, every Leil Shabbath (Friday night), to eat fruits between Qiddush and Ha<u>m</u>oṣi (the sanctification on the wine and the meal). But many Posqim do not approve of this custom.

It is best, therefore, to eat the fruits after reciting Birkath Hammazon (Grace after meals). If one were to eat all the fruits one eats on Ṭu Bishbaṭ before starting the meal, one would not be able to eat the meal with a hearty appetite. (If one were to eat them during the meal, there are different opinions as to the need to recite a blessing on them).

There is no problem of unnecessary blessings if they are eaten after the meal, since it is common practice in many homes to do this on a regular Shabbath in order to make up the additional Berakhoth (blessings) that we need on Shabbath.

(See Maamar Mordehai Hilkhoth Ḥaggim, 61: 10. Rambam Hilkhoth Tefillah 7:16, concerning making up blessings. Ben Ish Ḥai)

Ḥanukkah

Ḥanukkah: What's in a name?

The eight days of Ḥanukkah begin on the 25th of Kislew. During this time eulogies and fasting are not permitted. However Melakha (servile work) is performed as usual.

Women, however, do not do Melakha while the Ḥanukkah lights are burning (during the half hour that the lights are required to burn only), though there are women who have the custom of not doing Melakha on the first and last day of Ḥanukkah as well. This is, in fact, one of the explanations of the word Ḥanukkah, *"They rested on the 25th"* which is formed by splitting the word into *Ḥanu* (they rested) and *Kah* (the letters Kaf and Heh which equal 25).

The word Ḥanukkah in Hebrew is also an acronym for Ḥeth Neroth WeHalakha Kebeth Hillel (eight candles in accordance with the rulings of Hillel). The way we light, by adding one candle each day was the ruling of Beth Hillel, as opposed to the House of Shammai who ruled that we should light eight candles the first night and reduce one each subsequent night.

(See Shulḥan 'Arukh, 680: 1, Ben Ish Ḥai, yr. 1, Wayyesheb, 27. Kaf Haḥayyim 680, Oth 1 & 2)

Parallels between the the Ḥanukkah lights and our lives

The Shulḥan 'Arukh states that If a person did not kindle the Ḥanukkah lights at the appropriate time, he can light the whole night, but if the night has passed and he did not light, he can no longer make up for it.

We can understand this Halakha (law) as a parallel to our lives. A person who did not kindle the lights at the appropriate time can be compared to one who did not grow spiritually in his early years, as one is supposed to, but instead, chased after the pleasures of this world. The fact that he can, nevertheless, light the whole night tells us that he should not lose hope of repenting, because his whole life is still appropriate for repentance. This, however, is not the highest level of repentance because it was not done at the ideal time but, nevertheless, still counts.

But if his entire life was spent devoid of any Torah or Miṣwoth (commandments), once his soul leaves his body there is no longer any way to repent. It is too late. Once the night has passed he can no longer make up for the fact that he did not light when he was supposed to.

(Shulḥan 'Arukh, 672: 2. Dabar Be'itto, Rimzei Ḥanukkah)

The holiness of Ḥanukkah and a woman's advantage.

It is important to balance the happiness of Ḥanukkah with the seriousness and the important message that is connected with it. Rabbenu the Ḥida, 'a"h, states that one should not allow oneself to behave lightheadedly during these holy days. Rather, on days of miracles such as these, we must show our appreciation to the Al-mighty.

Ḥanukkah, as we know, is a particularly important time for women. It says in ‘Aṭereth Tifereth, that on Rosh Ḥodesh, Ḥanukkah and Purim, women receive a spiritual advantage and elevation. As such, they should not wear their everyday clothes but should dress in clothes befitting the holiday.

A woman who has gold jewelry should wear them on these days to make known the fact that women have this spiritual advantage.

(Moreh Be'eṣba', 9, Oth 303. Dabar Be'itto, Rimzei Ḥanukkah. ‘Aṭereth Tifereth, Kether Malkhuth, 206.)

Not speaking till all the Ḥanukkah candles have been lit

Even though only the first candle that we light each night of Ḥanukkah is the obligation for the day, nevertheless, from when one recites the Berakha (blessing) one must not speak till all the candles have been lit.

If after lighting the first light, however, one notices that there are insufficient candles or, perhaps, some were knocked over, the one who lights should not speak, but should wait silently till more are brought for him. If he did speak, however, the blessing is not recited again.

If one spoke between the recitation of the Berakha and the lighting of the first candle, about a matter connected with the lighting of the candles, the blessing is not repeated. But if the speaking was unconnected with the lighting of the candles, then one should say *Barukh Shem Kebod Malkhutho Le'olam Wa'ed* and recite the blessing again.

(See Ben Ish Ḥai, Wayesheb/Ḥanukkah, Oth 10. Maamar Mordekhai Ḥaggim 57:27)

The Special Torah readings for Ḥanukkah and if one read the wrong one

On Ḥanukkah, the reason that we read from the Torah portion connected with the gifts that the Nesi-im (Princes of Israel) brought to the Mishkan (Tabernacle), is because the Mishkan was completed on the 25th of Kislew, the day that Ḥanukkah starts. The custom of Sephardim is to start with the portion of the Birkath Kohanim (the Priestly Blessing), because the miracle of Ḥanukkah was performed through Kohanim. (Some Ashkenazim do the same while others start from *Beyom Kalloth Moshe*).

If a person made a mistake in the reading of the Torah, and instead of reading the portion for that day, read a portion for a subsequent day of Ḥanukkah, the reading still counts, because all the days are valid. However, if the Sefer Torah has not been returned and is still on the Teba, it is preferable to read the correct portion without the Berakhoth (blessings).

If the Torah was returned to the Hekhal, however, then the correct portion for that day is not recited. Neither is it read the following day when the Torah is taken out again. Rather the correct portion for that particular day is read. For example, if on the second day the portion for the third or fourth day was read, then on the third day the portion for the third day must be read and not the portion for the second day which was omitted in error.

(See Shulḥan 'Arukh, 684: 1. Rama, ibid. Kaf Haḥayyim ibid, Oth 1, 2, 4, 8.)

Lighting in the Synagogue on Ḥanukkah

Even though everybody lights at home, the Ḥanukkah lights are also kindled in the Synagogue between Minḥa and 'Arbith because of Pirsumei Nisa (publicizing the miracle). However, in the Synagogue, the Ḥanukkah (Menorah) is always lit on the Southern wall.

Even though the lights in the Synagogue are lit with a Berakha (blessing), a person does not fulfil his obligation with this lighting, but must light again at home. If there aren't ten men present in the Synagogue at the time of lighting, they are lit without a Berakha.

When the first night of Ḥanukkah falls on a Friday, and everyone present in the Synagogue has already lit at home prior to coming there, the Berakha of Sheheḥeyanu must be omitted since everyone has already said it at home.

(Shulḥan 'Arukh, 671: 7, with Rama. Kaf Haḥayyim ibid, Oth 65 and 72. Ben Ish Ḥai, Wayyesheb, Ḥanukkah, Oth 11.)

If someone lit Shabbath lights before Ḥanukkah lights in error

On Friday evening the Ḥanukkah candles are lit before the Shabbath candles. The question is, if someone were to light the Shabbath candles first in error, can the Ḥanukkah (Menorah) still be kindled?

If a man lit the Shabbath lights, since (provided) he did not specifically have the intention to accept Shabbath with the lighting of the Shabbath candles, he can still light the Ḥanukkah after the Shabbath candles. But this only applies to a man.

If it was a woman who was lighting the Ḥanukkah lights in her home, and she lit the Shabbath candles first in error, she may not light the Ḥanukkah. This is because women ordinarily accept Shabbath upon themselves with the lighting of the Shabbath candles and, as such, she is now forbidden to light the Ḥanukkah lights. Therefore, she should have someone else, who has not yet accepted Shabbath, light the Ḥanukkah and the person doing the lighting should recite the Berakha (blessing) of *Lehadliq Ner Ḥanukkah*. However she can still say the blessing of *She'asah Nissim* (and *Sheheḥeyenu* if it is the first day).

(See Shulḥan 'Arukh, 679: 1. Kaf Haḥayyim ibid, Oth 3 and 4)

Why do we not mention Ḥanukkah in the Hafṭarah blessings on Shabbath Ḥanukkah?

When Ḥanukkah falls on two Shabbaths (the first and last days fall on Shabbath), the prayers are identical on both Shabbathoth, except for the Hafṭarah which is different (*Ronni Wesimḥi* is read on the first and *Waya'as Ḥirom* on the second).

Why do we not mention Ḥanukkah in the blessings of the Hafṭarah on Shabbath? Normally, on a Holiday we mention the holiday when reciting the blessings of the Hafṭarah. The answer is that Ḥanukkah is different, because the Hafṭarah is not read on account of Ḥanukkah but, rather, because it is

Shabbath. Proof of this is that on the other days of Ḥanukkah, even though we read from the Sefer Torah, there is no Hafṭarah.

On holidays which are Yom Ṭob, however, a Hafṭarah is read irrespective of what day of the week it falls on. And since the Hafṭarah is read on account of the Holiday, the Holiday is mentioned in the blessings of its Hafṭarah.

(See Shulḥan 'Arukh, 684: 2. Kaf Haḥayyim ibid, 14)

Adar / Purim

Why is Shabbath Zakhor before Purim?

There is a commandment to remember 'Amaleq and to read the portion of Zakhor (remember) from the Sefer Torah. There is no specfic time connected with this commandment, so why do we read it specifically on the Shabbath before Purim?

It says in the Gemara of Meghilla that Zakhor is read before Purim because we wish to mention the eradication of 'Amaleq alongside the eradication of Haman, as it says in the Meghilla: "And these days shall be remembered and celebrated". The word remember (which is mentioned first) refers to reading Zakhor, and celebrate refers to the eradication of 'Amaleq. That is why Zakhor (remember) is read on the preceding Shabbath.

In addition, every miracle that occurs sees a re-awakening every year. That is why all the Holidays (Pesaḥ, Purim and so on) come around every year. This re-awakening always starts from the Shabbath before the Holiday. From the Shabbath before Purim there is a re-awakening of the actions that caused the repentance and the Geullah (redemption).

The Shabbath before Purim sees an amazing (spiritual) light that assists Israel. That is why the Jewish people must engage in the study of the Torah on that Shabbath, more than any other Shabbath, to awaken the redemption and the elevation of Qedu<u>sh</u>a (holiness) that arises on this day.

(See Meghilla 29a with Rashi. M.M 685: 1. Dabar Be'Itto, Derush on Zakhor/Purim)

Women and Parashath Zakhor

According to many authorities, the reading of the Parasha of Zakhor, *Remember what 'Amaleq did unto you*, is an obligation from the Torah (as opposed to from the Rabbis). So every man must ensure that he finds a Minyan where it will be read.

There is an opinion that women are obligated to hear the reading also, and this is the custom followed by most Ashkenazim. Sephardim follow the opinion that women are not obligated to hear the reading, even though they have an obligation to "remember". If a woman does come to hear it, she should have in mind that she is not taking it upon herself as a Neder (vow), so that she will not obligate herself to hear it the following years.

If she does hear the reading, however, she will get a reward for doing so, as one does in every case where one is not obligated to perform a commandment but still does.

(See Shulḥan 'Arukh, 685:7. Kaf Haḥayyim, ibid, 30. M.M. Hilkhoth Ḥaggim 62: 12, Torah Lishmah 187)

Fast of Esther on Thursday or Friday

Ta'anith Esther (the Fast of Esther) is held on the 13th of Adar, the day before Purim. The Shulḥan 'Arukh states that when this falls on Shabbath, the fast is brought forward to the preceding Thursday. This is because we may not fast on Shabbath, and we prefer not to fast on a Friday so as not to enter Shabbath while in an unpleasant state.

The Rama adds that if there is a Milah on that Thursday, the participants are permitted to eat at the Se'uddah (festive meal), but those who ate must fast on the following day (Friday). Some Aḥaronim state, however, that if there is a Milah on Thursday, the Se'uddah should be held at night as is done on other fast days. There are those who say that the parents of the child together with the Sandaq and Mohel are permitted to eat and do not need to fast on Friday.

If someone was traveling on that Thursday and forgot about the fast, but when he returned home at night realized his error, he should fast on Friday.

(See Sh. A. 686: 2 with Rama. Kaf Haḥayyim ibid, 24, 27, 28. M.B. ibid, 7)

Why were the miracles not open and wondrous?

Why did G-d cause the salvation in Purim to happen in a natural way and and not as an open miracle as happened in Egypt or with Sanḥerib (Sennacherib)?

Had the miracle been open and wondrous, the nations of the world, specifically the enemies of the Jewish people, would say that miracles do not happen on a regular basis. The reason it happened at that time was because there were prophets and righteous people then. It was in their merit that the miracles took place. Nowadays, there are no prophets, and there aren't individuals who are on such a high spiritual level. Therefore, miracles would not occur for the Jewish people nowadays.

That is why G-d caused the salvation to happen in a natural way, in accordance with the norms of nature. Nature exists all the time, and does not depend on the merits of individuals. The enemies of the Jewish people must be concerned, therefore, that the Jewish nation's protection is not dependent on the merits of specific individuals, but is there all the time.

(See Ben Ish Ḥayil, Derush Geemal, Zakhor)

Haman and the sea

Our Rabbis of blessed memory tell us that Haman, vis-a-vis the Jewish people, is likened to a bird who built its nest on the sea-shore. A wave came from the sea and flooded the bird's nest. The bird was very angry and swore to the sea that it would block up the sea, by filling it with dust and turn it into dry land.

So what did the bird do? It started to kick sand from the sea shore into the sea with its foot, but saw that all that was happening was that the sand just disappeared as soon as it reached the sea. He tried harder and harder till he was tired of trying and couldn't go on, but it was all to no avail. The sea said to the bird, "Even if all the creatures in the world would gather together, they would not be able to fill even one side of the sea with dust, so why are you being so foolish in your behavior?

Haman wanted to uproot Israel because of the fact that Shemuel Hannabi, 'a"h, (the prophet Samuel) had killed Aghagh his forefather. The Jewish people, however, are likened to the sea, because of their study of the Torah which, in turn, is called "longer than the earth and wider than the sea" (Iyyob). The word Purim is made up of the Hebrew words Pur and Yam (he threw lots to close up the sea [Israel]).

From this we see the importance of the study of the Torah. For when the Jewish people are involved in the study of the Torah, we are likened to the sea and, as a result, all Haman's machinations proved to be an exercise in futility.

(See Dabar Be'Itto, Zakhor/Purim)

When must the Meghilla be read?

Everyone is obligated to hear the Meghilla twice on Purim, once at night and once during the day. Contrary to what many think, the reading during the day is more important than the one at night and everyone must make the effort to hear it again then.

The reading at night must be done after the stars come out and may be done at any time until dawn. If, for whatever reason, the Meghilla was not read at night, it can not be made up by reading it twice during the day.

The reading during the day can be done at any time during the day, from sunrise to sunset. If, for some reason, it was read before sunrise but after 'Ammud Hashaḥar (dawn), one has fulfilled his obligation. If it goes into Bein Hashemashoth (between sunset and the emergence of three stars), however, since there is a doubt as to whether this time is considered to be day or night, it should be read without a Berakha (blessing).

(See Sh. 'A 687: 1. Kaf Haḥayyim ibid, 1-4, 7, 9, 10)

What should the Sheheḥeyanu on the Meghillah cover?

The Shulḥan 'Arukh states that the Berakha (blessing) of Sheheḥeyanu is said at night, over the reading of the Meghillah, but when it is read again during the day it is not repeated. This is the custom followed by Sephardim. The Rama adds that the custom in Ashkenazic lands is to repeat the Berakha of Sheheḥeyanu when reading during the day.

When one hears the Berakha of Sheheḥeyanu being recited over the reading of the Meghillah, it is appropriate to have in mind that it covers the Se'uddah (festive meal) and the sending of Mishlowaḥ Manoth as well. Sephardim should have this in mind when saying Sheheḥeyanu at night, and Ashkenazim should have this in mind when reciting the Berakha of Sheheḥeyanu during the day.

(See Shulḥan 'Arukh, 692: 1 with Rama. Hilkhoth Ḥaggim Maamar Mordekhai 64: 15)

Who should open the Meghillah like a letter?

The custom is for the Ḥazzan to spread out the entire Meghilla like a letter, in order to make the miracle known. Only the Ḥazzan (the one who reads it out loud) needs to spread it out before reading. Individuals who are following the reading with their own Kasher Meghilla (written on a parchment scroll) do not need to do so. The Meghillah must be spread out before the recitation of the Berakha (blessing).

According to the Maharil, if an individual is reading for himself to fulfill his obligation (not following the reading of the Ḥazzan or another person) he should also spread out the Meghilla before reading. Care should be taken not to let the

Meghilla drag on the floor, therefore, the reader must have a Bimah or chair in place for it to rest on.

There is an opinion that it is not necessary for the entire Meghillah to be spread out before reading. Rather, it can be unrolled, bit by bit, while one is reading it, but should not be rolled up again till after the entire reading is completed. The Meghillah must be rolled up before the final Berakha is recited.

(See Shulḥan 'Arukh 690: 17. Ben Ish Ḥai, Parashath Ki Thissa (Purim), Oth 4. M.B. 690, 55/56. Kaf Haḥayyim ibid, Oth 104. Maamar Mordekhai (Ḥaggim) 64:18)

Reading the Meghillah in a foreign language

If someone who does not speak Hebrew hears the Meghilla read in Hebrew, from a Kasher scroll written in Hebrew, he fulfills his obligation even if he does not understand what is being said.

It says in the Shulḥan 'Arukh that if a Meghillah is written in a non-Jewish language, only someone who is familiar with that language can fulfill his obligation by reading it. There are certain restrictions connected with this, however.

The universal custom that we follow nowadays, that we should not deviate from, is that the Meghilla must be written in the Holy Tongue (Hebrew) in accordance with the rules for writing a Meghillah, and must be read only in the Holy Tongue. This applies to everyone, men and women, even if they are not familiar with the Holy Tongue, as we mentioned above.

(See Shulḥan 'Arukh 690: 8, 9. Kaf Haḥayyim, ibid, Oth 56, Qiṣur Shulḥan 'Arukh, Ḥakham' Rafael Barukh Toledano, ibid, 17)

Giving Mattanoth La-ebyonim without a Blessing and not from Ma'aser

One reason, according to the Rashba, as to why we do not recite a blessing over the giving of Mattanoth La-ebyonim (gifts to the poor) and Mishlowaḥ Manoth (sending portions of food to our friends) on Purim, is because perhaps they will not accept them from us.

It is far better to increase the giving of Mattanoth La-ebyonim than to increase the food during the Se'uddah (festive meal) or the amount of Mishlowaḥ Manoth one sends to one's friends, because there is no greater happiness than when we make the hearts of those who are less fortunate than we are, happy.

In places where the custom is for members of the community to participate in giving gifts to the Ḥazzan before Purim, the money they give cannot be considered as Mattanoth La-ebyonim. One's Ma'aser money (tithes) cannot be used for Mattanoth LaEbyonim but must be in addition to one's Ma'aser. However, if one wishes to give more than is required, the additional portion may come from the Ma'aser. The money for the Maḥaṣith Ha<u>sh</u>eqel (half Sheqel) must also be in addition to one's Ma'aser.

(See Kaf Haḥayyim 694, Oth 4, 5, 14 & 16.)

Rosh Ḥodesh

Repenting before Rosh Ḥodesh

It used to be that people would fast before Rosh Ḥodesh (the new month). Nowadays, people find fasting much harder, so it is not that common.

Nevertheless, even if one does not fast, one should still make Teshubah (repentance) on the last day of the month before Rosh Ḥodesh and closely examine one's deeds. One should try to rectify all the wrongs that one committed that month, because it is the last day of the month, in the same way that the day before Rosh Hashanah, which is the last day of the year, is also a private fast day which is accompanied by repentance. The last day of the month, therefore, is also time for atonement.

There are those who do Tiqqun Kareth (stay up all night reading appropriate readings, such as Mishmereth Haḥodesh by the Ben Ish Ḥai), while others do so only till midnight. Each one according to his ability. This is a fine custom if one is able to do it.

(See Kaf Haḥayyim 417, Oth 25, 26)

Rosh Ḥodesh for Men and Women

Originally, Rosh Ḥodesh was to be given to the Jewish people as a Festival (in addition to the Festivals of Pesaḥ,

Shabu'oth and Sukkoth). But because of the sin of the golden calf, this holiday was cancelled for them. Women, however did not sin and it remained a holiday for them, though of a lesser magnitude than the three Reghalim (Festivals).

A man is forbidden to force his wife to do any Melakha (servile work) that she is not permitted to do on Rosh Ḥodesh, even in a place where it is not the custom to refrain. On the other hand, if a man wishes to take upon himself the restrictions of not doing certain Melakha on Rosh Ḥodesh, he may and it is considered to be a charitable deed. We do not apply to him the concept that one should not do something that one is exempt from doing.

From this we see how great the commandment of Rosh Ḥodesh is for women and how particular they should be about it. Even though in many commandments (Miṣwoth) it is the men who have the primary responsibilty, in this case it is the women who have the primary responsibility and men are only secondary.

(See Ben Ish Ḥai, Parashath Wayyiqra, Oth 1-2)

4

תעניות

Fasts

Not fasting on both the 9th and 17th of Tammuz

Even though, at the time of the destruction of the first Beth Ha<u>m</u>iqdash (Temple), the walls were breached on the ninth (9th) of Tammuz, since, when the second Temple was destroyed the walls were breached on the seventeenth (17th) of Tammuz, that was the day that was designated as a fast day. The reason being that the destruction of the second Temple is more serious for us.

Our Ḥakhamim of blessed memory could have also designated the 9th of Tammuz as a fast day since the walls of the first Beth Ha<u>m</u>iqdash were breached then, but did not wish to place an additional burden on us. Neither should a person take this fast upon himself as a private fast.

In addition, it is written in the Yerushalmi (Jerusalem Talmud) that at the time of the destruction of the first Temple the walls were also breached on the 17th of Tammuz, but because of all their suffering they erred in its calculation.

(See MM, Sefer Hilkhoth Ḥaggim, Maran Mordekhai Eliyahu, 'a"h)

Without fast days we would not remember what caused this exile

The fasts that all Jewish people are obligated to fast every year (other than Yom Kippur) are on the 9th of Ab, the 17th of Tammuz, the 3rd of Tashri (Ṣom Gedaliah) and the 10th of Ṭebeth.

Through these fasts that were established by our Rabbis of blessed memory, we remember what befell us and we understand that our sins are what brought this exile upon us. If it were not for these fasts, we would have forgotten by now all that transpired and we would not be moved to return to the right path.

As a result of these fasts that return every single year, however, we are conscious of the fact that repentance is the remedy for all our that has befallen us. And through it we will merit to receive all the good of this world and the world to come and see the coming of Mashiyaḥ Ṣidqenu (the Messiah), speedily in our days, Amen.

(See Shulḥan 'Arukh, 549:1. Qiṣur Shulḥan 'Arukh H' Rafael Barukh Toledano, 496, Oth 9)

One who is not fasting on a public fast

On the four public fasts, as long as there are six or seven members of the congregation who are fasting (presumably the others are unable to fast for health reasons), the Ḥazzan recites 'Anenu with its own Berakha (blessing) during the repetition of the 'Amidah, and the portion of *Wayḥal* is read from the Torah.

It is, nevertheless, preferable to try and have at least ten men who are fasting.

A Ḥazzan who is not fasting should not lead the prayer. If there is no one else to take his place he should lead the prayer but not say 'Anenu with its blessing, but rather say it like the other members of the congregation in the blessing of *Shomeya' Tefillah*.

One who is not fasting, or does not intend to complete the fast, should not go up to the Torah. If he is the only Kohen in the Synagogue, he should step out so that another who is fasting can go up instead.

Note: according to Sephardi custom, if a Kohen does not go up, only a Yisrael can go up in his place. In some Ashkenazi communities a Lewi is sent up instead if one is available, whereas in others, a Yisrael is sent up instead of a Kohen. One's Rabbi should be consulted.

The other honors, however, such as Pethiḥath Hahekhal (the opening of the Ark) and Haqqamah (called Haghbaah by Ashkenazim), may be done by one who is not fasting.

(See Shulḥan 'Arukh 566: 6. Kaf Haḥayyim ibid, Oth 32, 45, 48)

5

בית הכנסת

Synagogue

Is it better to walk to Synagogue on weekdays, or drive?

Is it better to walk to Synagogue on a weekday, or is it equally acceptable to drive? The following question was asked in Torah Lishmah:

A wealthy individual lived approximately half an hour's walk away from his Synagogue. He had no difficulty walking there but, in view of his important status in the town on account of his wealth, there was some concern that the non Jews (in particular) of the town would not understand this, because it would be expected that he would ride. Is it preferable for him to walk to Synagogue, or does he perform the Miṣwah (commandment) equally well if he rides?

In the Gemara of Soṭah it speaks about a widow who lived near a Synagogue but would walk to one further away in order to get Sekhar Peṣi'oth (reward for each step). This implies that in order to get the reward one must actually walk.

Also, in the case of the 'Aliyah Lareghel (pilgrimage to the Temple), those who lived very far away would obviously have to ride. But when they approached Jerusalem, they would dismount and complete the journey on foot. Those who lived within walking distance, even though it may have been a long walk, did not ride but walked the entire way.

In addition to the above, the Pasuq *Beth Elokim Nehalekh Bereghesh* (we will walk to the House of G-d), hints at the fact that going to Synagogue should be on foot whenever this is possible. And one must not be concerned about what others think even if he is rich and well respected.

(See Torah Lishmah, Oraḥ Ḥayyim 40)

Turning a Beth Midrash into a Synagogue

It is permitted to make a Beth Midrash (house of learning) out of a Synagogue. However, a Beth Midrash may not be turned into a Synagogue. The reason for this being that the holiness of a Beth Midrash is higher than that of a Synagogue and we have a concept that we can increase holiness but not decrease.

This applies to building a Synagogue that is used exclusively as a house of prayer with no Beth Midrash for Torah study. If, however, the Synagogue which was built in the place of the Beth Midrash will also contain a Yeshibah for the daily study of Torah, it is permitted to make such a Synagogue from a Beth Midrash.

(See Shulḥan 'Arukh, 153: 1. Kaf Haḥayyim ibid Oth 1 and 5)

When to show the Sefer Torah

It says in Ben Ish Ḥai about the custom in his city of Baghdad when taking out the Sefer Torah from the Hekhal (Aron), that they would open it and show it to the congregation from the Hekhal. However, not all the members of the congregation would be able to see it from there.

They would then take the Sefer Torah to the Tebah (Bimah) which is located in the middle of the Synagogue, and would open it there to show to the entire congregation. They would show it in all four directions twice. They would then place it where it would be read from.

After they finished reading they would close the case and would not show it to the congregation again when returning it from the Tebah to the Hekhal. He mentions Qabbalistic reasons why it should be shown before the reading and not after. This is the custom of Sephardim.

The Ashkenazi custom is not to show it when taking it out, but rather, to show it after the reading is completed, as is mentioned by the Rama.

(See Ben Ish Ḥai, 2nd year, Parashath Toldoth, Oth 16)

Can one Sefer Torah take precedence over another?

If a Sefer Torah was rolled to the place of that day's reading in preparation to be taken out and, by mistake, another Sefer Torah was taken out instead, the second Sefer must be read from. We cannot put it back in the Hekhal and take out the one that was prepared, even though the one that was taken out by mistake may be in totally the wrong place and require much rolling.

There are many Synagogues which have so many Sifrei Torah that they cannot all fit in the Hekhal. So they are locked in a separate storage room and when they are to be read from, they are removed from there and placed in the Hekhal. It happened once that one was brought to the Hekhal from the storage room and rolled to the correct place in preparation for taking it out that Shabbath. The Ḥazzan looked at it and thought that there was a problem with it that made it unfit for use (he thought that two letters were touching each other). As a result, another Sefer Torah was taken out of the Storage area and put next to it in the Hekhal and rolled to the correct position in preparation to be taken out instead.

Before taking it out, someone else re-checked the one that was prepared first and found that the letters were not touching. Which of the two Sifrei Torah should be taken out? It says in Torah Lishmah̲, that the one that was prepared first, takes precedence.

(See Torah Lishmah̲, Oth Nun Waw)

With which hand should you carry the Sefer Torah?

With which hand (against which shoulder) should a person carry a Sefer Torah? If we say that it must only be carried on the right, then what should a left-handed person do? Also, if a person is wearing Tefillin on his left arm, shouldn't the Sefer Torah be carried in the same arm because of its importance?

It says in Torah Lishmah̲ that the right is definitely the preferred side for carrying since it says in the Torah that G-d gave Israel the Tablets of Stone written (as it were) from G-d's right hand (מימינו). Indeed, not only a Sefer Torah, but all holy books should be carried in the right.

This applies all the more if a person is wearing Tefillin on his left arm. He should hold the Sefer Torah in his right, the same way that our Rabbis of blessed memory said that the Ḥanukkah (Menorah) should be on the left if the Mezuzah is on the right.

One who is left handed should also carry the Sefer Torah in his right hand unless his right arm is so weak that there is a risk that he would drop it, Heaven forbid. In such a case, he should carry it in his left hand.

(See Torah Lishmah̲, Oraḥ Ḥayyim, She-elah Kaf Beh)

The custom of the Ari z"l, when taking out the Sefer Torah

When taking out the Sefer Torah, the custom of the Ari z"l was to kiss it and to follow it from the Hekhal (where it was kept) to the Teba where it was read. He would remain next to the Teba till the Sefer Torah was opened and shown to the congregation.

He would then look at the actual letters of the Sefer Torah. He said that if one would look at the Sefer Torah from close so that one could actually read the letters clearly, it was beneficial to the person for Qabbalistic reasons.

After this he would return to his seat and remain seated there till the end of the Torah reading, and would not stand during the reading.

(See Sha'ar Hak̲aw̲anoth, Derush Aleph, Be'inyan Sefer Torah. See also Ben Ish Ḥai, Yr. 2. Toldoth, Oth 16)

6

תפלה

Prayer

If one did not hear the Barkhu from the Ḥazzan

When the Ḥazzan says the Barkhu, the congregation say the response of Barukh H' Hammeborakh... which is then repeated by the Ḥazzan.

What happens in a case where a person did not hear the Ḥazzan say the Barkhu, but only heard the congregation responding? There is an opinion that he should only answer Amen. However, this is not the generally accepted custom. The custom is that a person who did not hear the Ḥazzan but heard the congregation respond Barukh H'..., responds Barukh H'... with them

(See Shulḥan 'Arukh, 57:1. Ben Ish Ḥai, 1st year, Wayiggash, Oth 17. M.B. 57: 2. Kaf Haḥayyim, 57, Oth 1)

Saying the Qedusha and Torah phrases in the prayer with the cantillation notes

The Qedusha of Yoṣer (the Qadosh, Qadosh that is recited before the Shema' during Shaḥrith) should be recited together with the Ḥazzan. When one recites it on one's own, the

Zohar and Shulḥan 'Arukh state that it should be read with the Ta'amim (cantillation notes).

The Rama comments that the prevalent (Ashkenazi) custom is to read it without the cantillation notes, even when one prays by oneself. In 'Od Yoseph Ḥai, Ḥakham Yoseph Ḥayyim, 'a"h, mentions that this is, in fact, the custom of many Sephardim too, to read the Qedusha without Ta'amim even though they are reading it by themselves.

Since, however, it is possible to read it with the notes one should do so when not reading it with the congregation. This is especially true since, according to Rabbenu the Ari z"l, every verse from the Torah that appears anywhere in the prayer must be recited with its Ta'amim (cantillation notes) in the prayer.

(See Ben Ish Ḥai, 1st year, Parashath Shemoth, Oth 2. 'Od Yoseph Ḥai, ibid, 6 & 7)

Someone who is unable to complete the Hafṭarah

If the person who was called up for Mafṭir on Shabbath is reading the Hafṭarah and suddenly stops in the middle and falls silent, for whatever reason, someone else must take over from him. The one who takes over cannot continue from where the first reader left off, but rather, must start from the beginning of the Hafṭarah again.

Since there is a difference of opinion as to whether he should repeat the first Berakhoth (blessings) of the Hafṭarah or not, they should not be said. In addition, according to the Ari z"l, each person is obligated to read the Hafṭarah for himself, except for the blessings which the reader says on behalf of everyone. As such, the blessings that were recited at the beginning counted for the one who replaced the original reader also.

If the original reader stops at the end of the Hafṭarah, then the Ḥazzan or some other person should immediately rise and say the blessings that are after the Hafṭarah.

The Mafṭir is not repeated in these cases.

(See Sh. "A. 284: 5. Kaf Haḥayyim ibid, Oth 25 and 26)

Insufficient time to answer Barukh Hu Ubarukh Shemo

We mentioned previously that we have to be particular to answer Barukh Hu, Ubarukh Shemo when G-d's name is mentioned, and Amen at the end of a blessing, during the repetition of the 'Amidah. if the Ḥazzan does not give the congregation sufficient time to answer Amen to a Berakha (blessing) of the 'Amidah, before starting the next one, the congregation should not answer Amen.

It sometimes happens that the person reading the Ḥazarah (repetition of the 'Amidah) reads at such a speed that if a person would answer Barukh Hu, Ubarukh Shemo the Ḥazzan would have already finished the blessing. As a result he would miss the opportunity to say Amen at the end of the blessing, or it would come out as Barukh Hu Ubarukh Shemo Amen without a pause between them.

In such a case, the person should not answer Barukh Hu, Ubarukh Shemo, but should remain silent, so that he can answer Amen at the end of the blessing. The reason being that answering Amen is a greater obligation than Barukh Hu

Ubarukh Shemo. Clearly, all Ḥazzanim must be cautioned to give the congregation time to reply correctly to both.

(See See Ben Ish Ḥai, yr 1, Teruma, 12. Kaf Haḥayyim 124: Oth 28)

Studying Torah after prayers

The Shulḥan 'Arukh, quoting the Gemara, states that after leaving the Synagogue one should go to the Beth Midrash to study Torah. This is because, at the time, a Synagogue was only for prayer and a Beth Midrash was only for the study of Torah. One who does this has the merit to receive the Shekhinah (G-d's holy presence).

The Ṭur states that one should go to the Beth Midrash before going to work, and have a set time to study the Torah. This is based on Raba who states in the Gemara of Shabbath that when a person is judged on his judgement day, he is asked whether he conducted his business affairs faithfully (honestly) and whether he set aside a fixed time for the study of Torah.

The Gemara of Sanhedrin states that a person is judged first on his study of Torah.

(Shulḥan 'Arukh. 155: 1. Kaf Haḥayyim ibid 2. Mishnah Berurah ibid 1. Gem Shabbath 31a. Sanhedrin 7a)

Not saying "I prayed so well, I deserve to be answered"

Maran writes in the Shulḥan 'Arukh: A person must not think that G-d should fulfill his requests because he had the appropriate intent (Ka<u>w</u>anah) during his prayer. On the contrary, thinking this way is a reminder of a person's sins, since, because of this, they will look closely at his deeds saying, 'He seems very sure of his merits'.

A person must think, instead, that whatever the Holy One Blessed be He does for him, is out of His loving kindness, and he should say in his heart,"'Who am I, but a lowly individual, who is coming to make requests of the King of Kings, the Holy One Blessed Be He. And it is only out of His abundant kindness that he acts the way He does with His creatures".

It says in 'Od Yoseph Ḥai that this matter of saying in one's heart, "I deserve to get it because I prayed with the appropriate intent" ('Iyyun Tefillah), is one where many people stumble. Therefore we must be extremely careful in this area.

(See 'Od Yoseph Ḥai, Parashath Mishpaṭim, Oth Heh)

Not praying in vain

We are not permitted to utter a prayer in vain. A prayer over something that has already taken place, is considered to be a prayer prayed in vain.

The Shulḥan 'Arukh (Code of Jewish Law) gives examples of this. For example, if one were to enter a town and hear loud screams coming from within, one is not permitted to pray that those screams are not coming from his house. This is because the deed has already been done and the screams are coming from wherever it took place, whether from the person's house or somewhere else.

Similarly, if a woman is more than 40 days pregnant, by which time the gender of the baby has already been determined, one cannot pray for it to be a boy or a girl. We cannot pray for some sort of retroactive action to take place and change what has already occurred.

Instead, a person must pray for the future and thank G-d for what has taken place. For instance, a person should pray that he will arrive in peace at his destination. And when he does, he must thank G-d for it.

(See Shulḥan 'Arukh, 230: 1)

Praying in English

Nowadays, the level of Jewish knowledge is much higher than it was a generation or two ago. Nevertheless, there are people who are unable to pray in Leshon Haqqodesh (the Holy Tongue).

Someone who is unable to read Hebrew and pray from the Siddur (prayer book) should, nevertheless, pray in any language he is comfortable with, so that he will still have the opportunity of performing the Miṣwah (commandment) of praying. This situation is commonly found nowadays, when a person who was not observant and never prayed, starts getting closer to Judaism and wishes to pray on a regular basis, but is unable to read the prayers in the Hebrew Siddur.

It goes without saying, that a person should view this as a preliminary step, and make every effort to eventually pray all the prayers in Leshon Haqqodesh.

(See Shulḥan 'Arukh, 101: 4. Kaf Haḥayyim ibid, Oth 19)

Saying a prayer before a medical procedure

The Torah says: Rappo Yerappeh (you shall surely heal), from which we learn that we may go to doctors for treatment. However, one must always have in mind that they are the agents, and that the healing actually comes from G-d,

The Shulḥan 'Arukh states that when one goes to a doctor to let blood, as was common in those days (and some say for any medical procedure or treatment), one should say "Yehi Rason... Sheyihye 'Eseq Zeh Lirfuah Ki Rofeh Ḥinnam Attah" (May it be Your will... that this procedure will heal me, for You are a Free Healer"). According to the Eshel Abraham, this is said without G-d's name. After it is over he should say, "Barukh Rofeh Ḥolim" (Blessed is the One who heals the sick).

We must always put one's trust in the Creator and recognize that all healing comes ultimately from Him.

(See Shulḥan 'Arukh, 230: 4. Kaf Haḥayyim ibid, 16)

Praying in front of a mirror or pane of glass

It is forbidden to pray in front of a mirror, even if one closes one's eyes, because it appears as if one is bowing down to one's own reflection. The question is, does the same apply when one prays in front of a pane of glass?

The Ohr LeṢion says that a pane of glass is different because it does not appear that the person is bowing down to his reflection. Nevertheless, there is still the fear that by seeing his reflection in the window or pane of glass, he may lose his concentration.

Therefore, he must close his eyes if praying in front of a window, or turn away somewhat from the glass so that he will not see his reflection and become confused.

(See Ohr LeṢion, Responsa 2, ch 7:11)

Choosing between two different Ḥazzanim

Sometimes one has to make a choice between two individuals who wish to lead the prayers (be Shaliyaḥ Ṣibbur). One comes from an important family of fine pedigree but he himself is not so righteous, whereas the other comes from an inappropriate family, but he himself is very pious. Which of the two should one choose?

The Ṭaz says in the name of the Rosh that the praiseworthiness of the Shaliyaḥ Ṣibbur does not come from the family. Even if he comes from an unworthy family, but he himself is a worthy and righteous individual, he should be chosen over someone who comes from an important family but is, himself, unworthy.

It goes without saying, however, that if the two are on an equal level, that the one from the important family should be selected in preference to the one from the unworthy family, since the prayer of one who is righteous and the son of one who is righteous (Ṣaddiq Ben Ṣaddiq) is preferred.

(See Shebeṭ Mussar, Ch. 34, Oth 2)

A Ḥazzan who lengthens the prayer

If a Shaliyaḥ Ṣibbur (prayer leader) lengthens his prayer so that others will hear his pleasant voice, his intention as to why he does so, makes a difference. If the reason is that he has a happy heart that he is giving thanks to Haqqadosh Barukh Hu (the Holy One Blessed be He) in a pleasing way, he will be blessed, provided he prays in seriousness and fear.

If the purpose, on the other hand, is to have others hear his voice which makes him happy, it is considered to be shameful. In any case, one should not lengthen the prayer because it is a burden on the congregation. Even if he lengthens with the approval of the congregation he should not lengthen too much as it is considered shameful.

One who has a pleasant voice should use it to sing to Haqqadosh Barukh Hu and not for other songs.

(See Shulḥan 'Arukh, 53, 11. M.B ibid, 35, Kaf Haḥayyim ibid, Oth 55 & 57)

Will G-d cause us to sin?

How can we understand the statement in the morning blessings (Birkhoth Hashaḥar), *Al Tebi-eni Leedei Ḥeṭ* (do not cause me to sin)? Will G-d ever cause us to sin? G-d wants exactly the opposite. He wishes to see us follow His commandments.

Even though we say that if one desires to sin, the doors will be opened for him (to allow him to do his desires), it is still the individual's doing. Whatever path we decide to take, right or wrong, doors are opened for us to permit us to progress in the direction we have chosen. It is our decision.

Therefore, what we are asking for in this prayer, is that we should not be put in a situation where our own Yeṣer Hara' (evil inclination) may get the better of us and tempt or cause us to do something that is forbidden.

(See 'Od Yoseph Ḥai, Parashath Wayyesheb, Oth Yod Beh)

Making up the required 90 Amenim

The Shulḥan 'Arukh mentions a custom of taking turns to read the Birkhoth Hashaḥar (morning blessings) and each of the people present answer *Amen* to each of the Berakhoth. The Mishnah Berurah explains that those who do this do so in order to make their quota of 90 Amenim (Amens) that we are obligated to say each day.

It says in Ben Ish Ḥai that it is a good custom to say daily the Pasuq of *Barukh H' Le'Olam Amen WeAmen* forty five times. Since this will total 90 Amenim, it is good advice to make up the 90 that we are required to say daily, in a case where a person is unable to go to Synagogue because he is unwell or unable to go for an important reason out of his control.

He states that he, personally, had the custom to say this Pasuq that many times, every day, after the Birkhoth Hashaḥar.

(See Shulḥan 'Arukh 6: 4. Mishnah Berurah ibid 13. Ben Ish Ḥai, Yr. 1. Parashath Wayyesheb, Oth 15)

Not speaking from Barukh She-amar

One may not interrupt the prayer by speaking, from when one begins Barukh She-amar till the completion of the 'Amidah. Even if it's for the purpose of a Miṣwah, one may not speak between Barukh She-amar and Yishtabbaḥ.

The reason being that Barukh She-amar is the Berakha (blessing) before the Pesuqei Dezimra and Yishtabbaḥ is the final Berakhah. Nevertheless, if one did speak during between

Barukh She-amar and the Pesuqei Dezimra, or during the Pesuqei Dezimra itself, one does not need to repeat Barukh She-amar.

The above applies to talking. However, the Qaddish (until Be'alma), Qedusha and Barkhu may be responded to. This applies even if one is in the blessing that is within Barukh She-amar. However, one may not reply Amen to the portions after Be'alma in the Qaddish of Yehe Shelamah and 'Al Yisrael. Barukh Hu Ubarukh Shemo may not be said at the mention of G-d's Name in the blessings. The same rules apply when one is in the middle of the Pesuqei DeZimra.

(See Shulḥan 'Arukh 51:4 with Rama. Kaf Haḥayyim ibid, Oth 7, 11)

Women and the blessings of Barukh She-amar and Yishtabbaḥ

Are women permitted to say the Berakhoth (blessings) connected with the Pesuqei Dezimra, of Barukh She-amar and Yishtabbaḥ?

Women are exempt from all Miṣwoth Shehazzeman Gerama (positive commandments which are dependent upon time). The Pesuqei Dezimra which are part of the morning Shaḥrith prayer must be read by a specific time – before the Shaḥrith 'Amidah – which means no later than four hours into the day. If a man reads them after this time he may not recite the blessings. As such, this is a positive Miṣwah dependant upon time and women are exempt from praying the Pesuqei Dezimra.

This is as far as their obligation is concerned. However, if they wish to read it, including reciting the complete Berakhoth (blessings) of Barukh She-amar and Yishtabbaḥ, they are permitted to do so and will get a reward for doing it. This is a time-honored tradition even among Sephardim.

(See Ohr LeṢion Oraḥ Ḥayyim 2, 5: 3. Kaf Haḥayyim 70, Oth 1, concerning the prayer from the Aqedah till the end)

Saying Ashrei with the appropriate concentration

The more familiar one is with a prayer, the greater the danger that one will say it without the proper concentration. One such prayer is the Ashrei.

One must be careful to say the Pasuq (verse) of Potheyaḥ Eth Yadekha (You open Your hand) with concentration. If one did not concentrate when saying it, it must be repeated. One must also have the appropriate intent when saying Tehillah LeDawid. Ribbi El'azar states that one who says Tehillah LeDawid every day is assured a portion in the world to come.

And what is the essential aspect of the intent that one must have? One must understand the meaning of the words that Haqqadosh Barukh Hu (the Holy One Blessed be He) watches over all His creatures and provides their livelihood.

(See Shulḥan 'Arukh 51: 7. Kaf Haḥayyim ibid, Oth 31 & 34)

Saying the Shirath Hayyam as if one were there

The Shirath Hayyam (Az Yashir Moshe) must be said with great Ka<u>w</u>anah (intent). It is said that whoever says it every day with concentration will merit to recite it in the world to come and in the days of Mashiyaḥ (the Messiah).

Whoever says it in great joy, taking care to say each word correctly and with the Ta'amim (cantillation notes), and says it as if he himself came out of Egypt and and is crossing the Red Sea, will be saved by the Holy One Blessed Be He who will forgive him his trespasses.

(See Kaf Haḥayyim 51, Oth 40 and 41)

Not rushing when reading the Qaddish

One who is reciting the Qaddish, must do so in a calm temperate manner, and not hurriedly. This is because those who are answering the Qaddish should be able to answer from Yehe Shemeh Rabba till Be'alma (this refers to Sephardim – Ashkenazim only reply till either 'Almaya or Yithbarakh), without any interruption. They should then reply Amen when the reader says Berikh Hu (according to Sephardim. Ashkenazim answer Berikh Hu) before he says Le'eilla.

When many people are reading the Qaddish at the same time, they must be careful to ensure that they are reading together. We often hear people reading at very different paces and this only serves to confuse those who are answering.

In a case where people are not reading the Qaddish at the same speed, one should answer the the first one.

(See Ben Ish Ḥai, 1st yr. Parashath Wayḥi, Oth 11. Kaf Haḥayyim 56, Oth 30. Mishnah Berurah ibid, 15)

Speaking during the Qaddish

It is well known that there are people who talk during the prayers, the Derashoth (sermons) and the Qaddish. Not only do they sin themselves, but they cause the one to whom they are speaking to sin as well.

There is a story of a pious individual who saw another pious person who had died and was looking gloomy. He asked him why he was looking so sad. The person who passed away replied that it was on account of the fact that he used to speak while the Shaliyaḥ Ṣibbur (Ḥazzan) was reciting Waykhullu and Maghen Aboth (on Friday night), and Yithgaddal (the Qaddish).

Quoting a Midrash, it says in Maṭṭeh Moshe that a Ḥakham appeared before his student in a dream. His disciple noticed that he had a stain on his forehead and asked him why this happened to him. The Ḥakham replied that it was because he was not careful about not speaking when the Ḥazzan recited the Qaddish.

It says in the Kaf Haḥayyim of Ḥakham Falaji that this applies to any and all Qaddishim, and not only those which are part of the prayers.

(See Kaf Haḥayyim (Ḥakham Ya'aqob Ḥayyim Sopher) 56, Oth 2. Sefer Ḥasidim 58. Maṭṭeh Moshe 411)

The minimum one must have in mind when reading the Shema'

Ḥakham Yoseph Ḥayyim, 'a"h, states in Ben Ish Ḥai that before reading the Shema' one should have in mind that he is fulfilling the positive commandment of reading the Shema' twice a day. One should also have in mind that one is performing the commandment of the unification of G-d (Leyaḥed Eth Hashem) by saying the words of the Shema'.

As mentioned previously, the first verse of the Shema' and, some say, the second, require the appropriate concentration. At the very least, one must have the basic meaning of the words that one is reciting in mind (Hear O Israel, the L-rd our G-d, the L-rd is One), when reading the first verse. As we mentioned, if one did not have at least this basic intent in mind one must repeat the Shema'. However, since we do not want it to appear as if there are two separate entities (deities), Heaven forbid, one must remain silent the time that it takes to read the first paragraph and then start the Shema' again. If one wishes to read the first paragraph instead of remaining silent, before repeating the Shema', it is actually preferable.

The basic meaning of the second verse is: Blessed is the Name of G-d whose glorious sovereignty is for ever and ever.

(See Ben Ish Ḥai, 1st year, Parashath Wa-era, Oth 6)

Understanding the verse Shema' Yisrael

The Pasuq (verse) of Shema' Yisrael (Hear O Israel) has six words. They should be read in pairs, two at a time in order to have in mind the following meanings:

The word Shema' means accept. It also has the meaning of understand. So the meaning of the two words Shema' Yisrael is: Accept these words, understand them and believe in them. This is because the L-rd is our G-d and also He is One.

With the next two words, H' Elokenu (the L-rd our G-d), we accept the yoke of Heaven. We accept that He is our G-d and that we are His servants. The pair of words H' Eḥad (the L-rd is One) refers to the Unity of G-d, that He is One without any other partner.

(See Ben Ish Ḥai, Yr. 1. Parashath Waera, Oth 7)

Reading the Shema' without the appropriate intent

When reading the Shema', the Shulḥan 'Arukh rules that the primary concentration is in the first Pasuq (verse) which begins with the words Shema' Yisrael. Accordingly, if one read it without the appropriate intent, he did not fulfil his obligation and must read it again. Even those who are of the opinion that the performance of Miṣwoth (commandments) does not require intent, agree that the proper concentration is required for the first verse.

The Mishnah Berura writes that the same applies to the second verse, which starts with the words Barukh Shem, that if it is read without the intent it must be repeated.

In Ben Ish Ḥai it mentions that there are those who are of the opinion that if the second verse is not said with intent it must be repeated. He adds, however, that if one is repeating the verse of Barukh Shem, one one must repeat it starting with the first verse of Shema' Yisrael, on account of Qabbalistic reasons to do with the order.

(See Shulḥan'Arukh 63:4. M.B. ibid, 14. Ben Ish Ḥai, 1st year, Parashath Waera, 6)

Not understanding the 'Amidah and not being able to pray by heart

If people are praying by heart and there are no prayer books available and someone does not remember the 'Amidah by heart, he can rely on the Shaliyaḥ Ṣibbur's repetition. This is provided he concentrates from the beginning to the end of the repetition without any interruption or taking his mind off it.

This also assumes that the person understands the 'Amidah (i.e. what the Shaliyaḥ Ṣibbur is saying). If not, he cannot fulfill his obligation this way. It would seem that in view of this and the fact that he must concentrate fully on the words of the Ḥazzan, from beginning to end, which is something that most people are unable to do in our generation, it is unlikely that someone can fulfill his obligation this way nowadays. Therefore, he should make every effort to find a Siddur or always carry a small one with him.

Someone who is able to pray the 'Amidah by heart cannot rely on the repetition of the Ḥazzan. If someone who is praying from a Siddur is able to read correctly, but does not understand the meaning of the words, he nevertheless fulfills his obligation of praying the 'Amidah.

(See Shulḥan 'Arukh, 124:1. Kaf Haḥayyim ibid, Oth 1, 3, 4)

If you are unsure if you read an additional section in the 'Amidah

There are different opinions as to what one should do when one is not certain if he added the portion in the 'Amidah for a specific occasion, such as the request for rain (Mashib Haruwaḥ) or Ya'aleh Weyabo and the like.

The Mishnah Berurah says that if a person knows that he intended to say it during the prayer, but some time after he finished he is not certain if he said it or not, he does not repeat it. Only if his uncertainty arose immediately after the 'Amidah does he repeat it.

The Kaf Haḥayyim brings down that for the uncertainty to be of the type that requires the 'Amidah to be repeated, the doubt in one's mind must come during the specific Berakha (blessing) that the additional portion is in or, at the very least, during that 'Amidah. But if he had doubts after the 'Amidah was over (and especially if some time passed) he does not repeat it.

The Kaf Haḥayyim says further that there is a difference between Maran Yosef Qaro (the author of the Shulḥan 'Arukh) and the Rama in the matter of where there is a doubt if Ya'aleh Weyabo was recited or not on Rosh Ḥodesh. Because of that, the correct way to proceed on Rosh Ḥodesh, is to state when repeating that if it is not necessary to repeat it, it should be considered as a Nedabah (voluntary offering).

(See Shulḥan 'Arukh, 114: 8. M.B. ibid, 38. Kaf Haḥayyim ibid, Oth 48. Shulḥan 'Arukh, 422: 1 with Rama. Kaf Ḥayyim ibid, Oth 18)

Ḥakham who is taking a long time in the silent 'Amidah

If a Ḥakham or an important person who is taking a long time saying his 'Amidah, notices that the Ḥazzan and the congregation are waiting for him in order to start the Ḥazarah (repetition of the 'Amidah), what should he do?

If he sees the Ḥazzan is waiting for him, he is allowed to take three steps back after he says the first *Yehiyoo Leraṣon*, so that the Ḥazzan will see him take three steps back, assume that he has finished and start the Ḥazarah (the repetition). This is permissible, even though he has not said *Elokai Neṣor* and finished the 'Amidah.

(See Ben Ish Ḥai, 1st year, Oth 10, Parashath Terumah)

Waiting for those who pray a long 'Amidah

If there are (10 or more) individuals who finished their silent 'Amidah very fast, they may not start the repetition of the 'Amidah but must wait for the rest of the congregation.

This is probably the origin of the custom of waiting for the Ḥakham of the congregation before starting the repetition. However, the Rabbi should not draw out his prayer unnecessarily or, if he does, he should give instructions to the congregation not to wait for him.

In a case where there is no Rabbi present at the Minyan, or he has instructed them not to wait for him, the question is, when the Ḥazzan finishes his silent 'Amidah, can he begin the Ḥazarah right away, or does he need to wait for those who are taking a long time to finish their silent 'Amidah?

The answer is, if the people are taking an extraordinary amount of time in reading their silent 'Amidah with great intent, he does not need to wait. However, if the Ḥazzan finishes fairly fast and there are many there who are reading the 'Amidah silently, quietly, word by word, not rushing, but not taking an extraordinary amount of time reading it, in such a case, the Ḥazzan must wait for those who are reading it word by word, to finish.

(See Ben Ish Ḥai, 1st year, Parashath Terumah, 10. Kaf Haḥayyim 124: 3 Oth 12.)

Speaking between the silent 'Amidah and the repetition

The Ḥazzan must be very particular not to speak at all between the silent 'Amidah and the Ḥazarah (repetition). Of course, it is not only the Ḥazzan but all members of the congregation who must be very careful not to speak between the silent 'Amidah and the repetition.

Unfortunately, there are those who feel that the wait before the Ḥazzan starts the repetition is a perfect time to enter into discussions with the person standing next to them. The Gurei HaAri wrote that it is a very serious transgression, even for an individual, to speak at that time.

How much more so must the one who is leading the congregation be stringent not to speak between the silent 'Amidah and the repetition.

(See Kaf Haḥayyim, 53, Oth 16)

Answering Qaddish after starting the Minḥa 'Amidah

During the Minḥa prayer, if someone started the first verse, *Hashem Sefathai Tiftaḥ*, but had not yet started the first blessing of the 'Amidah, and heard a Qaddish, Qedusha or Barkhu, he should answer them. After answering he should then repeat the Pasuq (verse) of H' Sefathai Tiftaḥ, and continue with the 'Amidah.

Even though this Pasuq is considered part of the 'Amidah, we cannot make a comparison between it and the first *Yihyoo Leraṣon* that we say at the end of the 'Amidah, before which we may not answer the above-mentioned items.

The reason being that till one says the verse *Yihyoo Leraṣon* the 'Amidah has not ended and it would be a Hefseq (interruption). In the case of the opening verse, *H' Sefathai Tiftaḥ*, however, since we have not yet recited any of the blessings, answering is not considered to be an interruption.

As such, after answering, we simply start the 'Amidah again from *H' Sefathai Tiftaḥ*.

(See Ben Ish Ḥai, 1st year, Parashath Wayyaqhel, Oth 10)

Praying Minḥa without a Repetition

Ḥakhamenu z"l (our Rabbis of blessed memory) said that a man must be very particular about the Minḥa prayer in all its aspects, because it is a time of Din (judgement). It should be noted that the first prayer that was ever prayed was the Minḥa prayer by Adam Harishon (Adam).

Rabbenu the Ari, z"l, was very particular to never pray Minḥa without a Ḥazarah (repetition), first quietly (the Laḥash) and then repeated loudly, as is done during Shaḥrith. (It goes without saying that this requires a Minyan). He would do so even if it was quite close to sunset. Even on Friday evening before sunset, he would pray it first silently and then again repeat it out loud.

(See Moreh Be'eṣba' 3, Oth 128. Kaf Haḥayyim 232, Oth 9)

Why we must always have a Ḥazarah (repetition)

We mentioned that Rabbenu the Ari z"l was very particular to always have a Ḥazarah (repetition) after the silent 'Amidah (Laḥash) of Minḥa. He writes that one must never do away with the Ḥazarah during any of the three prayers which have a repetition, Shaḥrith, Musaf and Minḥa.

He revealed that that the Ḥazarah was at a higher level than the silent 'Amidah itself and that both the silent 'Amidah and the repetition were an obligation. Therefore, when the Ḥazzan was reciting the repetition, the Ari z"l would close his eyes and listen intently to the words of the Ḥazzan during the Ḥazarah.

It says, therefore, in Ben Ish Ḥai, that one must never omit the Ḥazarah when praying, except in a case where one has no choice, such as where there is no time left.

Note: A Ḥazarah, obviously, can only be done in the presence of a Minyan.

(See Ben Ish Ḥai, Parashath Terumah, Yr 1, Oth 2. Kaf Haḥayyim, 124, Oth 2)

Pay workers or pray Minḥa?

The importance of paying employees who are paid by the day can be best illustrated by the following story about Rabbenu the Ari z"l. He had the custom of never praying Minḥa till he paid the wages of all his workers who were employed on the basis of being paid daily.

When, on occasion, he did not have the money in hand to pay them, he would actually delay praying Minḥa till he would borrow the money he needed and would pay all of them their dues. He used to say: "How can I stand before G-d and pray Minḥa, when the opportunity to perform a very important commandment was in my hands and I did not fulfill it?" The holy Zohar was very strict about this also.

The Ḥesed La-alaphim adds that a woman who does your laundry is in the same category, and must be paid right away whenever she brings the clothes.

(See Kaf Haḥayyim 232:, Oth 12)

Can Minḥa and 'Arbith be prayed during the same time period?

The Shulḥan 'Arukh states that on Friday night, 'Arbith (the evening prayer) is prayed earlier than it is during the week. The Mishnah Berurah comments that, if 'Arbith is prayed before sunset, it is not appropriate to pray Minḥa in the same time period, i.e. between Pelagh Haminḥa (which is 1 1/4 Halakhic hours before sunset) and sunset, but should be prayed earlier. This is the custom prevalent in many Ashkenazi communities.

Ḥakham Yoseph Ḥayyim, 'a"h, writes in Ben Ish Ḥai that nowadays the common practice, even on weekdays, is to pray both Minḥa and 'Arbith, one immediately following the other, together after Pelagh Haminḥa (in the same time period). This ruling applies to both weekdays and Friday evening and is the common practice for Sephardim.

He adds, however, that this is only acceptable when praying in a Minyan. If one prays Beyaḥid (by himself) at home, if he prayed Minḥa after Pelagh Haminḥa, he must wait till nightfall before praying 'Arbith. Since the custom on Friday evening is to pray 'Arbith before nightfall, one who is praying by himself must pray an early Minḥa, before Pelagh Haminḥa.

Women, he rules, are exempt from this restriction, and those women who pray Minḥa and 'Arbith, may pray both together after Pelagh Haminḥa.

(See Shulḥan 'Arukh 267:2. Mishnah Berurah, ibid, 2. Ben Ish Ḥai, Yr. 1, Parashath Wayaqhel, Oth 7)

How to read the Shema' before going to sleep

Before going to sleep we read Shema' Yisrael. According to the Shulḥan 'Arukh, it is sufficient to read the first paragraph only.

The Sha'ar Ha<u>k</u>a<u>w</u>anoth says that nowadays we are not at the level of the righteous who lived in early times (Ḥasidim Rishonim) and must read the entire Shema'. According to Midrash Tanḥuma, we must complete the Shema' in order to have 248 words (like the number of limbs in our bodies). To achieve this we must start with the words E-l Melekh Ne'eman (according to Ashkenazic practice) or repeat the final words H' Elokekhem Emeth (which is the most common Sephardic practice).

Even though there are authorities who permit this Shema' to be read while lying down, according to the Mequbbalim (Qabbalists) one should read it while sitting.

(See Shulḥan 'Arukh 239: 1 with Rama. Kaf Haḥayyim ibid, 1, 11. Mishnah Berurah ibid, 1

7

ציצית ותפלין

Ṣiṣṣith & Ṭefillin

Pure thoughts when wearing Tefillin

When a man wears Tefillin he must have a Guf Naqi (clean body). This does not apply only to the physical aspect, but also to his thoughts. The Shulḥan 'Arukh states that one who wears Tefillin must take care not to have desirous thoughts about a woman.

Therefore, one must make every effort to purify his thoughts before wearing Tefillin and put the fear of Heaven in front of him so that he can wear his Tefillin in holiness. It goes without saying that one must have pure thoughts at all times. The Rama adds that if one is unable to rid his mind of these thoughts it is preferable to not wear Tefillin.

It is brought down in the Kaf Haḥayyim, however, that the person should know that if he does not rid his mind of thoughts that prevent him from wearing Tefillin, he will have to give an accounting on the judgement day. Strong words, indeed, which should make a person aware of the importance of pure thoughts and the necessity to wear Tefillin each and every day.

(See Shulḥan 'Arukh 38:4. Kaf Haḥayyim ibid, Oth 11 and 12. Mishnah Brurah ibid, 15)

Wearing Tefillin is an atonement for many sins

Raba said: "Whoever dons Tefillin, wraps himself in Ṣiṣṣith, reads the Shema' and prays, is certain to inherit the world to come". Abbayye stated: "I guarantee that the fires of Gehinnam (hell) will have no jurisdiction over him". Rab Pappa said: "I guarantee that all his transgressions are forgiven".

All this applies if a person is very careful in all these matters, not to denigrate them by speaking about profane matters or in any other way while performing these Miṣwoth (commandments).

Our Rabbis of blessed memory stated that the Tefillin that are worn on the head are an atonement for arrogance and Tefillin of the hand are an atonement for spilling blood. If so, it behooves every man to make every effort to get Tefillin that are worthy in every respect, as it says: *"This is my G-d and I shall glorify Him"*.

(See Kaf Haḥayyim 37, Oth 1, 3 & 4)

Eight positive commandments connected with Tefillin

Razal said (Menahoth 44a) that one who does not wear Tefillin transgresses eight positive commandments every day. This is because there are four Parashioth each in the Tefillin of the arm and of the head, and each one is a positive commandment, making a total of eight.

On the other hand, one who wears them every day fulfills eight positive commandments. Additionally, one who is particular about wearing Tefillin will have the scales tipped in his favor on the judgement day, but one who was not will find the scales tipped against him, Heaven forbid. Rabbenu Ḥayyim Wiṭṭal, 'a"h, cautions about the severity of not fulfilling the commandment of Tefillin.

As such, it behooves every man to be particular about this important commandment and he will, as a result, merit to receive all the good of this world and of the world to come.

(See Qiṣur Shulḥan 'Arukh, Ḥ"R Rafael Barukh Toledano, 32, Oth 3)

Writing the contents of the Tefillin in the correct order

Tefillin contain the following four Parashioth (sections from the Torah):

1. Qaddesh Li
2. Wehaya Ki Yebiakha
3. Shema' Yisrael
4. Wehaya Im Shamowa'

These sections must be written in the above-mentioned order. If they were written out of order they become Pasul (unfit for ritual use).

In addition, the Parashioth for the Tefillin Shel Yad (Tefillin worn on the arm) should be written before the sections for the Tefillin Shel Rosh (the ones worn on the head.) However, if they were not written in that order, after the fact (Bedi'abad) they may still be used.

(See Shulḥan 'Arukh, 32:1 with Rama)

Reciting a blessing over borrowed or stolen Tefillin

If someone borrows a pair of Tefillin he is permitted to recite the Berakha (blessing) over it, since we can fulfill our obligation of Tefillin using a borrowed pair.

The case is different if someone were to steal a pair of Tefillin. It is forbidden to recite a Berakha on stolen Tefillin because this is considered to be a good deed that comes through sinning (Miṣwah Haba-ah Min Ha'aberah). It says further in Tehillim that one who steals and says a blessing, insults G-d.

Even though the vast majority of people would never consider stealing, there are important ramifications to this. Borrowing without permission is considered stealing (unless one knows for certain that the owner does not mind). As such, one must not use someone else's Tefillin without permission. However, if you are in a situation where there are no other Tefillin available, and it is not possible to ask the owner, and if you would wait any longer it would become too late to perform the Miṣwah (commandment), then you are permitted to rely on the fact that another Jew would be happy to have a Miṣwah done with his property.

Even so, after the fact, one should still go to the owner (if he can be found), and ask his permission retroactively.

(See Ben Ish Ḥai, 1st year, Parashath Wayyera, Oth 14)

Using someone's Ṣiṣṣith (Ṭallith Gadol) and Tefillin without permission

Under normal circumstances we would assume that another person would be happy if we borrowed an item of theirs without asking, if it were to perform a Miṣwah (commandment or good deed). This should also apply to borrowing someone's Ṣiṣṣith (Ṭallith Gadol) and Tefillin in the Synagogue.

It says in Ben Ish Ḥai, however, that nowadays the majority of people do not want someone else to use their Ṣiṣṣith and Tefillin without permission. As such, if the Shammash of the Synagogue gives you someone else's Ṣiṣṣith or Tefillin without the permission of the owner, you should not take them unless you are absolutely certain that the owner has no problem with it. It goes without saying that you should not take them yourself if you are not absolutely certain that the owner does not mind.

We must be cautious in this matter since different people feel differently about others borrowing their items without asking. Interestingly, Ḥakham Yoseph Ḥayyim, himself, adds that he would not want others to use his Ṣiṣṣith and Tefillin in such a manner.

(See Ben Ish Ḥai, 1st year, Parashath Lekh Lekha, Oth 6)

Which side of the Ṭallith Gadol should be on top?

It says in the Mishnah Berurah that the custom is to add a piece of silk to the top portion of the Ṣiṣṣith (Ṭallith Gadol), so that it will always be worn in the same position with the same fringes always in the front. The Mishnah Berurah adds that the Ari z"l was not particular about this.

It says in Ben Ish Ḥai that one should not be particular to add a collar in order that the same side will always be on the head, since the Ari z"l stated specifically that we should not be particular about this but, rather, should wear it whichever way it comes.

The custom among Ashkenazim is in accordance with the Mishnah Berurah, and all the Ṣiṣṣiths (Ṭallith Gadols) that are sold today come ready made with the collar.

Sephardim who are concerned about the words of the Ari z"l and the Ben Ish Ḥai, remove the additional collar that comes with the Ṣiṣṣith (Ṭallith Gadol). This way it is worn the way it comes, without any preference given to a specific side.

(See Mishnah Berurah, Siman Ḥeth, Se'if Qattan Ṭeth, Ben Ish Ḥai, 1st year, Parashath Bereshith, Oth 8)

Does a garment with more than four corners require fringes?

Maran Yosef Qaro states in the Shulḥan 'Arukh that a garment with more than four corners requires fringes (Ṣiṣṣioth), but only on four of its corners, specifically on those that are farthest from each other. The Mishnah Berurah states that there are those who who exempt it (say that it does not require fringes) and, as such, one should ideally avoid making a garment with five corners.

Ḥakham Yosef Ḥayyim states in Ben Ish Ḥai that a garment with five or more corners does require fringes, but that one should avoid making such a garment because of the reason outlined above, even though they are only being placed on four of the corners.

Because of this, he adds that if a four cornered garment rips, effectively causing it to have six corners, it must be repaired right away, because of the opinion that it does not require fringes. This is in a case where the tear is reasonably small. If, however, the rip was across the majority of the garment, then the fringes must first be removed before repairing the garment and then replaced when it is fixed, because of the concept of *Ta'aseh Welo Min Ha'asooi* (you should make, and it should not be the result of something made previously).

(Sh. 'A 10: 1. M.B. ibid 3. Ben Ish Ḥai, Parashath Noah, Oth 6 and 8)

8

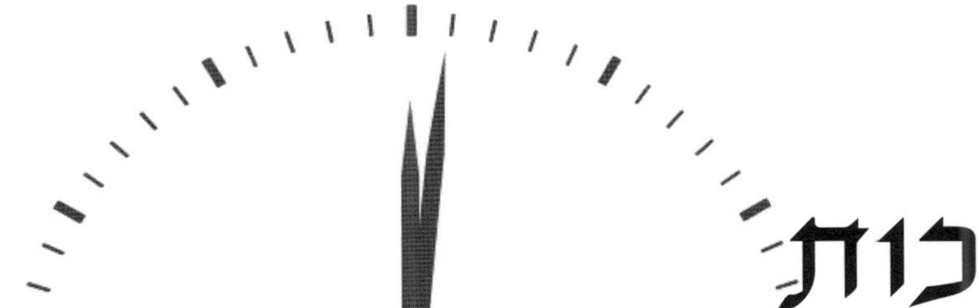

ברכות

Blessings

Importance of one hundred blessings a day

We are obligated to recite one hundred Berakhoth (blessings) a day. On Shabbath and Yom Ṭob as we know, there are less blessings in the 'Amidah and so we have to make them up by eating additional fruits and reciting Berakhoth on good smells, such as, *Boreh 'Aṣei Besameem* on Hadas (myrtle).

Rabbenu the Ari z"l explains, that the twenty two letters of the Hebrew alphabet depend on these one hundred Berakhoth. If a person does not recite one or more of these blessings or doesn't say them correctly or says them but without the appropriate concentration, the corresponding letters are negatively affected. From this we see how important these one hundred Berakhoth are.

(See Ben Ish Ḥai, 1st year, Parashath Wayesheb, Oth 14)

Reciting a blessing loudly or softly

The Zohar is very strict about a person who hears a Berakha (blessing) and does not answer Amen. This means, in practical terms, that if a person is reciting a Berakha and sees that, for whatever reason, the people there will not answer Amen – perhaps they are not paying attention, or do not understand – but it is clear to him that they will not recite Amen, It is better to say the Berakha quietly.

In this way people will not hear the blessing and come to stumble in this important matter by not answering Amen to the blessing. It is good to say a Berakha loudly when you know that the people present will answer Amen. But when you know that they will not, it is better to say it quietly to yourself.

(See Ben Ish Ḥai, Yr 1, Parashath Mas'ei)

If a blessing said on your behalf was not done correctly

When a group of people eat bread together, and only one person actually recites the blessing, when saying the blessing on behalf of all those at the table he must be particular to have in mind that his blessing includes all those at the table who are going to eat the bread. He must also say it out loudly and clearly so that they can hear every word.

For this reason, there are those who have the custom of saying, before reciting the blessing, that they intend to include the others with their blessing. Those who are at the table must also have the intent that his blessing includes them too, and must reply *Amen* after the blessing.

In view of this, if one of those at the table notices that the one who is reciting the blessing is not reciting it correctly, or fears that he does not understand that he has to have everyone else in mind, he should recite the blessing himself, on his own piece of bread. However, he should do this quietly, so that the host will not notice and become offended.

(See Ben Ish Ḥai, 1st year, Parashath Emor, Oth 9)

Answering Amen to one's own Berakha

A person must not answer Amen to his own Berakha (blessing). However if he says two or more blessings then he answers Amen after them. An example of this is the multiple Berakhoth (blessings) that we recite after the Hafṭarah on Shabbath to which the one reciting the blessings also says Amen.

If somebody hears another Jewish person saying any Berakha, even if he did not hear it in its entirety, from beginning to end, he must answer Amen. The person who answers Amen must also have in mind that he is answering Amen on behalf of the person reciting the Berakha. For this reason, he must answer loudly, so that the person who is reciting the blessing can hear the Amen.

For this to work, the person who is saying the Berakha must also have in mind that the Amen is covering him too. The person who answers Amen has to be particular not to answer Amen louder than the one who is making the Berakha.

(See Ben Ish Ḥai, Yr 1, Parashath Mas'ei)

Can we answer Amen to a Berakha of a child?

The Shulḥan 'Arukh tells us that one should not answer *Amen* to the Berakha (blessing) of a child who is being taught to recite blessings. This is so, even though children are taught to say the Berakha with G-d's name.

If a child recites the Berakha for its intended purpose, however, we do answer Amen if the child understands Whom he/she is blessing and has reached the age of instruction (Ḥin̲ukh), which is seven for the majority of children, or even six for a particularly bright child. The same applies when a boy of seven or so, recites the Mafṭir and Hafṭarah with the blessings in the Synagogue, that we respond Amen.

The Mishnah Berurah and Kaf Haḥayyim state that the implication is that if a child recites a blessing over food – one that he is supposed to recite – but has not yet reached the age of instruction, we do not answer Amen. Similarly, if one is uncertain whether one should answer Amen to a child's blessing or not, one does not answer, because we have a concept that when there is a doubt about an Amen, it should not be said.

It says in Ohr LeṢion, that when one does not answer Amen to a child's Berakha, it is good to say *Barukh H' Le'olam Amen WeAmen* while the child is saying the Berakha, with the last Amen being said after the child finishes. This way, he/she will not realize that we are not answering Amen.

(See Shulḥan 'Arukh, 215: 3. Kaf Haḥayyim ibid, 19, 21. Mishnah Berurah ibid 13-17. Ohr LeṢion 14, Oth 33)

Neṭilath Yadayim with or without a blessing

There are many different occasions when Neṭilath Yadayim (the ritual washing of the hands) is required, but no Berakha (blessing) is recited on it. The only times we recite a Berakha is in the case of washing one's hands after a night's sleep and when washing in order to eat bread. Even in these two cases, there are occasions when we do not recite a blessing.

If someone sleeps during the day, he should make Neṭilath Yadayim (as usual, three time alternately on each hand), even though there is an opinion that it is not necessary, but one should not recite a Berakha.

If someone gets up in the middle of the night and does not intend to go back to sleep, he makes Neṭilath Yadayim as soon as he gets up and recites a Berakha. If he intends to go back to sleep, however, he still must make Neṭilath Yadayim, but to avoid getting into a difference of opinion among Posqim, he should not say the blessing of 'Al Neṭilath Yadayim. Instead, he waits till he wakes up in the morning and says it then after washing his hands and going to the bathroom.

If his intention, however, is to remain awake for a while (to study Torah or recite Tiqqun Ḥaṣoth), and he says Neṭilath Yadayim and the Birkhoth Hashaḥar (the morning blessings), then when he wakes up again in the morning, he does not say a Berakha after Neṭilath Yadayim.

(See Ben Ish Ḥai, Parashath Toldoth, Oth 13. Ohr LeṢion 2: 1, Oth 2)

Neṭilath Yadayim using water whitened by air bubbles

The Shulḥan 'Arukh states that one may not do Neṭilath Yadayim (the ritual washing of hands) in water whose appearance has changed. Sometimes when pouring water out of a tap the water is white and cloudy in appearance, but when it settles down it regains its natural clarity. Is this water fit for doing Neṭilath Yadayim?

It says in Ohr LeṢion that in this case we do not consider that the appearance of the water has changed since the whiteness is not due to paint or coloring, but is due to small bubbles of air which cause it to appear white. When the air disappears from the water, it regains its natural look.

In view of this, one may use this water for Neṭilath Yadayim, even before the air has disappeared and while the whiteness is still apparent.

(See Shulḥan 'Arukh 160: 1. Ohr LeṢion, Ḥeleq 2, ch. 11, Oth 7)

When to say the blessing on Neṭilath Yadayim on bread

When eating a meal with a Kebeṣah (2 ozs.) or more of bread, one must do Neṭilath Yadayim (the ritual washing of hands) and recite the Berakha (blessing) of 'Al Neṭilath Yadayim on the washing. The first Kezayith (ounce) must be eaten within *Kedei Akhilath Peras.* There are different opinions as to how much time this is, varying from two to nine minutes, but a common opinion is four minutes.

If one eats less than a Kebeṣah, but at least a Kezayith (1 oz.), since there are different opinions as to whether he should recite the blessing or not, we apply the concept of *Sefeq Berakhoth Lehaqel* (when there is a doubt about a blessing we do not recite it). As such, Neṭilath Yadayim should be done, but without the blessing.

Maran Yoseph Qaro, 'a"h, states in the Shulḥan 'Arukh (Code of Jewish Law) that if one eats less than a Kezayith there is an opinion that Neṭilath Yadayim is not required at all. The Kaf Haḥayyim states that since there are differing opinions about this, the correct way to eat less than a Kezayith of bread is to do Neṭilath Yadayim but not recite the blessing.

He adds, however, that ideally, one should not eat less than a Kezayith, because unless one eats at least a Kezayith of bread, one will not have the opportunity to make Birkath Hammazon (the grace after meals) for which the minimum quantity is a Kezayith.

(See Shulḥan 'Arukh, 158: 1-3. Kaf Haḥayyim ibid: 8-11)

Immersing one's hands for bread if no vessel is available

When eating bread, if one is unable to do Neṭilath Yadayim (the ritual washing of hands) from a Keli (vessel), one can immerse one's hands in an appropriate body of water (such as the sea or certain rivers [a Rabbi should be consulted for specifics as to which bodies of water are acceptable]), or a Miqweh (ritual bath) that is Kasher for women to immerse themselves in.

Both hands must be fully submerged at the same time and the Berakha (blessing) of 'Al Neṭilath Yadayim is recited. Strictly speaking one need only immerse one's hands once and they do not need to be dried.

According to the Sod (Qabbalah), however, even when immersing one's hands, they must be immersed three times, rubbed together three times and then raised when saying the Berakha. They should also be dried for reasons of cleanliness.

(See Ben Ish Ḥai, 1st year, Parashath Tazria' Ṭaharoth, Oth 12. Kaf Haḥayyim 162, Oth 1)

Neṭilath Yadayim if dipping cookies in coffee

If someone dips his cookie into a cooked liquid, such as into a cup of tea or coffee, he must first do Neṭilath Yadayim (the ritual washing of the hands) as we do when eating bread, but without a Berakha (blessing). This assumes that the person actually touches the liquid.

If the person uses a spoon to eat the cookie and dips the cookie into the cooked liquid with the spoon, then Neṭilath Yadayim is not needed. Similarly, If a person dips a cookie into a cup of tea or coffee by hand, but is careful not to touch the liquid at all, then Neṭilath Yadayim is not required either.

(See Ben Ish Ḥai, Yr 1, Parashath Tazria', Oth 19. Kaf Haḥayyim 158, Oth 39. See also Ohr LeṢion 11:6)

Feeding someone else – who washes whose hands?

When someone eats bread he has to first make Neṭilath Yadayim (the ritual washing of hands) three times on the right hand followed by three times on the left, according to Sephardim, or twice each according to Ashkenazim.

When one feeds bread to another person, who is required to make Neṭilath Yadayim? The answer is that the one who feeds others is not required to wash his hands, but the one who is being fed must wash his, even though he does not touch the food with his hands. Similarly, when a person eats using cutlery and does not touch the food with his hands, he must still do Neṭilath Yadayim.

One may not give bread to someone to eat, if one is certain that he has not washed his hands, because of the prohibition of not placing a stumbling block before a blind person. This means that you may not cause someone to sin because of his lack of knowledge and it also applies to helping someone to perform a transgression that he would not have been able to do on his own.

(See Shulḥan 'Arukh 163: 2, with Rama)

Forgetting to recite the blessing till after drying one's hands

When washing one's hands (Neṭilath Yadayim) for bread and the like, one should, strictly speaking, say the Berakha (blessing) before washing. This is because the normal order is to say the blessing and then do the action.

We do not do so for various reasons and the custom has become, as stated by the Rama and also the Ari z"l, to first wash and then recite the blessing before drying one's hands. (One must be particular not to say the blessing while drying one's hands). If one started drying one's hands and then remembered to say the blessing while his hands were still partially wet, he may still say the blessing then.

If, however, one forgot to recite the blessing till after he dried his hands, there is a difference of opinion as to whether he is permitted to recite the blessing or not. As such, as in all cases where there is a doubt about a blessing, he should not recite the blessing. Instead, as mentioned in Ben Ish Ḥai, he should touch a portion of his body which will require him to do Neṭilath Yadayim (such as scratching one's head, etc.) and then do Neṭilah again with a Berakha (being careful to bless before drying)

Note: there is no issue here of causing an unnecessary blessing (which is not permitted), since he did not recite one in the first place.

(See Shulḥan 'Arukh 158: 11 with Rama. Ben Ish Ḥai, Parashath Shemini, Oth 7. Kaf Haḥayyim 158, Oth 83 and 85. Ohr LeṢion 11:4)

Stepping outside for a discussion during a meal requires Neṭilah

Someone who is having a meal with bread and takes his mind off the meal by stepping out and getting into a protracted discussion with his friend during the meal, must do Neṭilath Yadayim (the ritual washing of hands) again, because he took his mind off the meal. The Berakha (blessing) of 'Al Neṭilath Yadayim, however, should not be repeated.

It appears, however, that if one is holding a piece of bread in his hand, he does not need to do Neṭilath Yadayim again. This is because his mind is on it while he is holding it and he will not take his mind off it, as is mentioned by Rabbenu the Ḥida, z"l.

(See Shulḥan 'Arukh Siman 170, Se'if 1. Kaf Haḥayyim ibid Oth 11, 12 and 13. Mishnah Berurah ibid, 8)

Swallowing the bread before speaking

Once one says the Berakha (blessing) of *Ha<u>m</u>oṣi Leḥem Min Ha-areṣ*, one must eat the piece of bread immediately without interruption. In fact, not only must one put the bread in one's mouth, but one must actually chew and swallow a portion of it. Until that time a person may not speak.

If a person did speak, however, about matters unconnected with the eating of the meal, there is a question whether he needs to repeat the Berakha or not. The ruling mentioned in Ben Ish Ḥai is that he does not.

(See Shulḥan 'Arukh 167:6. Ben Ish Ḥai, yr. 1, Parashath Emor, 14. M.B. 167, 35)

Eating bread at the sea shore

If someone wishes to eat bread but the only water available is sea water, may it be used for Neṭilath Yadayim (the ritual washing of hands)?

The Shulḥan 'Arukh states that water that is salty, smelly or bitter, to the extent that a dog would not drink it, is unfit to be used for Neṭilath Yadayim, even though it may be used for Tebila (ritual immersion). As such, one can not use sea water for Neṭilath Yadayim.

If one has the opportunity to boil the water first, it then becomes fit for a dog to drink and, as such, can be used for Neṭilath Yadayim when it cools down. It is preferable however to immerse both hands in the sea instead, if this is possible.

If neither possibility is an option, one should use the sea water as it is and do Neṭilath Yadayim from a vessel. However, no Berakha should be recited and one must cover one's hands with a cloth while eating.

(See Shulḥan 'Arukh 140: 9. Ben Ish Ḥai, yr. 1. Parashath Aḥarei-moth/Qedoshim, Oth 13. Kaf Haḥayyim 140, Oth 42)

Coffee and doughnut for breakfast - what Berakha (blessing)?

When drinking a morning tea or coffee with a cookie, doughnut or danish (Path Haḇa-ah Bekhisanin - which is Mezonoth), the blessing (Berakha) or blessings one that recites depends essentially on the individual.

If the cookie or other similar Mezonoth that the person is eating is what is most important and the drinking of the tea or coffee is just to accompany it (on account of it) and is secondary, then the only Berakha that is recited is Borei Minei Mezonoth on the cookie, doughnut, or other similar Mezonoth and it covers the drink as well. But if the drink is what is most important and the Mezonoth is secondary and consumed simply to accompany (on account of) the drink, then the blessing of Shehaḵol should be recited on the drink and one must have in mind that it covers the Mezonoth also.

If, however, both the drink and the Mezonoth are equally important and neither is secondary to the other (as is common when a person settles down to drink his or her morning coffee and have a danish or doughnut with it and enjoys each one independently), then both blessings must be recited. First the Berakha of Borei Minei Mezonoth is recited on the Mezonoth and then Shehaḵol is recited on the drink.

(See Q. Shulḥan 'Arukh Ḥ"R Rafael Barukh Toledano, 167: 22)

What blessing on vegetables grown in water?

Nowadays, there are certain vegetables such as lettuce, that are grown in water and not in the earth, and are commonly found in our supermarkets. Does the Berakha (blessing) of

Borei Peri Ha-adamah (Who created the fruit of the earth) still apply, or, since it did not come from the earth should another blessing (Shehakol) be recited instead?

Even though the actual vegetable that one is eating was grown in water and not in the earth, nevertheless, the origin of the seed that was used in its planting, was from the ground. In view of that it is considered to be fruit of the earth and the Berakha (blessing) of Borei Peri Ha-adamah is recited as usual.

(See Ohr LeṢion 2, 14: 13)

If you only suck the juice out of a fruit, what blessing do you recite?

If you only suck the juice out of a fruit without eating it, do you recite a Berakha (blessing) of Borei Peri Ha'eṣ (as you would on any fruit of the tree that you eat), or Shehakol (which you would recite on juice)?

If you extract the juice by placing it in your mouth and chewing it, then you recite the blessing Borei Peri Ha'eṣ, as if you were eating it. If, however, you only hold the fruit in your hand and suck the juice out of it, the blessing is Shehakol.

There is also a difference concerning the blessing recited after drinking the juice (Berakha Aḥaronah). In the first case, it is treated as a regular case of eating a fruit, and requires a Kezayith (1 oz.) to be consumed within four minutes. In the latter case, however, since it is considered to be a case of drinking liquid only, we would be required to drink a full Rebi'ith (there are different opinions as to the volume of a Rebi'ith, from approximately 3 to 5.3 fluid ounces) in about half a minute. Since this is not possible when sucking juice out of a fruit, no blessing can be recited after drinking the juice, irrespective of how much juice one drank.

(See Ben Ish Ḥai, 1st year, Parashath Mas'ei, Oth 8)

Saying Shehakol on bread on someone else's behalf

If a person who is eating bread says the Berakha of *Shehakol* or *Borei Minei Mezonoth* or *Borei Peri Ha-adamah*, instead of the correct blessing of *Hamoṣi*, he has still fulfilled his obligation.

The complication arises when the person who says the wrong Berakha says it not only for himself, but also on behalf of others who are at the same table. Do they also fulfill their obligation with the blessing he recited instead of *Hamoṣi*?

The answer depends on how they reacted when he recited the incorrect Berakha. If they accepted it and still had their minds on the blessing he recited, then they fulfilled their obligation. If, on the other hand, when they heard him say the wrong blessing, they stopped paying attention, then they did not fulfill their obligation. The reason being that in order for someone else's blessing to cover another person also, both the one who blesses as well as the one who hears, require the concentration of the heart (Kawanah).

(See Kaf Haḥayyim, 167, Oth 77)

One who forgot to do Zimmun

Three or more people who eat a meal together (with bread) are obligated to say Zimmun (lit. "invitation", where they recite the Birkath HaMazon together). If they forgot and each one recited the Birkath HaMazon (Grace after Meals) on their own, they have lost the opportunity to say Zimmun and cannot say it together after the fact.

If only one of the three forgot and recited the Birkath Hammazon by himself, or even if he did so deliberately, the remaining two can include him in the Zimmun and fulfill their obligation. He, however, does not fulfill his obligation with this Zimmun even though he was included in it, because one cannot fulfill one's obligation of Zimmun Bedi'abad (after the fact). This also assumes that they are all adults with no boys under the age of 13.

The Rama adds that in a case where one of the three combined with two others for the Zimmun, the remaining two are unable to do a Zimmun. This is because he has already fulfilled his obligation

(See Shulḥan 'Arukh 194:1 with Rama. Mishnah Berurah ibid 4. Kaf Haḥayyim Oth 2, 4 & 5)

Saying Birkath Hammazon for one who does not understand

If two people ate a meal with bread together, it is preferable for each man to make his own Birkath Hammazon (Grace after meals). If one of them is not able to read the Birkath Hammazon, the other can read it and have the one who is unable to read fulfil his obligation through his reading.

This assumes that the one who is unable to read, nevertheless understands the Holy Tongue and listens word by word to what is being read. The one who is reading must have in mind that he is saying it on behalf of the other person also. But if the one who is listening does not understand what is being said, he does not fulfil his obligation.

The one who is reading Birkath Hammazon, however, fulfills his obligation even if he does not understand what he is saying.

(See Shulḥan 'Arukh, 193: 1 with Rama. Kaf Haḥayyim, 193: 4)

Birkath Hammazon with one's eyes open or shut

Making Birkath Hammmazon (Grace after meals), after eating the required quantity of bread, is a positive commandment from the Torah for men and, some say, for women also. There is an interesting difference of opinion concerning how it should be said.

The Mishnah Berurah says that one must read from the text and not say it by heart. This is the prevalent custom amongst Ashkenazim. Ḥakham Yoseph Ḥayyim, 'a"h, says in Ben Ish Ḥai that one must close one's eyes when saying Birkath Hammazon. This is based on what the Rashash (Ḥ"R Shar'abi) wrote in his Siddur. As such, this is the appropriate custom for Sefardim.

This assumes, of course, that one can read it correctly by heart. It is obvious, that one who does not know the Birkath Hammazon fluently by heart, must read it from the text. Additionally, if he feels that his Ka<u>w</u>anah (intent) would be hampered, or he would get distracted if he read it by heart, he should also read it from the written text.

(see Shulḥan 'Arukh, 185:1. Mishnah Berura, ibid, 1. Ben Ish Ḥai, 1st yr, Parashath Ḥuqqath, Oth 2)

Saying Shehaḵol on a fragrance

The Shulḥan 'Arukh states that if one makes the Berakha (blessing) of Borei Minei Besamim over any fragrance (even though this may not be the specific blessing for that particular fragrance) one will still have fulfilled his obligation. Therefore, if one is uncertain which blessing should be recited over a specific fragrance, the blessing of Minei Besamim should be said.

The Mishnah Berurah mentions that there are some Aḥaronim who are of the opinion that if the blessing of Shehaḵol were recited over a fragrance, one will have fulfilled his obligation after the fact. However, the Maghen Gibborim is of the opinion that Shehaḵol cannot be used for a fragrance at all, but applies exclusively to food and drink.

The Ben Ish Ḥai states, however, that if one recited the blessing of Shehaḵol on a fragrance, instead of 'Aṣei, 'Isbei or Minei Besamim, he has fulfilled his obligation.

(See Shulḥan 'Arukh 216:2. M.B. ibid, 13. Ben Ish Ḥai, 1st year, Parashath Wa-eth-ḥannan, 9)

Making a blessing over the fragrance of air freshener or perfume

In order to recite a blessing over a fragrance, the scent must be for the purpose of smelling and not for the purpose of masking a bad smell or the like. In addition, the fragrance must emanate from some substance and not just be a scent without a source.

As such, one does not recite a blessing over air freshener since it is used to mask bad odors. (If it was purchased for the purpose of smelling and reciting a blessing, and not in order to mask a smell, then one would say the blessing of Borei Minei Besamim over it).

One recites a blessing over perfume that is in a bottle, since the fragrance originates from the perfume itself and is used to provide a pleasant scent. If one pours the perfume onto one's hand, one recites the blessing as long as the hand is still wet from the perfume. If, however, the hand has dried, one cannot recite the blessing since there is only the scent that remained but without the substance from which it emanated. It should be noted that there are those who are of the opinion that, nowadays, one does not recite a blessing over perfume, but the Ohr LeṢion rules as mentioned above.

(See Shulḥan 'Arukh 217: 2, 3. Ohr LeṢion 14:35)

Sheheḥeyanu on a new home

Does someone who builds a new home need to say the Berakha (blessing) of Sheheḥeyanu or not?

Strictly speaking, when somebody builds a new home or even buys one, which is perhaps more common, that was built by somebody else, he should recite the berakha of Sheheḥeyanu, which of course is a very special blessing, thanking G-d for having given us life to be able to see this day.

However, the custom is not to say the blessing. Instead one should have a Se'uddah (festive meal) to give thanks to G-d for this wonderful good that He has done for us, and this meal is considered to be a Se'udath Miṣwah.

During the meal however, the custom is to wear an important new item of clothing, of the type that you would recite Sheheḥeyanu over, such as a new suit, and to say the Berakha of Sheheḥeyanu on this new item. One should have in mind while saying it that it covers the new home as well.

(See Ben Ish Ḥai, 1st year, Parashath Re-eh, Oth 6)

9

אכילה

Eating

Limiting one's food consumption during the week

Rabbenu the Ḥida, 'a"h, writes that any meal that one has during the week (excluding Shabbath) must be only what is required for one's health. Anything above this goes to the Siṭra Aḥara (the side of impurity).

It is said about Rabbenu the Ari, z"l, that he would only eat small portions. It says in Maggid Mesharim that the angel cautioned Maran Yosef Qaro, 'a"h, that he should not eat a lot of meat because it is harmful, or drink a lot of wine because one does not know where it may lead.

One must be careful to look after one's health. Each meal should be eaten at the correct time, and one should not wait till he is very hungry and feels week. One's intent when eating should be that it is for the purpose of being healthy because many of the illnesses that come are because of over indulging.

(See Kaf Haḥayyim 157, Oth 15, 33, 35)

Etiquette & cleanliness when eating

One must be particular not get one's clothes dirty when eating. It is preferable to eat with a spoon (or fork) rather than with one's fingers. But in a case when a person eats with his fingers, he must take care to only dirty the tips of the fingers and not his whole hand.

We must not put large amounts of food into our mouths. If the person who is eating has a beard, he must be careful not to spill food on his beard and dirty it. If his mustache is long, he must push it aside so that it will not get very dirty.

Obviously these rules apply when a person is eating with others, but they also apply when one is eating at home at one's own table.

(See Ben Ish Ḥai, Parashath Behar Sinai/Beḥuqqothai, Oth 5)

Salt and spirituality in eating

Eating, which is a physical act, also has a spiritual side. One should be more particular about the honor of one's soul than the honor of one's body. Therefore, before eating a meal, one should study some Torah.

When eating a meal, one should always place salt on the table and leave it there till after Birkath Hammazon (Grace after Meals). The bread must be dipped in it as soon as we recite the blessing of Hamoṣi. The reason is that since, for our sins, the Beth Hamiqdash (Temple) is not standing, the table at which we eat is likened to the altar and the food is in place of the offerings. And it is written, *"Upon all your sacrifices you shall offer salt"*. In addition this a Tiqqun (rectification) of the soul.

If one recites the blessing of Ha<u>m</u>oṣi and finds there is no salt on the table, he must not wait, but breaks and eats the bread immediately. When salt is brought later he should dip the bread in it.

According to the Sod (Qabbalah), the bread must be dipped three times into the salt and there are Qabbalistic reasons for this. It should be noted that the words Leḥem (bread) and Melaḥ (salt) are made up of the same Hebrew letters.

(See Ben Ish Ḥai, 1st year, Parashath Emor, Oth 10. Kaf Haḥayyim 157, Oth 8 & 9)

Not throwing bread to others

It says in Ben Ish Ḥai that when a group of people are eating together and one person recites the Berakha of Ha<u>m</u>oṣi and breaks the bread on behalf of the others, he must be particular not to throw the bread to those seated at the table. Instead he should place it in front of them as far as he can reach.

He should not hand it to another person either (hand to hand) because we only give bread into the hands of a mourner (Bar Minnan). Because of this one must be particular not to give children bread in their hands, but rather, one should place it in front of them so that they will take it themselves.

(See Ben Ish Ḥai, 1st year, Parashath Emor, Oth 11)

Serving food to someone who will not say the blessing

Maran states in the Shulḥan 'Arukh that one should only give food to a person if he knows that he will recite a Berakha (blessing) over it. The Rama adds that if it is given to a person as charity, there are those who are lenient and permit it. This applies when one is uncertain as to whether he will recite a blessing or not.

If one knows for certain that he will not, one should not give him food. There are those who say that this only applies if the poor person will not recite the blessing out of wickedness, but if it is because of for reasons out of his control ('Oness), then one is permitted to give it to him. The Kaf Haḥayyim states that it appears from the words of the Posqim that one should not give food to any person who one knows for sure will not recite the blessing. If, however, he knows that it is not out of wickedness but due to 'Oness, he should give the poor person a type of food that does not require Neṭilath Yadayim (the ritual washing of hands) or Birkath Hammazon (grace after meals).

Cafes and restaurants, however, are not forbidden to serve cutomers who eat bread without doing Neṭilath Yadayim or reciting the Berakha of Hamoṣi.

(See Shulḥan 'Arukh 169: 2 with Rama. Kaf Haḥayyim ibid Oth 15, 163, Oth 17)

Baking meat and fish together in an oven

The Shulḥan 'Arukh states that one may not eat meat and fish together because it is considered dangerous to one's health. The Rama adds that, a priori, they should not be roasted together either.

Meat and fish may not be baked uncovered in the same oven. The reason for this being that when two different foods are baked in the same oven at the same time, each food absorbs taste from the other food.

As a result, if meat and fish were baked together in an oven, and both of them were uncovered, they both become forbidden.

(See Shulḥan ‘Arukh, Yoreh De’ah 116: 2)

Taking on a stringency of keeping 24hrs between milk and meat

A question is asked in Torah Lishmah̲ about someone who had the custom of waiting 24 hours after eating meat, before having any cheese or other dairy. In addition he also kept 24 hours after eating cheese before eating meat. Is this Ḥumra (stringency) one he should continue to keep?

The response quotes sources in the Gemara and the Ari, z"l. We do see from the Gemara of Ḥullin that Mar Uqba's father kept 24 hours after eating meat. This only applies to cheese after meat and not the opposite. Any day that the Ari z"l ate cheese he would wait till the night, before eating meat (but not 24 hours). It would also appear that he did not keep more than this between meat and cheese.

After quoting several other sources including the Yerushalmi, Rama and Beth Yoseph, he concludes that this stringency, which not even the Ari z"l followed, is inappropriate to keep.

(See Torah Lishmah̲, Yoreh De’ah, She-elah Rosh Yod Beh)

10

מעגל החיים

Life Cycle

A pregnant mother's actions affect the baby

A woman must be careful during pregnancy concerning what foods she eats. The wrong foods can harm the baby because the baby tastes (absorbs) whatever the mother eats.

The pregnant mother should not go to any place that contains Tum-ah (uncleanliness) or a bad smell, because the unborn child is affected by it. Our Rabbis of blessed memory stated that ten things adversely affect one's learning, and one of them is passing through a place where there is a bad smell. When a pregnant mother passes through such a place, it has an adverse effect on her unborn child.

Instead, she should make a point of spending her time during her pregnancy in holy places such as at the Synagogue or Beth Midrash and to see Talmidei Ḥakhamim and hear words of Torah, because the words that enter her ears sanctify the, as yet, unborn baby. It says in Pirqei Aboth (the Ethics of the Fathers) concerning Ribbi Yehoshua Ben Ḥananya, that his mother caused him to become a Ḥakham, because as soon as he was born, she took him to the Beth Midrash so that he could grow up hearing words of Torah. Words of Torah enter the child's ears and cause all his limbs to become holy.

(See Horayoth 13b. Aboth 2:8. Shebeṭ Mussar 24, Oth 16. Ben Yehoyada‘, 'Erubim, 18b)

Milah and Pidyon on the same day. Which takes precedence?

A Milah (circumcision) is normally held on the eighth day, unless the child is not well enough. A Pidyon Habben (redemption of the first born) is done on the thirty first day. If the child was not well enough for the Milah at the correct time, and the first opportunity to perform it is on the thirty first day, which one should be done first? Should we do the Milah, because it is ordinarily done before the Pidyon? Or should we do the Pidyon first because this is the correct day for it?

It says in Yede Ḥayyim and Torah Lishmah̲, based on the Gemara of Pesaḥim about Birkath Hammazon, that the Milah should be done first because that is the normal order.

An additional reason is that we have a concept that something that comes regularly (Tadir), takes precedence over something that comes occasionally (Eino Tadir). A Milah must be performed on all baby boys. A Pidyon is far less common since in order to have a Pidyon, the boy must be a first-born with no miscarriages before his birth, it must have been a natural delivery and neither parent may be a Kohen or Lewi (Cohen or Levite).

As such, a Pidyon is far less common than a Milah and the Milah takes precedence.

(See Yede Ḥayyim, Section Torah Lishmah̲, She-elah Meem Zahn, and Torah Lishmah̲, Yoreh De’ah, 246)

A Pidyon Habben that falls on Shabbath

It is a commandment upon every man to redeem his son if he is a first born of the mother, unless either parent is Kohen or Lewi. The Pidyon (redemption) must be held on the 31st day and not before.

The redempton is made with coins or other vessels that have the silver content of 5 holy Sheqels. If the 31st day is Shabbath then the Pidyon is delayed to the following day (Sunday). The Pidyon may not be performed on Shabbath, even if using a vessel, because it resembles a business transaction.

Even though there is an opinion that when the 31st day is Shabbath, if the baby is more than 29 days, 12 hours and 40 minutes old on the Friday preceding it, the Pidyon can be made on that Friday, others, including the Maghen Abraham, reject this because a month as stated in the Torah is 30 days and therefore, the Pidyon cannot be till the 31st day.

If the Pidyon was performed on a Friday under these circumstances, it should be made again after Shabbath, but without the blessings.

(See Shulḥan ‘Arukh, Yoreh Deah 305: 11. Maḥaziq Berakha, Oth 15. Shulḥan ‘Arukh, Oraḥ Ḥayyim 339: 4. Kaf Haḥayyim ibid, Oth 55)

Celebrating Birthdays

It says in Ben Ish Ḥai that there are those who celebrate their birthdays every year. Ḥakham Yosef Ḥayyim, 'a"h, adds that it is good to do so and that this is the custom in his home.

He adds further, that there are those who have the custom of having a Se'uddah (festive meal) every year on the date of their Milah, and that it is a fine custom which he finds very positive, even though it was not his custom.

He did, however, say a special prayer every year on that day, which can be found in Ben Ish Ḥai, Parashath Re-eh, 1st Year.

(See Ben Ish Ḥai, Parashath Re-eh, 1st Year, Oth 17)

The younger boy becomes Bar Miṣwah before the older

As we know, a Shanah Me'ubbereth (Jewish leap year) contains an additional month of Adar. Let us look at a case of a boy who was born on the twenty-ninth day of the first month of Adar during a Shanah Me'ubbereth, and another boy who was born after him on the first day of the second month of Adar. If the year in which they become Bar Miṣwah (thirteen years of age) is not M'eubbereth and contains only one Adar, then the older boy becomes Bar Miṣwah after the one who was born after him.

The one who was born first, on the 29th of the first Adar, has to wait till the 29th of the (only) month of Adar that year to become Bar Miṣwah. The boy who was born after him on the first day of the second Adar, however, becomes Bar Miṣwah virtually a full month earlier, on the first of (the only) Adar that year.

If their thirteenth birthday was in a Shanah Me'ubbereth (which contains two months of Adar), however, they would be Bar Miṣwah in the correct order – the first on the 29th day of the first Adar and the second on the first day of Adar II.

(See Shulḥan 'Arukh, 55:10. Kaf Haḥayyim ibid, 59)

Performing a wedding without a Minyan

The wedding ceremony consists of two parts, the Erusin (also known as Qiddushin) and the Nisuin (sometimes also referred to as Ḥuppah). At one time they were held at different times (such as a year apart). Nowadays, they are both done together (one following the other) under the Ḥuppah.

The blessings of the Erusin (the first portion) should be done in the presence of a Minyan (quorum of 10 males), however, if a Minyan is not available, they may be recited with less than ten. The 7 blessings (Sheba' Berakhoth) of the Nisuin, however, require a Minyan and may not be made with less.

Nowadays, it is a fairly simple matter to get a Minyan in most places or to travel to a place where there is one in order to perform the wedding. But what if the couple wishing to get married are in a place which does not have ten males in the whole land, and are unable to travel to another location? In such a case, where they really have no alternative, they can rely on the lenient opinion and perform the second portion of the wedding ceremony with just one Berakha (Asher Bara). However, after they are married, when they are able to go to a place where there is a Minyan, they should go to a Ḥuppah in that town and listen to the full Sheba' Berakhoth and have in mind that these blessings apply to them also.

(See Ben Ish Ḥai, Yr. 1. Parashath Shofṭim, Oth 14)

May a bridegroom leave on a business trip during the first year?

There are those whose business commonly takes them on extended overseas trips throughout the year. The Radbaz was asked whether a Ḥathan (bridegroom) in his first year of marriage is permitted to go overseas on a business trip.

The basis of the problem is that is says in the Torah (Parashath Ki Theṣe), "When a man marries a new wife ... he shall be free for his home for one year and shall make his wife happy". This sounds like the husband must be available for his wife throughout the first year.

In a decision in his work of Responsa, Rab Pe'alim, Ḥakham Yoseph Ḥayyim, 'a"h, quotes what many Posqim have mentioned and reaches the decision that if the bridegroom is travelling for his livelihood, then this prohibition mentioned in the above-mentioned verse, does not apply.

(See Ben Ish Ḥai, 1st year, Parashath Shofṭim, Oth 19 and Rab Pe'alim Ḥeleq 3, Eben Ha'ezer, Pereq 9)

11

דיני ממונות

Financial

Returning a stolen item that dropped in value

If someone stole an item worth, let us say $100, and the value of that item drops to say $50, does he have to return the original value or the current value?

If he returns the item itself, the question would be, does he return the item plus $50 to compensate for the loss in value from when he stole it, or does he simply return the item, because that is what he stole, irrespective of its current value?

The answer is that, provided he is not responsible for its loss in value, but rather market conditions are what brought about the change in value, then he only returns the item itself. However, if he returns the monetary value of the item, then he must repay the value of the item as it was at the time he stole it.

(See Shulḥan 'Arukh, Ḥoshen Mishpaṭ, 354:3, 362:11, 363:1)

Opening in competition with another Jew

If a person wishes to open a store in a certain area where there already is an existing store in the same line of business, he is permitted to open his store next door to the existing one.

This is not considered to be Hassaghath Gebul (encroaching on the other person's territory).

A person is permitted to lower his prices vis-a-vis what others in the trade are charging, and the others do not have the right to complain about this. However, if a Jew does work for a non-Jew, it is forbidden for another Jew to offer do the same work at a lower price, so that he will get the job instead of him.

(See Ben Ish Ḥai, 1st. year, Parashath Ki Thabo, Oth 11)

Can a dispute between two Jews be taken to secular court?

If there is a dispute between two Jewish individuals in a civil matter which they cannot resolve themselves, they must take the matter to a Beth Din (Jewish Rabbinical Court). They may not go to a secular court, even if both parties agree, because it would imply rejection of the Torah.

If one of the two parties refuses to appear before the Beth Din, the common practice is for the Beth Din to summon him three times. If, after that time, the recalcitrant party still refuses to appear, the Beth Din can give permission to the plaintiff to take the case to the secular courts.

When the plaintiff receives this permission he is fully permitted to go to the secular courts without any concern of transgression.

(See Shulḥan 'Arukh, Ḥoshen Mishpaṭ 26: 1, 2)

12

מוסר

Mussar

Shalom (peace) is necessary for the world to exist

Shalom (peace) between people is a very important quality, because the existence of the whole world depends on it. When there is unity there is peace. The reverse is also true, division causes separation.

If all the objects that exist in the world were able to behave like human beings we would immediately see that the world could not survive. For example, if there is a wall built of stones that fit closely together, the wall will stand. If, however, one of the stones would complain that it was unfair that it was below certain other stones and was able to leave its position to go to the top, the whole wall would collapse.

If the parts of the body behaved the same way, with the heart saying that it was more important than the brain and would somehow be able to leave its place to sit on the top, the person would not be able to survive.

From this we see how great peace is. If we nullify peace by seeking separation and causing strife, we must understand that we are destroying the foundation of Creation.

(See Shebeṭ Mussar, 37: 15)

Bringing empty boxes

There is a Mashal (parable) of servants who were expected to bring presents to their master the king. Some brought casks full of wine, others brought containers of oil, yet others brought barrels of honey, while some brought packages of silk and embroidered clothes.

There were others, however, who brought large boxes and containers which were empty. Clearly, those who brought fine gifts would be rewarded and those who brought large empty containers would pay the price for their actions, even more than if they had brought nothing.

So too with our Tefilloth (prayers). When we pray to G-d and praise Him, it is like a present that we are bringing to Him. There are those who come to Him with Torah and with a desire to serve Him. Others come with prayer with Kawanah (dedication of their hearts) or with praise. A person and his limbs are like the containers. The Kawanah and the desire to praise Him are the bundles of silk and the fine embroidered clothes that we bring.

Others, however, bring themselves (the containers) to pray, but their hearts are not with them. What is the point of bringing our containers (our bodies) but leaving the contents out? G-d, unlike earthly kings, judges the contents – the heart. So when we make the effort to pray to G-d, it is important to make the additional effort to pray with devotion, to ensure that G-d receives the gift He is expecting.

(See Qol Sasson, 10)

Love and caring will bring the redemption

Each of the Jewish people is commanded to do *Ramaḥ* (248) Miṣwoth 'Aseh (positive commandments). Of course, it is not possible for each individual to perform all 248, because not all apply to each person.

The only way, therefore, for it to be possible, is through the love that exists between one another. In this way, each person completes his Ramaḥ (248) positive commandments through the actions of his fellow Jew. That is why Ramaḥ is made up of the same Hebrew letters as *Raḥem* which is one of the interpretations of the word *love*.

This hints to us that the 248 commandments will be considered performed by every single individual through the love between one another. And the performance of all 248 positive commandments helps to bring the Geullah (final redemption). From this we see how important love and caring are among the Jewish people.

(Ben Ish Ḥai, Yr 1, Parashath Wa-era, introduction)

What can we learn from the bees?

We humans are the most advanced of all the species in the world. We are endowed with wisdom and understanding and the ability to communicate, more than any other species on earth. Yet we have much to learn from lesser creatures around us.

In Qol Sasson it says there are things to learn from animals who do not speak. From the bees we learn Derekh Ereṣ (the proper way of behaving with each other).

Bees are united and stick together. In fact, they build their homes one next to the other in a hive. Not only that, but you will not find them trying to outdo each other with the size of the homes they build. Each bee's home is the same size as its neighbor's. Their homes are not spacious but the just right size to hold them.

Human beings, on the other hand, are constantly trying to build homes that are larger than the other person's and go out of their way to have something unique about it that no one else has.

(See Qol Sasson, ch. 39)

What's in it for me?

When looking for a job, it is normal to want to know what your renumeration will be before accepting it. You want to be rewarded for your efforts. But should the same apply to the performance of the Miṣwoth (precepts)?

We must learn a lesson from fruit trees. They give their fruit, year in year out, even though they receive absolutely no reward for doing so. Humans beings, are required to add bundles upon bundles of new Miṣwoth every year. We should really do this, like the trees, with no desire to receive a reward in return. If the trees can do it, surely we can too.

But, as we know, Haqqadosh Barukh Hu rewards us for each and every Miṣwah that we do, be it in this world or the hereafter. We should be very appreciative of this extra mercy He does for us and do each Miṣwah with a happy heart, knowing that this is an extra kindness that we should not ordinarily expect to receive.

(See Shebeṭ Mussar, 9: 11)

Learning to cope with life, from the plants

It says in the Ashrei, *WeAttah Nothen Lahem Eth Okhlam Be'Itto* (You give them their food at the right time). It is well known that G-d doesn't make all fruits appear at all times. Rather, some are summer fruits, others appear in the winter or the fall. Some appear when the weather is warm, others thrive when the weather is cool. The reason for this is that G-d knows what is most beneficial for people at that particular time.

Even plants that do not appear to have any useful purpose, are needed in the world, perhaps to grind as medication or for some other purpose. That is why it says when the Creation of the world was completed (on the sixth day) that *G-d saw* ***all*** *that He created, and it was exceedingly good*. This means that even a thorn has a purpose when the time is right.

Just as plants can, at times, harm a person, and yet at other times the same plants are used to heal people, so too when a person sees that times do not appear to be so good, we must realize that they have their uses. People go through good and bad times. It would help us to understand that bad times can be compared to plants that appear to be harmful. Therefore, much as we hope never to have bad times, we must know that if they come, they might be required to help a person, even though the reason may not be apparent till later.

(See Tehillah LeDawid, 'Einei Khol Elekha)

The importance of being happy when serving G-d

A person must be particular to perform every commandment with great happiness. Rabbenu the Ari z"l wrote about its importance, adding that through serving G-d in happiness, he himself, merited to have Ruwaḥ Haqqodesh – the spirit of Divine Inspiration. On the other hand, he states that one who does not do this is punished, because it is says in the Torah *"Because you did not serve the L-rd your G-d in happiness"*.

The Alsheikh Haqqadosh states that even among those who serve G-d in happiness, there are differences. Some serve Him with only a limited amount of happiness, while others serve Him with much more joy. The basic principle is that the more happiness one has when serving Him, the more reward one receives for it. A servant who knows his master and understands that he only wants good for him, realizes even when his master appears to be harsh (like a parent must sometimes appear to a child), it is only for his own good, and he will surely always serve him with a happy heart.

(See Shebeṭ Mussar, Pereq 20: 8)

Overcoming anger

Anger is a most serious character trait. The Ari z"l was more strict about the need to avoid anger than any other negative character trait. One must make every effort to overcome one's natural tendencies to get angry.

If a person is angry but contains his anger and doesn't say anything, he will overcome it more easily than if he speaks out of anger. The Qol Sasson brings a comparison to hot water and fire to explain this. In order to cool down water that is hot, you pour cold water into it. This has the effect of cooling it down, silently, without any visual signs. If, however, it is a coal fire that you wish to extinguish, and the fire is, of course, very visible to the eye, pouring water on it causes much reaction in terms of noise and steam and the like, which emanate from it.

We learn from this, that when something is already visible to the eye and made known, the reaction is much greater. Our first endeavor must be to eradicate anger altogether. But if we find that it has crept up on us, we must keep it internalized and not speak words out of anger. This is because it is easier to be appeased if the anger was not made public, than to overcome anger that was accompanied by inflammatory words. But clearly, our ultimate goal must be to train ourselves not to feel anger at all.

(See Qol Sasson, ch. 35)

Anger: eliminating it at all costs

A person must be very careful to avoid anger altogether, at all times. Our Rabbis of Blessed Memory told us, *"Whoever gets angry, if he is a wise person, his wisdom leaves him..."*.

Rabbenu the Ari z"l, was stricter about anger than any other transgression, even if the anger was over a Miṣwah (commandment) as happened with Moshe Rabbenu, 'a"h, who got angry for G-d's sake and, nevertheless, forgot Halakha as a result.

He states that one who gets angry has no rectification for his sin till he tries with all his might to overcome this trait and does not get angry at all.

(See Pesaḥim 66b. Wayyiqra 10:17. Kaf Haḥayyim 170, Oth 30)

Looking at the one covered in soot

In order to better understand how to be good Jews and serve G-d, we must see ourselves as if we are lacking in the area of service towards G-d.

There is a Mashal (parable) of two people who went to a copper foundry which was fired by coal. One of them was not careful to keep away from the coal, and his face soon became black. The other was very particular to keep clean and he didn't get any coal on himself.

When they finished and were about to leave, the one whose face was clean went and washed his face thoroughly. The other one, whose face was blackened by the coal did not wash at all. Why was this? The answer is that the one whose face became black did not see himself. He only saw his friend's face which was perfectly clean. On the other hand, the one with the clean face only saw his friend's face and saw that it was covered in soot, so he quickly went to wash his own face.

The same applies to a Rasha' and Ṣaddiq (wicked person and a pious individual). The Rasha' whose face became black because of his deeds, does not see himself, but looks at the one who is righteous and feels he is just like him. The righteous person should not see himself as being righteous, but should look at the the Rasha' and feel that he looks him and, as such, will constantly strive to improve and cleanse himself.

(See Qol Sasson ch. 5 'Abodath H')

13

מִגְוָן דַקּוֹת

Various Torah Minutes

The Torah is the remedy for all transgressions

The Torah is the remedy for all transgressions. We have proof of this from the Zohar which says:

Anyone who studies the Torah even if, because of his transgressions, retribution was already decided for him in Heaven, will find that his diligent study of the Torah will be more beneficial to him than any sacrifice or other offering that could have been brought in the days of the Beth Hamiqdash (Temple). The punishment that was decreed gets torn up, provided he studies Torah Lishmah (for its own sake and not for the purpose of some other gain) and the Holy One Blessed be He becomes appeased.

The reason why a person can become purified through the study of Torah is because the Torah cannot become Tameh (impure). On the contrary, it purifies the impure and, as such, the remedy to all transgressions can be found in the Torah.

(See Shebeṭ Mussar, 21: 19)

The Torah is the continuity of the Jewish people

This Torah Minute was written the day the holy sage and revered Rabbinic leader, HaRab Haggaon, Ḥakham Mordekhai Eliyahu, 'a"h, passed away. He wrote the following in his work on the laws of Jewish Holidays:

Long before the commandment was given over to Moshe Rabbenu, 'a"h, Ya'aqob Abinu, 'a"h, (our father Jacob) had already kept the important Miṣwah (commandment) of teaching Torah to one's sons. He taught Torah to all of his sons, and especially to Yoseph Haṣṣaddiq, 'a"h (Joseph). Not only that, but he ensured that Torah would be taught to his subsequent generations, even though they would be in Egypt, by sending Yehudah, his son, to form a Yeshibah in the land of Goshen. This is because he understood that the study of Torah is critical for the survival of the Jewish people.

That is why, when the prophet Mikha enumerated the thirteen attributes of mercy of G-d, he said: "Titten Emeth LeYa'aqob, Ḥesed LeAbraham, Asher Nishba'ta La-abothenu Mimei Qedem" (give 'truth' to Ya'aqob, kindness to Abraham , that You swore to our forefathers all those years ago).

"Truth" is the Torah that the Jewish people received through the merit of Ya'aqob Abinu, 'a"h. And it is in his merit that the Torah has been given to his generations.

(See Ḥ"R Maran Mordekhai Eliyahu, 'a"h, M.M., Hilkhoth Ḥaggim, introduction)

Studying Ḥoq LeYisrael every day

Every man is obligated to study, each day, the Written Law (Torah, Nebiim and Kethubim) as well as Mishna, Gemara and Posqim (Halakha).

The custom nowadays amongst Sephardim and many Ashkenazim who follow the teachings of the Ari z"l, is to study the Ḥoq LeYisrael every day, in Synagogue, after Shaḥrith. It permits one to study, in a short time, Tanakh, Mishna, Gemara, Zohar, Mussar and Halakha. It is said that the Ari z"l used to say it while still wearing his Ṣiṣṣith (Ṭallith Gadol) and Tefillin.

The ideal way for it to be studied in Synagogue, is for a Talmid Ḥakham to read it aloud and explain the portions of the Gemara and Zohar where there are lessons to be learned, as well as the Musar and Halakha (laws). And the G-d fearing people there gather around him to learn.

(See Mishnah Berurah 155: 1, 3. Kaf Haḥayyim ibid, Oth 3.)

Washing hands after touching socks

It says in the Shulḥan 'Arukh (Code of Jewish Law) that one who removes his shoes (touching them) and one who touches his feet must do Neṭilath Yadayim (the ritual washing of one's hands). The question is whether touching one's socks also requires one to do Neṭilath Yadayim.

The Kaf Haḥayyim mentions different opinions, implying that it is appropriate to be particular to do so, but that according to the strict Halakha (law) it is not necessary. The Kaf Haḥayyim states further, that they heard directly from Ḥakham Yoseph Ḥayyim, 'a"h, himself (the Ben Ish Ḥai), that according to the strict interpretation of the law it is not necessary.

The Ohr LeṢion says that if one touches the portion of the socks that is inside the shoe, where the feet perspire, one must do Neṭilath Yadayim, but the portions that are outside the shoe do not require it. In all the above-mentioned cases, the Neṭilah is done without a Berakha.

(Shulḥan 'Arukh, 4: 18. Kaf Haḥayyim, ibid, Oth 72. Ohr LeṢion 2:1, Oth 12)

The correct way to put on clothes - and head covering for men

We have to be particular not to wear two garments together, meaning one inside the other and put the two on together because this is considered to be harmful for the memory. Also articles of clothing must be put on the correct way, meaning, if you put them on inside out, you must remove them and put them on the right way.

One should not walk with one's head uncovered and should also be careful not to sit with an uncovered head even for a moment, unless it is necessary. G-d's name may not be mentioned with an uncovered head, and placing one's own hand on one's head does not constitute a head covering. However, somebody else's hand on one's head does.

I would like to point out at this time, that these rules apply to both to Sefaradim and Ashkenazim as far as men are concerned. The situation for women is somewhat different. There are differences of opinion between Sefaradim and Ashkenazim, as far as mentioning G-d's name with an uncovered head is concerned, and we will Be'ezrath Hashem discuss this matter on a different occasion.

(See Ben Ish Ḥai, 1st year, Parashath Wayyishlaḥ, Oth 16)

Cutting hair and nails on Thursday

There is an opinion that nails and hair should not be cut on Thursday. The reason, as mentioned by the Ṭaz, is that since nails start growing again on the third day, this would cause them to start growing on Shabbath. And the same applies to cutting one's hair.

The Kaf Haḥayyim brings opinions disputing this. In particular, since kings cut their hair daily, this is proof that hair grows constantly and not just on the third day. If that were not so, they would have no hair left. Even though the Be-er Heṭeb mentions this also, there are some Ashkenazim who do not cut their hair on Thursday. Each one should follow his own custom in this matter. Sephardim, however, need not be concerned about this opinion and may cut their hair and nails on Thursday.

It should be noted, however, that the Dabar Be'itto states that for Qabbalistic reasons, nails should only be cut on Friday and not on any other day of the week.

(Kaf Haḥayyim, 260: 15. Be-er Heṭeb ibid: 2. Ohr LeṢion, 47: Oth 4, Dabar Be'itto, Yom Hashishsi, Qesisath Haṣṣippornayim)

Cutting nails in order

There are some differences between the customs of Ashkenzim and Sephardim when it comes to cutting one's nails.

The Rama states that one's nails should not be cut in order. Rather one should start with the ring finger (counted as #4) on the left hand in the the following order: 4, 2, 5, 3, 1. The nails on the right hand are then cut in the following order starting with the index finger (counted as #2): 2, 4, 1, 3, 5. This is the custom for Ashkenazim. In addition, the Mishnah Berurah adds that there is an opinion that one should not cut the nails of both one's feet and hands on the same day.

For Sephardim the case is different. Rabbenu the Ḥida states that the Ari z"l, himself, used to cut his nails in order and cut both the nails of his hands and feet on the same day and was not concerned about either. The Ḥida adds that this is the Minhagh Pashuṭ (widespread custom). The Ohr LeṢion states that Sephardim may cut the nails of their hands and feet on one day and also need not be concerned about cutting their nails in order.

(See Shulḥan 'Arukh and Rama, 260: 1. Mishnah Berurah ibid: 6. Kaf Haḥayyim ibid: Oth 11, 17. Ohr LeṢion, 47: Oth 4)

Placing a Mezuzah too high or too low

Since a Mezuzah must be placed at the bottom of the upper third of a door post, a Mezuzah which was placed below the upper third of the door post is Pasul (ritually unfit). Even though there are those who permit it, this opinion should not be accepted except in a case of extreme need.

If, however, the Mezuzah was affixed in the top third, but not at the beginning of the top third, as it should be, but higher up, perhaps even touching the lintel, then even though this is not the ideal position it is, nevertheless, Kasher (ritually fit) according to all opinions.

Even so, one should still remove it (if this is possible) and place it in the correct spot at the bottom of the upper third, and should not say that since it has been affixed there and, Bedi'abad (after the fact) it is still Kasher where it is, it need not be moved. Rather, since one is in a position to put it in the correct location, one must do so.

(See Ben Ish Ḥai, 2nd year, Parashath Ki Thabo, Oth 7)

Positioning and repositioning a Mezuzah

A Mezuzah must be placed in the upper third of the doorpost, irrespective of the height of the door. If a person recited the blessing and placed it below the top third, and later realized, or was made aware of the error, he has to remove it and reposition it in the top third.

In such a case, he should not recite the blessing again when moving it. One of the reasons is that there is an opinion that if it is placed below the top third it is still valid. And even though we do not follow that opinion, since there is a difference of opinion we apply the concept of *Sefeq Berakhoth Lehaqqel* (when there is a doubt whether a blessing should be recited or not, we do not recite it).

Therefore, in this case of moving the Mezuzah to a higher position on the doorpost, it should be repositioned without a blessing.

(See Ben Ish Ḥai, 2nd year, Parashath Ki Thabo, Oth 8)

May you remove your Mezuzoth when moving?

A question that is asked fairly regularly concerns what one should do with one's Mezuzoth when moving out of a house or apartment. May they be removed or not?

If someone rented a house or apartment from a Jew, even if he himself put up the Mezuzoth, he may not remove them when he leaves. The Gemara says very harsh things about one who does.

If someone rents a house or apartment from a non Jew, obviously when he moves in he has to put up Mezuzoth. What he does with them when he leaves, depends on who will be moving in after him. If a Jew moves in after him, he is obligated to leave them there. If a non Jew moves in he takes them with him.

(See Ben Ish Ḥai, 2nd year, Parashath Pinḥas, Oth 11)

Must we honor our in-laws?

Everyone is aware that we are obligated to honor our parents. Perhaps less well known is the obligation to honor one's in-laws. We see from King David, 'a"h, that a person is obligated to honor his father-in-law, as he called Shaul Hammelekh, 'a"h, (king Saul - his father-in-law), *"my father"*.

The same applies to honoring one's mother-in-law and the requirement to honor one's in-laws applies equally to men and women.

A person is also obligated to honor his grandparents as well as his uncles from both his father and mother's sides. And he will be blessed for doing so.

(See Ben Ish Ḥai,2nd year, Parashath Shofṭim, Oth 30)

Making a vow in a dream

Someone who has a dream, and in the dream makes a vow or an oath, does not need to be concerned about the vow or oath since he did not have the intent of the heart nor were the words actually uttered.

There is an opinion, however, that such a dream does require Hattarah (annulment). And even more than that, according to this opinion, since this came from Heaven, three men are not sufficient to annul the dream, but one must have ten who are literate in the reading of the Torah. Since there is such an opinion, we must be concerned about it and follow it, except that in a situation where one is unable to find ten men, one may use three. Even if one dreamed that it was annulled, one must still have it annulled as described above.

Likewise, a woman who had a dream of this nature must have it annulled by ten men and cannot have it done by her husband. Furthermore, if someone has a dream that someone else made an oath or a vow, the person whom he dreamed about must have them annulled by ten men.

(See Ben Ish Hai, 2nd year, Parashath Re-eh, Oth 15)

Why is Heh the abbreviation for G-d's Name?

Why is the abbreviation of G-d's Holy Ineffable Name the letter Heh? In view of the fact that His Name actually begins with the letter Yod, we should logically use a Yod as an abbreviation. In fact, the Heh is actually the last letter of His Name.

Heh is the letter with which the world was created, as it says: *Behibbar-am* (when they [the contents of the Heavens and the Earth] were created). Rashi says that by pronouncing it slightly differently we read it: *BeHeh Bera-am* (with the letter *Heh* He created them). This is one reason for its importance.

Another explanation in Torah Lishmah is that the letter Heh is different from all the other letters of the Hebrew alphabet. When you pronounce any other letter, you feel the letter on your lips or on your tongue, but the letter Heh doesn't touch anything and is completely pure (because it is essentially only air).

This shows us the importance and uniqueness of the letter Heh and why it is the most fitting to be used as an abbreviation for G-d's Ineffable Name.

(See Torah Lishmah, She-elah Taw Kaf Geemal)

Treating the Western Wall with respect

The Kothel Hama'arabi (Western Wall) is the only remnant that has remained for us, of the destruction of the Beth Hamiqdash (Temple). The holy Zohar tells us that the Shekhinah (G-d's holy Presence) has not departed from it.

The Kothel Hama'arabi (Western Wall) must, therefore, be treated with the utmost respect. We are not permitted to destroy the smallest portion of it (hammering a nail into it would be forbidden) or treat it in an undignified manner. Nowadays the Kothel is well lit with electric lighting, but in the days when people only had candles, there were some people who would place a candle on the wall for light. This is forbidden because it blackens the wall, in addition to the fact that we may not use the wall for any purpose.

Apparently, some people would also write their names on the stone of the Kothel itself, and this was forbidden for the same reason. Today, the authorities would be quick to prevent people from writing on the Kothel or defacing it in any manner, however, we must be particular to behave appropriately there, not only because it is a remnant of the Beth Ha<u>m</u>iqdash, but especially since the Shekhinah is present.

(See Kaf Haḥayyim 151, Oth 76)

5th of Ab - Anniversary of the Ari z"l

Rabbenu Yiṣḥaq Luria Ashkenazi, more commonly referred to as the Ari z"l, passed away on the fifth of Ab. Many have the custom of reading a special Tiqqun every year on that night, which was written by the great Qabbalist, Rabbenu Ḥakham Yoseph Ḥayyim, 'a"h.

The Ari z"l was born in Jerusalem to Rabbi Shelomo Luria who was a very pious individual. It is said that Eliyahu Hannabi zl"t (Elijah the prophet) used to reveal himself to him. His mother was also extemely pious. When the Ari z"l was born, Eliyahu Hannabi appeared to his father and instructed him not to perform the Milah (circumcision) till he sees him in the Synagogue. On the eighth day the father did not see Eliyahu Hannabi in the Synagogue and would not proceed. The congregation did not understand why there was a delay, but he would not be rushed.

Eliyahu Hannabi deliberately delayed coming, in order to see if the father would follow his instructions. When he finally arrived he instructed the father to sit on the chair with the child in his hands. Eliyahu Hannabi sat on the father and took the baby into his own hands. No one, not even the Mohel could see Eliyahu Hannabi, except the father.

When the Milah was completed, he returned the baby to the father and told him that a great light would shine forth from this child which would illuminate the whole world.

(See Tiqqun Hamisha BeAb of Rabbenu Ḥakham Yoseph Ḥayyim, 'a"h)

14

פרקי אבות

Pirqei Aboth

Pirqei Aboth 1:

(See Parashath Shemini)

Pirqei Aboth 2: The smallest are on top

In the Ethics of the Fathers it says: *Da' Mah Lema'alah Mimmakh* - Know what is above you; an eye that is watching and an ear that is listening. This obviously refers to the Holy One Blessed be He who sees and hears everything. However, there is another important lesson to be learnt from this.

The word *Mah* alludes to something that is small. A person should look at his eyes and ears which are small parts of his body and are situated on top. Conversely, larger parts of his body, such as the arms and legs, are situated further down. In addition, the eyes and ears which are very small are extremely important because their actions are very powerful.

A person should learn a great lesson from this. One must be humble, because the body depends heavily on these organs through which one sees and hears, which are very small, yet are positioned on top. *Know what is above you; an eye that is watching and an ear that is listening.*

(See Birkath Aboth Pereq 2, Mishnah 1)

Pirqei Aboth 3: Why we must receive everyone with happiness.

"Receive (Meqabbel) all men with happiness". The Gemaṭria (numerical value) of the word Meqabbel is equal to the value of the word 'Eqeb.

The Rishonim explained the word 'Eqeb (in the Parasha of 'Eqeb) to mean humility. Therefore, one can understand from this that one should always be humble and, as a result, receive all men with happiness. Even if a person is complete and important, he should not feel superior to others who are not on the same level, but should receive each of them in happiness.

The last letters of the names of the Aboth (our Patriarchs) which are Abraham, Yiṣḥaq, Ya'aqob and Yisrael (Abraham, Isaac, Jacob and Israel) also spell the word Meqabbel (to receive). We, who are their children must, therefore, also receive everyone with happiness.

(See Pirush HaḤida on Masekheth Aboth, Ch. 3, 12)

Pirqei Aboth 4: How do you calculate your wealth?

There is a story about a king who asked his deputy, "What is your net worth, including all the money and land that you possess?". His deputy replied, "Your majesty, I have $30,000". The king became very angry because he knew that his deputy was extremely wealthy and had much more money than that.

His deputy, upon seeing the king's anger responded as follows:

"Your majesty, please do not be angry with me. Your majesty asked me how much I possess. My answer was the truth because I see from my records that I gave $30,000 in charity and that is what is mine. I do not know to whom the rest of the wealth, which is currently in my possession, belongs."

There are many who are blessed with much wealth, but they will be unable to take it with them when they go. They will have to leave it to those who inherit it, and they have no way of knowing what will become of it after they are gone. Therefore, this money cannot be considered as belonging to them.

Who can be called a truly rich person? The one who is happy with what possesses. And what does he unquestionably possess? Only what he has given in charity and acts of kindness can be considered truly his.

(See Rab Ḥida, Kissei Raḥamim)

Pirqei Aboth 5: When one's livelihood is a struggle

10 things were created on 'Ereb Shabbath Bein Hashemashoth (at twilight). One of them was the manna. Why was the manna created at this time?

In this, the final exile that we are in, many face financial difficulties and find it a challenge to put adequate food on the table. If one remembers the manna that G-d gave the Children of Israel in the desert, which was bread from Heaven that had every possible taste one could wish for, it will help a person develop his trust in Haqqadosh Barukh Hu (the Holy One blessed be He). If in the desert, where there is no possibility of finding food, G-d provided for all our needs, how much more so can we depend on Him in our own lives.

By trusting in G-d, not only does a person overcome feelings of sadness and depression, but if he truly trusts in Him, G-d will surely take care of his livelihood because He can provide something from nothing as He did for us in the desert. In times of financial difficulties, it behooves us to bear this in mind.

(See Birkath Aboth on Pirqei Aboth 5: 6)

Pirqei Aboth 6: Chapter six didn't exist

"The Sages taught in the language (style) of the Mishna".

Pirqei Aboth (Ethics of the Fathers) comprises, as we know, six chapters. Rabbenu Yehuda Ha<u>n</u>asi, its author, only compiled 5 chapters in the Tractate "Aboth". This hints at the Hebrew letter Heh (whose numerical value is five) which hints at the Shekhinah (G-d's Holy Presence). The Rambam and Rabbenu 'Obadia MiBartenura, 'a"h, only wrote an explanation on the five chapters. It appears that the explanation of the Rambam on the sixth chapter is really not his, but is taken from Rashi's explanations.

Rabbi Yoseph Ḥayon from Lisbon, wrote in his explanation to Pirqei Aboth that the custom spread to read one chapter of Pirqei Aboth every Shabbath between Pesaḥ and

Shabu'oth. Since the sixth week had no chapter, the sixth chapter was gathered from the sayings of our Rabbis of blessed memory from the Gemara but written in the style and language of the Mishna. That is why this chapter begins with the words, *The Sages taught in the language of the Mishna.*

They entitled it *Pereq Qinyan HaTorah* (chapter of the acquiring of the Torah), and specified that it should be read the Shabbath before Shabu'oth which is the day of the giving of the Torah.

(See Aboth 6. Ḥida on Masekheth Aboth 6)

Women's Corner

Rabbanith Ruth Menashe

Women's Corner

"Much can come from the woman"

The story of Qoraḥ and his followers reveals to us the power embedded within each one of us.

Who ignited the fire of jealousy in the heart of Qoraḥ, an important man who reached high spiritual levels, which ended in destruction?

Who, with wit and courage, performed an act unheard of - that of uncovering her hair in public - and prevented On Ben Peleth from joining the rebels and saved his life?

The answer to both questions is identical: his wife,

Ḥakham Yoseph Ḥayyim 'a"h relates the following story. One man dreamt of a king climbing up a very tall ladder, reaching the 500th rung, which was approximately the middle of the ladder. The next morning he went to the king and shared his dream with the king. The king instructed his servants to give him a thousand gold coins.

When the neighbor's wife heard the story of the success of this man, she advised her husband: "Our neighbor who saw the king climbing halfway was granted one thousand gold coins. Go and tell the king a similar dream, but tell him that in your dream the king reached the top of the ladder. He will surely give you ten thousand gold coins."

The man followed his wife's advice. How did the king react? He commanded his servants to throw him out of the palace. Why did he do that?

The second dream meant that the king had reached the top and could now only go down, whereas the first dream, in which he had reached only half the height of the ladder, was a sign that he would continue to rise and increase his power.

Much depends on us, the women. We have an incredible power to build, nurture, and elevate, or Heaven forbid - to destroy. May the Holy One Blessed be He grant us the wisdom to be builders; builders of our homes, builders of our palaces.

The meaning of life

Let us imagine the following scenario, a group of soldiers betrayed their king and joined the army of the enemy. After some time, they regretted their actions and decided to return to their homeland and beloved king.

What should the king's reaction be? we would agree, unanimously, that he should punish his disloyal soldiers and never consider the possibility of returning them to their former positions.

This parable can provide us with an insight into the incredible concept of Teshubah (repentance). The Al-mighty awaits our return. He wants His children to return to Him. No matter how far we have gone or how grievous our sins are, His arms are open to embrace us.

Why is it that Hashem acts in such an unimaginable way and almost begs us to do Teshuba? Why is it that the gates of repentance are open forever? (Debarim Rabba 2,12)

Perhaps one of the answers to these questions will give us an insight into the meaning of life. While we are all busy with our daily lives, attending to our basic needs, we rarely find the time to examine the meaning of life and to introspect. If we seek the true essence of life we, inevitably, find that life without Torah is meaningless, we can even say lifeless.

When we give a present to a person we dearly love, we hope that he/she will cherish it, use it and appreciate it. Don't we feel disappointed when they don't?

Our Father in Heaven, in His infinite love for us, gave us the gift of life. The instructions of how to operate the gift were included in our Torah. In His kindness, he added to His gift, a magical tool, a tool that can fix the gift in case something goes wrong. This magical tool is Teshuba.

My prayer for us all is, that we may have the merit of strengthening our connection with our loving Father in Heaven, to add more depth and meaning into our lives, and be able to use and appreciate the precious gift that we have been given – our life!

Mothers and Torah

Learning Torah is often associated with men and boys. As women, we often wonder what role we play in the arena of Torah learning. Ḥakham Yoseph Ḥayyim 'a"h, in his holy work 'Od Yoseph Ḥai, sheds light on the connection between Torah and women.

When G-d gave the Torah to the Jewish people, He did not send it through His messenger, Moshe Rabbenu 'a"h, who would be the intermediary between G-d and the Jewish people. Rather, He Himself revealed His glory to the entire Jewish nation: men, women and children, at Har Sinai (Mount Sinai). The Children of Israel saw with their own eyes, the awesome sight of thunder and lightning. They heard the voice of G-d with their own ears. Their receiving of the Torah was not done in a theoretical or philosophical way, but rather, in a clear obvious manner which cannot be misinterpreted in any way.

The Ben Ish Ḥai compares the obvious validity of the Torah to a mother and her baby. Who the mother is, is not a debatable matter since she was the one from whom the baby came - from her womb. The father, on the other hand, we cannot be quite as certain about. The same way we are certain about the mother, we know that the Torah is true since our entire nation heard the voice of G-d telling us the Torah. The validity of our Torah is irrefutable because of the fact that we got it directly from Hashem Himself, not even through Moshe Rabbenu 'a"h. In addition, every Jewish soul was present at that time.

Reading about this awesome occasion, the giving of the Torah to the Jewish people, often inspires a journey to our own personal Mattan Torah (receiving the Torah). Isn't it heartening to know that such an analogy between us as mothers and the special present that Hashem gave us – His holy Torah – exists?

Faith: our Strength

On Shabbath Sheqalim, the first of the four special Shabbaths, two Torah scrolls are taken out from the ark. We read the Mafṭir from Parashath Ki Thissa. It recounts the commandment of the yearly contribution of a half a Sheqel for the purchase of the offerings in the sanctuary.

Ḥakham Sasson Mordekhai Moshe a"h writes that there is a hint here, connected to the fact that the Jewish people were commanded to bring specifically half a Sheqel. A man is considered incomplete without his wife. According to the holy Zohar, a husband and wife are two halves of one soul. They obtain perfection and completion when they get married. Since only the men, and not the woman sinned in the sin of the golden calf, they alone had to bring a half a Sheqel as an atonement for their sin. Men representing half of a whole were, therefore, commanded to bring specifically the amount of half a Sheqel.

My dear friends, as woman, we possess an incredible ability to lead our families and thereby the entire Jewish nation through the path of Emunah (faith) in the Al-mighty. The women resisted giving their gold jewelry for the construction of the golden calf. They didn't lose their faith and, on the contrary, had complete faith that Moshe Rabbenu 'a"h, their leader, would return after ascending to Heaven.

As we read the special portion of the Torah about the obligation to contribute the half Sheqel, let us remind ourselves who we are and what our strength is. Let us spread the seeds of our unshaken faith and instill them in our family and those around us.

Not a Wasted Time

Ribbi Ṭarfon says: ...The reward is great. (Pirqe Aboth 2,15)

Ḥakham Yoseph Ḥayyim 'a"h expounds on this Maamar (saying), guiding us to find a proper balance between the spiritual and physical worlds. The time we dedicate to connecting with the Al- mighty is actually immeasurable quality time. Only one or two hours of Torah study, can build unimaginable spiritual worlds in Heaven.

When Moshe Rabbenu 'a"h spent forty days and forty nights on Har Sinai he refrained from sleeping. The Ben Ish Ḥai says that it is likened to a servant whose master told him to collect as many gold coins as possible within a limited amount of time. Would it be sensible for him to take a break and go to sleep? Of course not. So too, Moshe Rabbenu 'a"h didn't want to lose any of the precious gems of the Torah. We too, must realize that the reward we get for investing in spiritual matters is immense and out of all proportion to the time that we put into it.

My dear friends, during the time between Pesaḥ and Shabu'oth, we are required to consciously elevate ourselves to be fit to receive the Torah. Let us be inspired by Moshe Rabbenu, 'a"h, who did not want to waste any precious moments to be side-tracked from reaching new spiritual heights. Setting aside time for prayer every morning or joining Torah classes is not a waste of time, even if our daily "to do" list is endless. On the contrary, the reward is priceless. Spending time to visit a sick friend, or a lonely elderly person is a profitable investment. Let us grab these priceless opportunities and go higher and higher.

Character Traits - Is it possible to change them?

Can we change our habits and improve our natural inclinations? While there may be a range of opinions, Ḥakham Yoseph Ḥayyim 'a"h answers the debate with the following story:

There was a Torah scholar who had a profound knowledge in the art of reading palm and forehead lines. It happened, that a foreigner visited his city, who claimed to be an expert in the very same "art". The Torah scholar sent his students to the man to test his expertise. He asked them to show the visitor their palms, and sent an imprint of his own forehead and palms. To their amazement, the visitor unfolded past events and appeared to be an expert in the field. When they showed him their Rabbi's imprints he told them that this man has a bad temper, and that he is a liar and a cheat. This completely changed their opinion of the visitor! They all knew their Ḥakham to be an righteous, upright individual.

The students told their Ḥakham what had transpired. To their amazement and total disbelief, the scholar told them that the visitor was indeed correct! His palm lines revealed his true nature. However, with intense work, he was able to overcome his inclination and break through his desires.

The Ben Ish Ḥai gives us priceless advice. Yes! - if one wants, he can change his bad habits. But the secret to a smooth and easy change is to start at a young age. The earlier we start, the easier it is. Change at a later stage in life requires hard and intense work.

The Ben Ish Ḥai adds that as mothers and future mothers, we must invest in the upbringing of our children from a young age. We must be aware of their strengths and their shortcomings and take an active approach. We should guide and teach them to adopt good habits and work on their character traits.

"Where Are You Going to?" (Pirqe Aboth 3,1)

Ribbi Aqabia says: "...Know where you are going to..." (at the end of your days). Ḥakham Yoseph Ḥayyim, 'a"h, in his explanation to the Ethics of our Fathers says that keeping this powerful statement in mind will assist us in overcoming jealousy. Wealth only lasts for a limited amount of time. When we leave this world we leave it empty handed.

The Ben Ish Ḥai relates the following parable to illustrate his message. A man was passing a group of people and decided to tease them. What did he do? He told one of them, in the presence of the others, "Take this gold coin and share it with all your friends". In reality, he did not give him anything. Each of the people in the group started shouting: "Where is my share?". They got into a big argument.

We are like that group of people, feeling jealous of those who have more than we do. In truth, those whom we perceive to be far richer than we are have no more than we do. When we leave this world, we do not take riches, glory or the like with us. We are all equal in this respect.

My dear friends, the message is clear and simple. Let us gather and collect our riches for the next world in heaps, riches of good deeds, acts of kindness, and bundles of Miṣwoth. Physical wealth is limited in time. Our spiritual wealth is eternal!

Our own personal "gates"

Parashath Shofṭim begins with the following verse: "You shall appoint judges and officers in all your gates". The literal meaning of this verse refers to the importance of establishing a court system in Israel. Ḥakham Yoseph Ḥayyim, 'a"h, in his holy work 'Od Yoseph Ḥai, presents a different outlook on this verse. He explains that the word gates may refer to the openings, or gates, that we have in our body.

What are those gates?

There are three main parts of our body which have an opening and a gate: the eyes, the mouth and our ears. If we examine them, we notice that each one of them is attached to a specific "gate". The eyelids serve as "gates" for the eyes, the lips for the mouth and the earlobes for the ears. Can you think why these particular parts were assigned gates?

The Ben Ish Ḥai expounds on this idea saying that the eyes, the mouth and the ears are all tools used more than any other for the study of the Torah. And it is for this same reason that the evil inclination tries to make us stumble through the use of these three parts of our body. The gates should be shut when the evil inclination tries to make us use the tools for the wrong purpose. Now we can understand better why they were assigned gates.

In his book "The Laws for Women" the Ben Ish Ḥai expounds on the topic of the mouth and its use for speech. If we look at the way we were created we notice that we have two ears and only one tongue. What lesson can we derive from this? Needless to say, we should spend more time listening than talking. Speech, he continues is likened to salt. When overused, it spoils everything, but when used in small quantities, it improves the taste of the dish.

My dear friends, speech is a powerful tool , especially for us, women. We must use it wisely and ensure that we do not say things which we will regret later on. If the value of speech can somehow be measured, we can say that keeping silent (at the right time) is priceless. May the Al-mighty give us all the wisdom to know when to talk and when not to.

The tongue, the arrow and the bullet

What is the connection between the tongue, the arrow and the bullet? Are there any similarities or differences?

Ḥakham Yoseph Ḥayyim 'a"h, says that all three have the power to shoot. They can all hit. We can easily understand the arrow and the bullet shooting at a distance and hitting, but what about the tongue?

The tongue, he says, can reach from one end of the world to the other end of the world. A person who speaks evil of another, might be in New York, but his words can reach as far as China. Moreover, the speed at which speech travels is unimaginable. The Ben Ish Ḥai compares it to a galloping horse, only much faster. Even the analogy of the fastest aircraft is too slow. In fact, in today's world we are all aware of the speed and impact of just one email.

The Ben Ish Ḥai relates a story about a wise man, who asked his servant to get for him something tasty. The servant returned home with a tongue. The next time the man asked the servant to buy for him some food which is not considered to be good. What do you think the servant brought back with him? A tongue!

When the man requested an explanation, he wisely said: "My master, when the tongue is good, nothing is compared to its goodness. However , when it is bad, it is the worst of all!"

My dear friends, Hashem gave us a precious gift, the ability to express ourselves through speech. We must be aware of its strength and take charge of our tongue and the words which come out of our mouths. Next time when we use our mouth, let us find those comforting, pleasing and complimentary words and make a difference in the lives of those who are around us.

To Say it With Love

Sefer Debarim is a collection of Moshe Rabbenu's words to his beloved people. Our Rabbis of blessed memory commented that the first verse "These are the words that Moshe spoke to all Israel" (Debarim 1,1) denotes words of rebuke. Five weeks before his death our faithful shepherd, Moshe Rabbenu, 'a"h, reminds the Jewish people of the sins they performed in various places in the wilderness.

If we would have to guess what the words that our leader would communicate to his Jewish nation weeks before his death would be, would we ever imagine that they would be words of rebuke? Moreover, if he had some "words" to share with Bene Yisrael of misdeeds that happened years prior, why wait?

As parents, friends, spouses and other similar roles, we find ourselves in the position of having to rebuke. In fact, the Torah tells us that we have an obligation to rebuke our fellow man. (Wayyiqra 19,17)

Let us explore what rebuke is all about based on the actions of Moshe Rabbenu 'a"h. Ḥakham Yoseph Ḥayyim 'a"h explains that from the fact that Moshe Rabbenu 'a"h spoke to all Israel, we learn the important lesson of how careful we must be not to embarrass the "sinner". Moshe Rabbenu 'a"h made a point of gathering all of Israel, even though, different groups transgressed in different areas. Although they were not all to be blamed for every single transgression, they were all present. This is how nobody was put to shame.

In addition, the Ohr Haḥayyim Haqqadosh expounds on the question of why it was done at that particular time. Why wait till now to mention the sins that took place years ago? Moshe Rabbenu 'a"h waited for the right opportunity and for the right time for his words to be accepted by the Jewish people and penetrate their hearts.

My dear friends, let us take these powerful lessons to heart. When we want to "tell off" our children, siblings, friend, or our husbands, let us speak with love and not out of anger or frustration. Let us find the right time, so our words have an effect and not build resentment. And never ever put someone to shame or embarrass them in front of others.

We are unique and important, despite our failings

When we read about the blessings which Ya'aqob Abinu 'a"h gave his children before he passed away, we notice the uniqeness of each blessing, designed to meet the mission of each one of them. When we examine each Berakha, we realize that the shortcomings of Reuben, Shimon and Lewi are clearly mentioned. We can even find words of rebuke for his three elder children.

We might wonder what kind of feelings Ya'aqob Abinu had for these children. Were they considered outsiders in the family? Is there any message for us to be learnt?

The portion of the section of the benedictions is concluded with the following phrase: "All these are the tribes of Israel, twelve..." (Bereshith 49,28). According to the Alshikh Haqqadosh, Ya'aqob Abinu was particular to make known that every single one of his children was an integral part of the twelve tribes of Israel. None of them was excluded. Each one was righteous in his own right, and fit to be counted amongst the tribes of Israel.

Ḥakham Yoseph Ḥayyim 'a"h comments in his holy work "Addereth Eliyahu" that the name Yisrael (Israel) denotes importance. It is only when we follow the path of the Torah and the will of Haqqadosh Barukh Hu that we deserve this title "Yisrael".

My dear friends, our father Ya'aqob Abinu 'a"h transmitted to us an important value. When we see in people around us – particularly those who are close to us (our children, our spouse, etc.) – a characteristic which requires improvement, or a trait which is imperfect, we must remember that we are all descendants of our forefathers. We are all part of the tribes of Israel. Different as we are, we are all unique and must be equally included, just like Ya'aqob Abinu blessed each one of his children with his special customized benediction and included them all equally in the twelve tribes of Israel!

And Yisrael Loved Yosef More Than All His Children

We are all familiar and intrigued by the story of Joseph (Yosef Haṣṣaddiq 'a"h) and the coat of many colors that was given to him by his loving father, Ya'aqob Abinu 'a"h (Jacob). Our Rabbis of blessed memory extracted from this an important and essential rule in parenting: a person should be careful not to act in a way that will create jealousy amongst the siblings in the family. They state that the multi-colored coat initiated the process which eventually ended in the exile to Egypt. Rabbenu the Ḥida (in Naḥal Qedumim) goes even further and says that all the four exiles were a result of the preferential love of Ya'aqob Abinu to Yoseph, 'a"h. We are not attempting to analyze Ya'aqob Abinu's actions, however, we can derive a lesson for ourselves as parents.

In the Gemara of Shabbath (10, 2) our Rabbis warn us parents, not to differentiate between our children, or to display more love to one of them. It is important to consciously understand the different natures, qualities and strengths of each of our children. The Gemara of Berakoth tells us, "Just as there no two people whose faces are identical, so too, there are no two people whose ways of thinking are exactly the same." We all know this, but must also appreciate the uniqueness of each child. Our goal, as parents and teachers, is to encourage our children to develop and fulfill their potential. Each one is blessed with his or her own talents and each is valuable and precious. One may be a math wiz, the other a creative artist, and the third, a "people person". Every gift is precious and welcome.

When our children get such a message, they learn to be tolerant of others and to appreciate the uniqueness of those around them. They learn that differences are not a source of division, but rather a creation of harmony and perfection.

How happy are those who brought them into this world

In the Parasha of Wayyelekh, Moshe Rabbenu, 'a"h, commands the entire Jewish nation to gather, once every seven years, to hear the king read to them portions from the book of Deuteronomy. Men, women, children, and converts were present at this auspicious event.

A question is raised in the Gemara (Ḥaghigha 50a) concerning the purpose of bringing little children to this gathering. Since, obviously, they cannot participate in the process of learning and understanding, why bring them?

The Gemara answers that by bringing the children, we, the fathers and mothers who bring them get a reward for this deed. "What is the reward for this deed?" questions Ḥakham Yoseph Ḥayyim, a"h; we all know that young children cannot understand and appreciate the portion which is read.

The Ben Ish Ḥai explains that it was said about Moshe Rabbenu, a"h, "Happy is the one who gave birth to him". He expands on this point saying that Moshe Rabbenu's glory was a result of the righteous and pure intentions which were instilled in him by none other than his mother. His righteous mother guided him from childhood. Therefore, we must take to heart that if we train our children from childhood to serve the Al-mighty, go to Synagogue, hear words of Torah, etc., then by doing so they acquire the habit of following the right path, and they will continue to do so. Naturally, we will be rewarded by having children who walk in the path of our holy Torah.

My dearest friends, we live in a world that demands of us to shield and protect our precious children. Let us start molding their behavior from a young age. We are their first and most influential teachers. Our teaching must start from infancy in order for it to be everlasting. May we all merit to see our children grow in the path of Torah and follow our holy traditions. Then we will merit to hear people say "how fortunate and happy are those who brought them to this world".

Dress to Impress

The episode of Dina, the daughter of Ya'aqob Abinu, 'a"h, and Leah Immenu, 'a"h, serves as a springboard to explore the topic of modesty and self respect. The Abarbanel, in his commentary on Parashath Wayyishlaḥ, stresses the fact that Dina was, in fact, as modest as her righteous mother Leah and her father Ya'aqob, 'a"h. We are told that her mother Leah Immenu would not leave her home even when taking care of the cattle, while her father, Ya'aqob Abinu is known for "one who dwells in tents". He states, that Dina's intention was "to look over the daughter's land" (Bereshith 34, 1). Meaning, because she was the only girl in her household, she wanted to see other girls' clothing and jewelry.

Other commentators, however, interpret her behavior as an expression of a lack of modesty. The Midrash explains that the word Lir-oth, to see, can also be read as Le' raoth, to be seen. Implying that Dina went out adorned to be seen.

Mode of dress and general appearance are of great importance to any woman, and so they should be. We must make a conscious effort to look beautiful in the presence of our husbands, inside our homes. It is a crucial component in building close relationships with our husbands. At the same time, every single one of us should be aware of the immeasurable impact we have on others. We are constantly seen by other women and examined by our friends. The way we dress affects the decisions that other women make concerning what they will wear, how they will cover their hair and so on. The unspoken statement of "if it's good for her, it's good for me" must not be ignored.

My dear friends, I hope and pray that each and every single one of us will find the inner strength to raise ourselves to new levels of modesty. Each small step higher that we take will have a ripple effect on thousands. This area, though challenging, is our unique territory. May we each find and reveal our true beauty.

Prayer: the vessel for our blessings

On the third day of Creation, we are told that the Holy One Blessed be He created the herbs, vegetation and fruit trees. Later on, (Bereshith 2:5) the Torah states: "The shrubs of the field were not yet on the earth and the herbs of the field had not yet sprung up".

Rashi comments and explains, based on the Gemara of Ḥullin, that even though the trees, the shrubs, the herbs and all vegetation were created, their process of growth came to a halt. They all remained beneath the surface of the earth, waiting to break through.

What were all the trees, shrubs and herbs waiting for? Why hadn't they all appeared above the ground?

"And there was no man to work the ground". Hashem was waiting for the prayer of Adam!

Only when he prayed for rain and acknowledged the fact that the actual growth of the vegetation is dependent on the Al-Mighty, did it had happen. Moreover, even though the gift of the fruit trees, the grass and the flowers was right there, it only broke through and became part of Adam's world, after he had asked for it.

The great sage, Ḥakham Yoseph Ḥayyim, 'a"h, expounds on this thought and poses the following question: Doesn't the Al-Mighty know what our needs are and even better than we do? Why, then, do we need to pray?

We need to create vessels, he explains, to "hold" the blessings and the abudance that He wants to bestow upon us. When a poor person asks for food, he must bring a vessel with him to place the food in. The letters of the words of our Tefilloth have the power of creating such vessels and pipes through which an abundance of good will flow. This clarifies why the Holy One Blessed be He desires the prayers of the righteous!

Let us pray, pray and pray.

Precious advice in difficult times

During difficult times, when people face financial hardships, as well as many other challenges, it is perhaps worthwhile to explore the words of Ḥakham Yosef Ḥayyim 'a"h.

Even though his words were recorded over 100 years ago, we can all relate to them today. This is true, even though certain circumstances are different today. For instance, it is very common that both husband and wife need to work today, whereas 100 years ago, the wife depended exclusively on the husband.

He says that a woman who is fortunate to have a generous husband, who does not withhold anything from the needs of the household, must be sensitive to the value of even a piece of vegetable, a small quantity of food, or a bit of a drink. She must be careful not to waste them unnecessarily just because he is generous. The Ben Ish Ḥai goes on to speak about instances that we may find incomprehensible. It is, perhaps, worthwhile to spend a minute thinking about them. It may serve as an eye-opener and give us an indication of how far we have gone.

He speaks figuratively, about a person who found some apples and other fruit in the garbage. He was asking how these items found their way into the garbage, and was told that they were not important enough in the eyes of their owner and were discarded.

I wonder what this person would say today, if he passed by homes that have many items, from furniture to electronic items, in excellent condition, waiting at the curb for the garbage truck to pick them up. Just because we are blessed with the means to buy new items, does not mean that we should discard that which has value.

An additional practical piece of advice that the Ben Ish Ḥai shares with his readers is to work according to a plan, thereby eliminating any possible waste. One example he gives is of women who can cook seven types of tasty and delicious dishes out of just two pounds of meat. Whereas there are those who would cook four pounds of meat – but the outcome would not be appealing even to a hungry man. If we are organized and plan ahead, we can not only avoid waste, but can make what we have more meaningful.

My dear friends, I think there is a message here that we cannot ignore. Thank G-d, many of us do not experience, and I pray never will, real poverty. However, no matter what our financial situation is, we must develop sensitivity to appreciate what we have, avoid waste at all cost, and always be grateful for what we have. There are many who have a lot less than we do.

And Sara is in the tent

When the three angels came to Abraham Abinu's tent, they asked concerning Sara Immenu, 'a"h: "Where is Sara, your wife?" The obvious question is, didn't the angels know where Sara Immenu, 'a"h, was? They undoubtedly did know. However, our Rabbis tell us that their whole purpose in posing the question was to cause Sara Immenu, 'a"h, to become more beloved in the eyes of Abraham Abinu, 'a"h.

How can such a question enhance the emotions of love and intimacy between Abraham Abinu and his wife? The answer can be found in Abraham Abinu's reply, "Hinne Ba-ohel" (she's in the tent). The essence of our mother Sarah can be extracted from these two words, from which we learn of her extreme modesty. And it is precisely this quality that endeared her to her husband.

Let us try and explore this virtue, even though our explanation might only be a drop in the bucket compared to all there is to say. Our Rabbis of blessed memory tell us that modesty is precious in the eyes of Hashem, to the extent that it is said, "there is nothing that Hashem loves more dearly than modesty". Women who possess this quality are known to generate respect and dignity. Such women infuse their homes with holiness and blessings. In fact, the entire Jewish people benefit from an elevated level of modesty displayed by the Jewish women.

Though many people associate the word "modesty" with clothing (long sleeves, long skirts etc.) it is actually an all encompassing term. It is connected with every aspect of our life, with the way we eat, think, behave and talk.

We live in a world that promotes the exact opposite of the quality of modesty. Today's role models are Hollywood stars and T.V. actresses. We must not lose track, but rather, return to our sources. Let us learn about dignity, nobility and beauty from our mothers. We are the royal descendants of our Mother Sara, and should be proud of this important and precious lineage.

What's in a Home?

When Yiṣḥaq Abinu, 'a"h, (Isaac) brought his new bride Ribqa (Rebecca) into Sara Immenu's tent, he knew that she was fit to continue in the path of his mother. What was the proof of that?

There are three miracles which are associated with Sara Immenu's tent,

1. Her Shabbbath lights remained burning from one Friday to the next,

2. Her dough was blessed, and

3. A cloud (referring to the Holy Presence) rested upon her tent.

What is the significance of these three miracles and is there any relevance to us, women, in our own "tents" (homes)?

Sara our Matriarch created a home which was founded with the same attributes as the Beth Ha<u>m</u>iqdash (the Temple). In the Temple, the lights of the Menorah remained lit from one Friday to the next; the show bread remained fresh from one Friday to the next, and of course, the Divine Presence rested upon this holy place.

We women are referred to as the "essence of the home", Aqereth Habbayith. In fact, the root of the word "Aqereth" (essence) in Hebrew has two contrasting meanings. One denotes, essence, while the other implies uprooting. This is the power that we have in our possession. It all depends on us.

It is up to us to create a home which resembles Sara Immenu's tent, as well as the Beth Ha<u>m</u>iqdash. Our mission in our miniature temple is a holy one, it can be overflowing with blessings, holiness and purity. We can bring G-d's presence into our home. It is in our hands.

Like a Rose Between the Thorns

Ribqa Immenu, 'a"h, was a righteous woman and a prophetess. She was also the one suitable to be the wife of our Patriarch Yiṣḥaq Abinu 'a"h (Isaac), who willingly and happily cooperated with his father when he bound him as a sacrifice on the altar. Such an incredible woman we may think, must have been raised in a special home and holy environment.

What kind of home did she have, and who were her father and brother?

"Rebecca the daughter of Bethuel the Aramean...sister of Laban the Aramean" (Parashath Toldoth, 25:20)

Our Rabbis of blessed memory, describe Ribqa Immenu's father Bethuel as a dishonest and evil person, who tried to poison Eliezer. Laban, her brother, is the epitome of trickery and deceit. This was her daily environment and exposure. In fact, the Alshikh Haqqadosh and the Ohr Haḥayyim Haqqadosh both comment that the reason Ribqa Immenu was barren for twenty years, was as a direct result of her ancestry - her father Bethuel and brother Laban. She is likened to a rose between the thorns.

The Midrash (Bereshith Rabbah) explains that the reason the Torah repeats Rebecca's genealogy at the beginning of

Parashath Toldoth, after mentioning it in the previous Parasha, was to praise her. Ribqa, the daughter of a wicked man and the sister of a wicked one was not influenced by them and did not learn their bad ways.

There is a commentary which suggests that one of the reasons for having Ya'aqob Abinu, 'a"h, and 'Esaw (Esau) as twins is to give us and the entire world an incredible message. We should not say that Ya'aqob Abinu's righteousness was achieved because of the kind of parents he had, the constellation at the time of his birth, or other forces. Both he and 'Esaw were born to the same parents, at virtually the same time.

My dear friends, there is a powerful message for us here. In every one of us there is a hidden potential to become a great woman. It is not dependent on who our parents are, or our birth place. Haqqadosh Barukh Hu gave us the tools we need to become great women. The rest is up to us. We have to refine our character tenaciously, to increase our devotion to Torah life, and strengthen our connection with out Father in Heaven. Then, we will actualize our potential and become the great women we are destined to be.

Who is Raḥel Immenu (our Mother Rachel)?

What is it about Raḥel Immenu, 'a"h (the matriarch Rachel), that makes our heart beat and our eyes tear? Who is this very special women?

After the destruction of the first temple, the prophet Jeremiah called out to our forefathers and Moshe Rabbenu 'a"h, asking them to plead for the anguished Jewish people.

Abraham Abinu, 'a"h, wept and reminded the Al-Mighty of the awesome moment when he brought his only son as a sacrifice before G-d, at the age of a hundred. "In this merit, will You have compassion for my children?"

Yiṣḥaq Abinu, 'a"h, (Isaac) came before Hashem begging that He grant mercy to his children on account of his willingness to bind himself and stretch out his neck to be slaughtered at the age of thirty seven.

Next, Ya'aqob Abinu, 'a"h, (Jacob) spoke and poured his heart out before the Creator saying that when his brother 'Esaw (Esau) wanted to kill his sons, Ya'aqob Abinu, 'a"h, was ready to give his life for them. "Will You have compassion for my children who are being slaughtered like sheep?"

Moshe Rabbenu, 'a"h, our beloved shepherd pleaded to Hashem, But G-d remained silent.

At that moment, Raḥel Immenu, 'a"h, prostrated herself in front of the Holy One Blessed be He and said, "My Father in Heaven, when my father gave my sister Leah as a wife to my beloved man, after he had worked for seven years so that I would be his wife, I made sure that she would not be put to shame. I shared the secret signs I made with Ya'aqob. In spite of my pain, I, a human being made of flesh and blood did not display the remotest feelings of jealousy. And You, a merciful Al-mighty, are jealous of idols, made by man out of stone and wood? You exiled my children?"

Instantly, our Merciful Father in Heaven replied, "Refrain your voice from weeping and your eyes from tears, for there is a reward for your labor... and your children shall return to their borders/boundaries."

Her compassion for her children knew no boundaries, her refined character and selfless personality is a true inspiration for all. Let us connect with her by trying to emulate her and follow in her path. Let us use our unimaginable strength to bring the redemption closer. Our forefathers did not have the power of soliciting from our G-d what she did. As her daughters, we can continue her work.

Who was Leah the Matriarch?

Leah Immenu, 'a"h, was an extremely righteous woman. In fact, we are told that her eyes were tender due to her excessive crying. She cried for years, with a fervent prayer to change the decree of her marriage to , 'Esaw (Esau). Rashi in his commentary explains that people would say that Rebecca the matriarch had two sons. The older one, Esau, will marry the older daughter of Laban (Leah), while the younger son (Ya'aqob), will marry Raḥel, the younger daughter of Laban.

Such was the level of Leah's righteousness, that she wept continuously to annul the Heavenly decree to marry the wicked Esau and merited to connect with the righteous, Yaaqob Abinu, 'a"h.

How then, did she tell her childless, pained sister, "Was your taking my husband insignificant?".

Ḥakham Yoseph Ḥayyim, a"h gives us a deep insight into this perplexing statement. Leah Immenu's intention when saying these harsh words, "Was your taking my husband insignificant?", was a hidden and lofty one – that of praising her sister. She wanted to publicize her sister's greatness. When Raḥel Immenu asked Leah for the Dudaim (good smelling plants), and Leah replied with harsh and painful words, we would have expected Raḥel to cry out, "Is he your husband-or mine? Didn't I selflessly give him to you to prevent any embarrassment caused to you?"

But Raḥel, the noble Raḥel accepted Leah's provocative statement quietly and did not respond. She accepted her sister's words, and therefore offered to let Yaaqob go to Leah's tent in exchange. Leah was able to show the entire world who her sister was, her nobility, righteousness, and admirable inner qualities.

"And the midwives feared G-d"

Imagine a mighty king, a ruler of a most powerful country, and on the other hand of the scale two women, a mother and her daughter, serving as midwives. Can we, for a brief moment, put ourselves in those women's shoes? How would we react to the command of such a ruler, demanding of us to join in the secret plan of killing all the Jewish male babies? Would we find the courage to defy the order of the king, or perhaps display signs of fear and succumb?

Yochebed and Miriam (mother and sister of Moshe Rabbenu 'a"h), the two Jewish midwives "feared G-d". Not only did they not obey the cruel decree, thereby risking their own lives, but they went out of their way to take special care of the newborns.

Ḥakham Yoseph Ḥayyim 'a"h, in his commentary on Pirqe Aboth (Ethics of Fathers) writes that there are those who display their fear of Heaven like a man who carries his wallet in his pocket. Needless to say, the only time he sees his wallet is when he needs to purchase an item. Similarly, these people do not remember the obligation to be a G-d fearing individual. It is only if he sins, G-d forbid, that feelings of fear may arise within him – fear of punishment.

Our fear of Heaven, however, should be likened to the clothes we wear, which are constantly in contact with our eyes! It must always be there, even when times are difficult or when it contradicts our nature.

And the reward?

The Al-mighty rewarded Yochebed and Miriam by having their offspring become Kohanim (Priests), Lewyim (Levites) and kings. May we all merit to reach the level Heaven desires, with courage and deep faith, just like our Jewish heroines, Yokhebed and Miriam.

Miriam – a Role Model

Water is one of the most essential and important commodities in the world. All humanity, as well as animals and vegetation, are dependent on it. During the forty years of the traveling of the Jewish nation in the desert, their only source of water was a mobile well, known as the Well of Miriam (Be-er Miriam). The entire Jewish people, a couple of million people, at least, satiated their thirst day after day, from Miriam's well.

In what merit did Miriam deserve to be the one to provide water for the entire Jewish people? Miriam, a six year old girl, impressed upon Amram, her father, the importance of remarrying his wife Yokhebed, from whom he separated. The decision to separate was in response to Pharaoh's decree to kill all the Jewish baby boys. Why remain married under such devastating circumstances? Miriam claimed that this act made her parents worse than Pharaoh, for as a result of this decision no girls could be brought into this world.

Amram, a leader of the Jewish people, followed his daughter's advice. When the baby boy Moshe was born and had to be hidden from Pharaoh's officers, he was placed in a basket on the River Nile. And who was the one who watched over him? His loving sister, Miriam.

There is an opinion, that because of this kind act connected with water, Miriam merited to provide the Children of Israel with water in the desert. When she passed away, (on the 10th of Nissan, according to some opinions) as mentioned in the Torah, the well stopped giving water. As it says, "And Miriam died there... and there was no water for the congregation".

My dear friends, every single one of our actions is recorded, an act of kindness never goes unnoticed. A small step of growth results in extreme joy in Heaven. Miriam, in her courage and wisdom, is a true role model of inspiration.

The Wife Behind the Torah Giant - Ribbi 'Aqiba (Part 1)

During the 'Omer, the period between the holiday of Pesaḥ and Lagh La'omer, 24,000 students of Ribbi 'Aqiba passed away. Ribbi 'Aqiba, a shepherd who did not know the alphabet, rose to become an outstanding Torah scholar. He stated that his entire knowledge of Torah and the knowledge of his disciples were his wife's.

Who was this heroine Raḥel and why did she deserve such glorious recognition?

Raḥel was the only daughter of one of the richest men in Yerushlayim, who was known for his extreme generosity and open house. Raḥel observed her father's shepherd 'Aqiba, and valued his refined and noble character. She might have sensed his hidden potential for spiritual heights, and therefore suggested that they marry on condition that he goes to study Torah. He agreed and they married secretly. When her distinguished father found out that his only daughter married his illiterate shepherd, he asked her to leave his home and made a vow to disown her. Needless to say, they lived in extreme poverty. After sometime 'Aqiba went, as planned, to study Torah. Raḥel supported herself selflessly – we are told that at some point she was even forced to cut off her beautiful hair and sell it. To her great joy, however, her husband was living her dream.

Ribbi 'Aqiba studied in the Yeshiba of Ribbi 'Eliezer, where he remained for twelve years. During this period of time he rose to unimaginable heights in Torah study. Twelve years after his departure from his beloved wife, Raḥel, he returned home accompanied by 12,000 students. Upon reaching his home he heard an old man taunting his wife, asking her: "How much longer will you have to suffer like a widow on your own?"

My dear friends, how would you have answered such a provocative question? What would you have replied? Raḥel's response was what made her deserve that glorious recognition of her husband.

The Wife Behind the Torah Giant - Ribbi 'Aqiba (Part 2)

Raḥel, whose whole being was devoted to her husband's growth in Torah, answered the evil question without any hesitation. She replied: "I wish he could hear me and remain in his Yeshiba twelve more years!". Hearing his wife's words and her verbal permission, Ribbi 'Aqiba turned back to continue his learning.

Twelve years later, he returned to his hometown, accompanied by 24,000 disciples! When Raḥel heard the news about her husband, she ran outside to greet him. She refused the kind offer of her neighbors to borrow nice clothing. When she saw him she fell upon her face, while his students tried to push her away. Ribbi 'Aqiba said to them: "Leave her alone. My Torah knowledge and yours are all hers!"

Raḥel's father, Kalba Sabuwa', also heard about the arrival of the outstanding Torah scholar. Not knowing who he really was, he decided to go to him. He was hoping the scholar would be able to help him find an opening to annul the vow he had made, over two decades earlier, to disown his daughter, Raḥel. Ribbi 'Aqiba asked him if he would have made his vow if his son-in-law was a knowledgeable man. Kalba Sabuwa' replied: "Even if he knew one chapter or one single Halakha, I would not have made that vow". Ribbi 'Aqiba humbly said: "I am that man..." His father in law fell upon his face and kissed his feet. He gave Ribbi 'Aqiba and Raḥel half his wealth.

Now Ribbi 'Aqiba was able to fulfill his promise to his beloved wife, a promise he had made, to comfort her, when they lived in extreme poverty. He gave her a gold ornament of Jerusalem, which women were accustomed to wear.

My dear friends, many lessons can be learnt from this extraordinary story. Each one of us can derive her own personal one. If we would only remember, that every single one of us possesses the hidden power to leave indelible impressions on those around us: the ability to change an illiterate shepherd into a Torah giant.

A Precious Gift

The commandment of keeping Shabbath is mentioned in the Parasha of Ki Thissa: *"The children of Israel shall observe the Sabbath..."* (Shemoth 31, 16).

In the Gemara (Shabbath 10b) we are told that G-d told Moshe Rabbenu 'a"h the following: *"I have a precious gift in My treasure house, called the Shabbath. I desire to give it to the children of Israel, go and tell them"*.

The Ohr Haḥayyim Haqqadosh comments that the use of the verb *Weshamru* (observe) alludes to the fact that we have to anxiously wait for the Shabbath. This special day must not, G-d forbid, be a burden. On the contrary, it is a day to look forward to. Ḥakham Yoseph Ḥayyim 'a"h writes that we should start our mental preparation for Shabbath from the Wednesday preceding that Shabbath.

As women, our role in creating an atmosphere of anticipation for Shabbath is essential. To a large extent, the association of pleasant and exciting feelings for the coming of this holy day is dependent on how we prepare for Shabbath. Do we hear voices singing and music playing or people shouting and screaming? Do we feel tension in the air or are we surrounded by a calm and relaxed atmosphere? Do we receive the Shabbath, the queen, like an important guest, or light the candles in our work clothes?

My dear friends, I know it is the dream of every Jewish woman, to build a home where Shabbath is a day to look forward to by the entire family. With proper planning and organization it can be achieved. Your Shabbath can be a manifestation of *"a precious gift from His treasure house"*.

The Pesaḥ challenge

The holy books mention that the preparations for Pesaḥ should start thirty days before the holiday. Ḥakham Sasson Mordekhai Moshe writes that when Moshe Rabbenu, 'a"h, informs Bene Yisrael about Pesaḥ Sheni, he announced it thirty days before the holiday. Even though Pesaḥ Sheni did not require the process of cleaning the house of Ḥameṣ, still preparation for thirty days was required. How much more so Pesaḥ itself!

The thirty day period prior to Passover is considered to fall into the category of 'Ereb Pesaḥ – the eve of Passover. That is why it is important to be actively involved in getting ready for this awesome holiday. In fact, part of the preparation is to review and study the laws concerning the holiday.

My dear friends, Pesaḥ is a holiday which sometimes women view with some trepidation. As women, and mothers, we must always remember that it is our responsibility to ensure that our family feels excited during the period of time leading to Passover. Organization and priorities are some of the main essentials and ingredients necessary in avoiding tension and confusion. Starting the preparations early, especially the cleaning process, will ensure a smooth and pleasant experience and a thorough job.

Please set deadlines for yourself in regards to cleaning different rooms and parts of your home. Decide by which day the entire house should be completed and when you can begin cleaning the kitchen.

Please remind yourself constantly that Pesaḥ is about cleaning Ḥameṣ. "Spring cleaning" is not required. Additionally, dust is not Ḥameṣ. Let us not get carried away, but rather, focus on our goal. We must do what is necessary based on the guidelines of the Halakha, yet, within a happy home and relaxed environment. It is in our hands.

Getting rid of our internal Ḥameṣ (leaven)

Our Rabbis of blessed memory tell us that just as our forefathers were redeemed in the month of Nissan, so too the future Geulla (redemption) will be in the month of Nissan. In addition, the deeds that brought about their Geulla will be the same ones that bring about the future one. One such act is that of Teshuba (Repentance). This is precisely why our Rabbis of blessed memory instructed us to examine ourselves at the time of Bediqath Ḥameṣ (searching for leaven) and remove not only our physical Ḥameṣ (leaven), but also the spiritual Ḥameṣ from our souls.

It says in the Torah: *Ushmartem eth Ha Maṣṣoth* - and you shall safeguard the Maṣṣoth (unleavened bread) (Exodus:12:17). Since the word Maṣṣoth can also be read as Miṣwoth (commandments), our sages conclude this refers to the importance of safeguarding the Miṣwoth i.e. showing diligence and enthusiasm. Ḥakham Yoseph Ḥayyim 'a"h expounds on the meaning of this point by saying that G-d created a few main limbs in our body for the use of performing the Miṣwoth: eyes, ears, mouth, tongue, heart, hands and legs. One must pay special care not to bring any impurities upon these parts of the body with forbidden things, but rather should sanctify and purify them.

My dear friends, in the midst of our Pesaḥ preparations and cleaning, let us set aside a few minutes to focus on the fact that Pesaḥ is a holiday which symbolizes our redemption from Egypt and slavery. While yearning for the coming of Mashiyaḥ, let us safeguard the Miṣwoth with zeal and eagerness, sanctifying our bodies which clothe the soul. We should not look at that which is improper, hear or speak Lashon Hara', or desire what is not ours. Rather, we should make a conscious commitment to do the opposite; especially we, as women, about whom it says *"in the merit of righteous women our forefathers were redeemed from Egypt, and in their merit we will be redeemed."*

"So that you tell in the ears of your son and your son's son"

Why are we commanded to tell our children the story of the Exodus from Egypt? Why is there so much emphasis on children during the seder? The Ohr Haḥayyim Haqqadosh poses a similar question. He asks why it is necessary to tell our children about the miracles and wonders that Hashem performed for us.

He explains that the whole purpose of the miracles, as witnessed during the ten plagues, was to strengthen the faith in the hearts of the Jewish people. The impression of Hashem's greatness had to be indelible, imprinted deep within their hearts and everlasting.

The Alshikh Haqqadosh expounds on this point saying that the fact that the Jewish people witnessed Hashem's greatness with their own eyes, reinforced their Emunah (faith). This powerful experience must be passed on to the next generations. It is a powerful tool to bring us closer to our Creator and follow His path.

Different communities have different customs and traditions concerning the involvement of the children at the seder. However, they all have one common factor - the evening revolves around the children. What a fantastic and amazing way to instill the faith in our children and nurture it.

This is a generation where many of us are experiencing hardship and pain in the process of trying to keep the flame of faith burning. Pesaḥ is a wonderful opportunity to inspire our children, involve them and answer the unique needs and questions of each and every one of them.

Finding G-d at Times of Distress

The period between the Seventeenth of Tammuz and the Ninth of Ab is called Yeme Ben Hameṣareem, which literally means *the days between the narrow straits*. The term is taken from one of the verses of lamentations in Meghillath Eikha, which we read on the ninth of Ab: *All her pursuers overtook her in narrow straits* (Lamentations 1,3). The word Meṣareem (narrow straits) can also be interpreted as distress. Hence, we can understand this verse from a different angle: *All her (the Jewish nation's) pursuers overtook her during the days of distress.* Days of distress are the twenty two days between the Seventeenth of Tammuz and the Ninth of Ab, which are known to be times of great sorrow and affliction for the Jewish people. Many tragedies and calamities befell us throughout our history.

Our Rabbis of blessed memory, based on the Qabbala, explain that these days have another deep meaning. The term (one word in Hebrew) *her pursuers* (Rodfe-ha) can be divided into two separate words: *Rodfe* and *Y-ah* – those who search for G-d. It is during these days that we can truly search for G-d and find Him! This is the time to consciously make an effort to connect to our Father in Heaven.

How? Through focusing on the needs of the Jewish people as opposed to our own personal needs. Rather than feeling pity for ourselves for not being able to wear new clothing, we should focus on the lack of a temple and the destruction of Yerushalayim. Instead of feeling sorry for not being able to swim during the nine days (between the first of Ab and the ninth of Ab), let us pray for the redemption to take place.

The more we think and pray for the Geulla (redemption) of our Jewish people and the pain of our Father in Heaven the closer we get to Him. This way we will become *Rodfe Y-ah*, those who truly search G-d and find Him. In this merit may we see the coming of the Mashiyaḥ speedily in our days, Amen!

Our Mouth, the "Battle Field" (the 17th of Tammuz)

The Seventeen of Tammuz is a fast day and the first of the twenty two days of the saddest period in the Jewish history. Naturally, a fast day signifies refraining from the consumption of food. The tool used for the action of eating and drinking is the mouth.

It is interesting to note that one of the ways the prophet Yeshayahu (Yeshayahu 41,14) refers to the Jewish people is: *Tola'ath Ya'aqob*, (worm Jacob). One may wonder about the unusual connection between the two seemingly unrelated words. Ḥakham Yosef Ḥayyim 'a"h, brings an insightful explanation to this question. He explains that just as the power of a worm is in its mouth – a soft worm can easily consume hard wood – so too, the power of the Jewish people lies in their mouth. The study of the Torah is done through the use of the mouth. The mundane act of eating and drinking, which can be a holy act when done according to the guidelines of the Torah, is done with the use of the mouth as well. Of course, our Tefilloth (prayers) emanate from the mouth too.

Now we can understand why so many of us struggle in the area of eating. Since the mouth has the ability to lift us to incredible levels of Qedu<u>sh</u>a, holiness, it is the most obvious place for our evil inclination to "get us" and make us stumble. The mouth may be described as a "battle field". Reciting blessings over the food and keeping in mind that we eat in order to serve our Creator are some of the tools to win the "battle".

From one perspective, a fast day is a day when we are detached from the physical, everyday act of eating and drinking. Perhaps, specifically on such a day, when there is a "cease fire" between us and the evil inclination, we should make a conscious effort to remind ourselves of this powerful weapon; our mouths.

Naḥamu Naḥamu, but let us still remember

One day after, and it seems as if it has all been forgotten. This is how the human mind works. Two days earlier we were sitting on the floor, wearing cloth shoes, crying for the destruction of the two Temples and today, the music is blasting, we're going on shopping sprees and dancing at weddings.

On the Shabbath after the Ninth of Ab we read the first Hafṭarah of the seven prophecies of consolation, which are read between the Shabbath following the Ninth of Ab and the Shabbath preceding Rosh Hashana. The message is clear, it is time for spreading hope and light. We should be consoled and comforted.

Yet, as many of us know, we must always display a firm belief in the future redemption and anxiously await it. It is, in fact, one of the thirteen principals of our faith. The Gemara in tractate Shabbath states that one of the questions that every single one of us will be asked on our day of judgment is: "Did you anxiously await the Geullah, the salvation?"

The Pele Yo'eṣ, (Ḥakham Eliezer Papo, 'a"h, from Turkey), writes that it is not sufficient to just utter the words, rather, we must feel it with our hearts and await the redemption wholeheartedly. He adds that a person's way of speech is an indication of his sincere expectation of the Geullah.

How so? When someone who makes plans for the future says: "May the Holy One Blessed be He bring the Geullah before that", this is a testimony to his true longing for the Geullah. For example, if we are planning a wedding or a trip that may take place a few months down the road, we should use this form of speech. Perhaps we should accustom ourselves to think and speak in this fashion.

The Pele Yo'eṣ shares another interesting point. Those of us who live outside the land of Israel, should refrain from building big homes with fancy and elaborate decorations. The constant daily longing for the land of Israel and for the redemption, does not go hand in hand with living in big comfortable houses.

A point to ponder...

Elul – a time for Introspection

Elul is the month of mercy and forgiveness. Rosh Ḥodesh Elul falls 40 days before the Day of Atonement – Yom Hakippurim. It is incumbent upon each of us, my dear friends, to take a few minutes out of our hectic schedule to prepare ourselves for this period of time when the focus on the act of repentance is most pronounced and emphasized.

Ḥakham Yoseph Ḥayyim 'a"h tells of a couple who had the following conversation. The husband asked his wife for her age, to which she replied "twenty-five." "Not possible" the husband exclaimed, "we've been married for twenty years." His wife explained by saying that only the years in which she followed the path of the Torah can be counted as her meaningful years. The rest of her life was wasted and therefore could not be added to her age.

The Ben Ish Ḥai comments on the above advising us to introspect and examine our life on this earth. The only element which determines the quality of our life is serving our Creator, which is done by following the path which He has paved for us. All other matters such as money, physical pleasures and the like, last for only fleeting moments. The only real benefit is gained by surrounding ourselves with an abundance of acts of kindness and Miṣwoth. As Hillel the Elder said in Ethics of the Fathers "...if not now, then when?"

Our sages teach us that when a chicken rolls on the ground and is covered in dust, nobody has the ability to clean it; even if much time and effort is spent in the cleaning process. Only the chicken itself can do it and the cleaning can be done in no time.

So it is with us. We alone know what is in our hearts and what our sins are. We know which areas require improvement, which character traits need to be refined. No one, other than ourselves, can cleanse us and our souls. When we do so, our loving Father in Heaven will forgive us and accept His returning daughters with open arms.

Our Heart – A Precious Gem and the month of Elul

If you had to choose the one part of your body which is most crucial for the process of repentance, what would it be?

Ḥakham Yoseph Ḥayyim 'a"h, in his book Mayim Ḥayyim, writes that this organ is the heart. Any thought or action that we do that is associated with Teshuba must emerge from the depth of our hearts. Those who fast, cry out, and beg – must do so with a contrite heart. In fact, there are a number of verses in the bible which support this idea. For example, when Moshe Rabbenu 'a"h guided the Children of Israel to repent (Parashath 'Eqeb 10:16) he said: "You should cut away the barrier/covering of your heart." Symbolically, Moshe Rabbenu 'a"h describes the heart of those who sin as being blocked by a covering which separates them from the Master of the universe.

We must pay close attention to our heart and its level of purity. The heart is likened to a king who rules over his servants. The heart is in charge of all the body organs. If the king lacks wisdom, what benefit is there in having smart servants? So too, the heart which is in charge of the rest of the body must not be blemished, otherwise, the whole body will be affected.

My dear friends, our heart is a shining gem, pure and bright. Its level of cleanliness determines our closeness to the Al-mighty. Our sins coat our heart, this precious gem, with layers which create separation and detachment between us and our Creator. During the month of Elul, we must focus on brightening and shining our hearts, and remember that our Sages tell us: "G-d seeks the heart" (Sanhedrin 106:)

Bringing blessings into our homes during the Ten Days of Repentance

One of the three special commandments for women is the one of separating "Ḥallah" (Hafrashath Ḥallah). In the past, women used to be engaged in the act of making bread on a daily basis. This was an integral part of their daily schedule. Ḥakham Yossef Ḥayyim a"h writes in his holy work Ben Ish Ḥai, that women who do not have the opportunity to perform this commandment on a regular basis, should separate the Ḥallah at least once a year. Since during the 'Aṣereth Yeme Teshuba (the Ten Days of Repentance) we make a conscious effort to increase our Miṣwoth (good deeds), this is a perfect time to engage in the process of kneading, baking, and of course performing this precious Miṣwah.

The prophet Ezekiel says, (44: 30) "the first yield of your dough, you shall give to the priests, to make a blessing rest upon your home".

The Ben Ish Ḥai and other authorities state that the Miṣwah (commandment) of separating the Ḥallah brings blessing into our homes. Many of us have heard about the blessed tent of Sara Immenu (our matriarch). Her bread remained fresh from one Friday to the next. Her home is a symbol of holiness and blessings. We, as her descendants carry within us an incredible potential to be like her. Just like a mother leaves an indelible impression on her beloved children, so did she, our matriarch Sara.

As we know, bread is the sustenance of life. People can live by consuming bread and water alone and many serve bread on a daily basis. Our Father in Heaven gave us a special commandment connected with this daily activity, the separation of the Ḥallah, in order to elevate the physical act into a spiritual one.

I pray, that in the merit of this precious commandment, our homes will be blessed abundantly. May we all, the daughters of our mother Sara, be living proof of our ability to bring holiness and the presence of G-d into our homes. May each one of us, through the acts of sifting, kneading, baking and separating the Ḥallah, reach new heights of closeness with our Creator.

To sit or not to sit (in the Sukkah)

Women are known to be the foundation of the Jewish home and, therefore, due to their numerous responsibilities, are exempt from time bound positive commandments. For instance, the commandment of sitting and dwelling in the Sukkah is just such a commandment, since it has to be performed on a particular date (from the fifteenth of Tashri for seven days).

There is an additional explanation for the exemption of women from these time bound commandments. The Torah views time as a holy and precious commodity. One of the ways to instill the value of time is through the time bound commandments which serve as a reminder of the importance of time. Women, who are created with an internal biological monthly clock, do not require an additional "external" reminder, while men do.

Ḥakham Yoseph Ḥayyim 'a"h writes in his holy work "Laws for Women" , that women who wish to perform these time bound Miṣwoth, may do so (with the exception of Tefilleen and Ṣiṣṣith), and will, in fact, be rewarded by the Creator for their deeds. He adds that women should accompany their husbands at night to sleep in the sukkah, and of course join him for the meals.

Ḥakham Ya'aqob Ḥayyim Sopher, known as the Kaf Ha'Ḥayyim, adds that the act of sitting in the Sukkah purifies the souls and gives a message of recognition of Hashem's kindness to us.

My dear friends, may we have the Zekhuth (merit) to appreciate the holiness of the precious Miṣwah (commandment) of dwelling in the Sukkah, which represents the clouds of glory surrounding the children of Israel in the desert. May this commandment nurture and increase our gratitude of Hashem's continuous kindness to us, then and now.

Women and Ḥanukkah

The performance of any commandment is considered to be a complete act, when the three following areas are covered: speech, action and intent. How do we acquire this level when lighting the Ḥanukkah candles? We read the blessings (speech) and we light the candles (action). Let us explore the intent that we should have during this time.

Ḥakham Sasson Mordekhai Moshe 'a"h explains that while darkness symbolizes our sins, the performance of the

Miṣwoth illuminates our soul and the entire world. When we light the Ḥanukkah lights, we should repent and regret bringing darkness into the world. We should strive to increase the spiritual light.

This was the act of Deborah the Judge, who was a prophetess as well as a leader of the Jewish people. She prepared special thick wicks for her husband to deliver to the Temple in Shilo. She wanted her wicks to be used for lighting the Menorah. Her wicks were so thick, that they were actually torches; when they were burning they produced immense light.

In addition to creating a magnificent physical light, she also had the special intention to increase the unification of G-d's holy name. Her entire act was for the sake of Heaven, "Leshem Shamayim." Therefore, the Holy One Blessed be He said to her, "You intended to increase my light, (therefore) I will illuminate you with the power of prophecy".

My dear friends, just as we add one more candle every night, so too, may each of you grow spiritually by expanding the light around you. May your performance of the Miṣwoth be complete on all three levels with a pure intent to multiply your own personal light, thereby expanding the light in the entire universe.

To be like a vine

The month of Shebaṭ is associated with water and growth. The seven species associated with the Land of Israel are an essential part of this month as well. All seven are special in their qualities and each one represents a deeper meaning. Let us try to explore one of them: Gefen (vine). What are some of the unique attributes of the vine?

The fact that grapes, the fruit of the vine, can be consumed in their entirety, and have neither a peel nor a pit gives this fruit special importance. In adddition, this is the only fruit that has its own individual blessing: Bore Peri Haggefen. However, outwardly, the vine is the least impressive tree of all: a low tree with thin branches.

Ḥakham Sasson Mordekhai Moshe, 'a"h, explains that the tree is likened to the physical body of a person. When a person does not chase after the physical pleasures of the world, but rather focuses on the spiritual aspect, he/she produces delicious fruit, (the performance of the Torah commandments). Then he is similar to a magnificent vine tree bearing sweet grapes. However, when we accentuate the physical, pursuing our bodily desires, then our fruit, our spiritual product is limited.

We, the Jewish people, are likened to the Gefen the vine. We must not lose focus, but must remember who we are. Though external beauty is important, it is secondary. Spiritual growth should be placed at the top of our priorities. May the Al-mighty grant us the clarity to make the right choices and may we, our children and all future generations, merit to flourish like a fruitful and gracious vine.

What it takes to save a nation

"And he brought up Hadassah..." (Esther, 2,7).

The word that is used in the Meghillah for bringing up can be translated as training. After Esther's parents passed away, Mordekhai, the leader of the the generation, took upon himself to bring up his orphaned niece and train her. In spite of his important and demanding role in the Jewish world, he invested in his "adopted" child.

Bringing up children involves continuous training and teaching. Our job as parents is to mold, refine and perfect our children's character. It goes without saying that it is our personal obligation as well – conscious and continuous effort must be made to polish our own character traits.

When Mordekhai heard that the two guards of the king plotted to kill King Aḥashwerosh, he told Esther. Esther informed the king in Mordekhai's name. It might seem unimportant to specify the fact that Esther informed the king in Mordekhai's name. A minute detail, with a powerful message. Esther, in her piety, made sure she mentioned Mordekhai's name, in connection with the "latest news". She did not reserve the glory for herself. Our Rabbis of blessed memory tell us that this seemingly unimportant act brought about the salvation of the entire Jewish nation!

This unbelievable outcome was a direct result of Esther's fine and polished character. Only a person with the proper upbringing, based on the foundation of our holy Torah, can reach this level of sensitivity and consideration.Such a person has the potential and the power of saving our nation.

...And you can do it too!

Daughters of the King, every one of us.

As Purim draws near, the image of the heroine of the Purim Story, Esther the queen, is what comes to mind and stands out. Little girls are fascinated by the role of a queen or princess. The crown, scepter, and glamorous royal clothing captivate their hearts.

Perhaps it would be appropriate to explore the outlook and the role of a princess from a different perspective. If you were asked to define yourself with a one or two word phrase, what would you choose? I would suggest *Bath Melekh* (daughter of a King). King David wrote in Tehillim (45:14), about the essence of a princess: *Kol Kebudah Bath Melekh Penima*. All the honor of a princess lies within.

We are composed of two opposing elements, body and soul. The body gets its importance by serving as a dwelling place for our holy Neshama, our soul. While the outside world emphasises our external appearance, the Torah view is the opposite, and focuses on the internal. Drawing attention to our outside appearance sends a message that we consider our body to be superior to our soul. Our essence is *Penima*, within, and our beauty is illuminated from within.

King David completes the verse with how a Jewish woman, a princess should be dressed: *Mishbeṣoth Zahab Lebushah* her clothing is of wrought (beaten) gold. The attire of a Jewish woman, a daughter of a King must be regal, compared to the glorious clothing of the Kohanim (Priests).

My dear friends, let us stand in front of the mirror and examine ourselves and how we dress; "Do I look like a regal queen, do I present myself in a respectable manner like a priest in the Beth Hamiqdash?". Let us all – each of us, at our very own personal level – make a commitment and go one step higher in how we dress.

It is difficult to do, but let us consider what we can improve. If you wear mostly pants, choose one day a week to wear skirts or dresses. If you only wear skirts and dresses, do they cover the knees even when seated? If you wish to focus on your arms, are they covered till past the elbows? For others, a step higher may be wearing less tight clothing. If you are married, consider if your head covering is as modest as it should be. I know how challenging it is. I also know the immense blessings and holiness every small victory generates.

Women and the gift of Rosh Ḥodesh

Rosh Ḥodesh, the first day of the month, is considered to be a special day for women. The festive meaning of this day is, in fact, of even greater importance for women than it is for men.

The reason for this can be found in an event in the history of our nation, over three thousand years ago: the sin of the golden calf. The men demanded that the women remove their gold jewelry for the creation of the golden calf. The women refused saying: "You want to build a statue, which is powerless and devoid of the ability to save us!" The men, however, volunteered their gold, thereby losing the privilege to benefit from twelve holidays (for each of the twelve months), which correspond to the twelve tribes.

On this account G-d rewarded the women doubly, both in this world and in the world to come. Women refrain from sewing and washing clothes and were promised to be renewed in the world to come, just like the moon, which is renewed each and every single month.

Ḥakham Sasson Mordekhai Moshe 'a"h, adds and comments that it would have been appropriate for women to avoid any type of Melakha (servile work), similar to the ones which are forbidden on the holidays. However, to avoid embarrassment to the men, whose privilege to celebrate Rosh Ḥodesh was taken away from them, we only refrain from the above mentioned two. He advises women to dedicate the day of Rosh Ḥodesh to the collecting of charity for poor Torah scholars as well as other worthy causes.

My dear friends, Rosh Ḥodesh is a unique day with an enormous spiritual potential imbedded in it and we should make a conscious effort to maximize it. We can honor it by wearing special clothing and preparing a delicious selection of foods. On the eve of Rosh Ḥodesh we have the custom of lighting candles, and should dedicate time to introspect and examine our deeds during the past month and search for ways to improve ourselves.

Transliteration Table

The following is the method of transliteration used by Midrash BEN ISH HAI. It reflects the Babylonian Jewish pronunciation, generally considered to be the most authentic.

Hebrew Letter	Description	Transliteration
א	**Alef**. Alef does not have its own sound per se. It is essentially a vowel sound which varies depending on the Nequddoth (vowels) that accompany it.	Various
בּ ב	**Beh** - Beh. Always a "B" sound. However, when there is a Ḥizzuq (Daghesh) the "B" sound is emphasized in accordance with the rules of the Daghesh for all letters.	B
גּ	**Geemal**. The sound of a "G" as in "Good".	G
ג	**Gheemal**. A sound made from the back of the palate, similar to a French "R".	GH
דּ	**Dahl**. A "D" sound, but not as hard/sharp sounding as in English.	D
ד	**Dahl/Ðahl**. Always pronounced "D" except in G-d's name when it is pronounced like "TH" as in "The", but accompanied by a sound from the back of the throat.	D In G-d's name: Ð
ה	**Hé**. An "H" sound.	H
ו	**Waw**. A "W" sound	W
ז	**Zahn**. A "Z" sound.	Z

ח	**Ḥeth**. Likened to an "H", but actually much sharper sounding and emanates from the back of the throat. Totally dissimilar to the Khaf sound.	Ḥ
ט	**Ṭeth**. Similar to a dull "T" sound accompanied by a sound from the back of the throat..	Ṭ
י	**Yod**. A "Y" sound.	Y
כּ	**Kaf**. A "K" sound.	K
כ	**Khaf**. Similar to the Welsh "ll". Totally dissimilar to the letter Ḥeth.	KH
ךּ	**Kaf Sofith** (Mithlu Kaf). Same as Kaf.	K
ך	**Khaf Sofith** (Mithlu Khaf). Same as Khaf.	KH
ל	**Lamad**. A pure "L" sound, which does not contain the accompanying throaty sound that is found in the English "L".	L
מ	**Meem**. An "M" sound..	M
ם	**Meem Sofeeth** (Mithlu Meem). Same as Meem..	M
נ	**Noon**. An "N" sound.	N
ן	**Noon Sofeeth** (Mithlu Noon). Same as Noon.	N
ס	**Simmakh**. An "S" sound.	S
ע	**'Ahn**. A guttural sound (from the back of the throat) which is attahed to an accompanying vowel sound.	'(& vowel)
פּ	**Peh**. A "P" sound.	P

פ	**Feh**. An "F" sound.	F
ף	**Feh** Sofeeth (Mithlu Feh). Same as Feh.	F
צ	**Ṣahd**. An "S" sound accompanied by a sound from the back of the throat.	Ṣ
ץ	**Ṣahd Sofeeth** (Mithlu Ṣahd). Same as Ṣahd.	Ṣ
ק	**Qoph**. A "K" sound accompanied by a sound from the back of the throat.	Q
ר	**Rosh**. Likened somewhat to a Spanish "R" but gentler and not rolled as much.	R
שׁ	**Sheen**. A "SH" sound	SH
שׂ	**Seen**. An "S" sound.	S
תּ	**Taw**. Similar to a "T" but duller and not as sharp sounding as in English.	T
ת	**Thaw**. A "TH" sound as in "Th"ank you.	TH

Letters that have a Daghesh for emphasis (Ḥizzuq) are either doubled or underlined.

More information on the transliteration used, may be found at:

www.midrash.org/atorahminute/transliteration